Courage 101

True Tales of Grit & Glory

Introductory Lessons in Heroism

By

George M. Spencer

www.365courage.blogspot.com

The cowards never started,
and the weak ones died by the way.

—American pioneer saying

Dedicated to My Children—
Henry, Eleanor, Margaret, and Page

TABLE OF CONTENTS

76. Sealing the Deal — Brownie Wise

77. Hooked — Harold Russell

78. Clocks Were Striking — George Orwell

79. Hewer of Steel — Dwight Eisenhower

80. Holey Man — Henry Moore

81. Jailed, Not Imprisoned — Nelson Mandela

82. Greatest Unconcern — Julius Caesar

83. August Decision — August Landmesser

84. Not Such an Unsufferable State — Alexander Selkirk

85. Explosive Idea — Edward Cave

86. Prayer on a Wing — Eilmer of Malmesbury

87. Man in Gear — Henry Ford

88. Faithful Dog — Captain Greg and His Companion

89. Real McCoy — Elijah McCoy

90. Start Swinging — Henry Kaiser

91. Likeness of the Truth — Charb

92. Dragon Slayer — Xernona Clayton & Calvin Craig

93. Clean Hands, Clean Conscience — Ignaz Semmelweis

94. Saintly Coincidence — Frederic Gehring

INTRODUCTION

Without fear, there is no courage; courage is the will to conquer fear. Courage and fear—flip sides of the same coin, brothers.

"I learned that courage was not the absence of fear, but the triumph over it," said Nelson Mandela, a man who knew something about courage. He spent 28 years in prison, unjustly convicted for wanting to bring liberty to his nation.

"Courage is being scared to death, but saddling up anyway," said John Wayne, a man who also knew something about perseverance. He made more than 80 of the worst westerns ever filmed before becoming a star.

Franklin Roosevelt's smile said it all. His wife Eleanor Roosevelt put it another way. "Courage," she said, "is more exhilarating than fear, and in the long run, it is easier. We do not have to become heroes overnight. Just a step at a time, meeting each thing that comes up, seeing it is not as dreadful as it appeared, discovering we have the strength to stare it down."

"Take heart, it is I. Do not be afraid," said Jesus, who brought hope to the hopeless, even in the face of death.

Courage is having heart—A brave heart, a stout heart, a strong heart. The word comes from the Latin word *cor* and then from the Old French *couer.* Both words mean heart. "Have the courage to follow your heart and your intuition," said Steve Jobs.

If the brain is cool and rational, the heart is hot and irrational. The brain may have the idea, but the heart must fire up the blood. After all, being courageous may sometimes seem mad. The vigor to fight against all odds—whether in war, in love, in business, or against illness—that is the essence of courage.

"Success is not final," said Winston Churchill. "Failure is not fatal: it is the courage to continue that counts."

Know courage, and you are the king of your soul, the queen of your one true self. Read on, and learn how 101 people—famous and little known—conquered fear. Whether they won or lost may not matter all that much. It's better to take a stand than to sit it out. What counts is that they tried and were true to humanity's highest ideals.

There are different types of courage—Physical courage in the face of fear or suffering, spiritual courage on behalf of high ideals, social courage that allows one to defy social norms, and intellectual courage. Is one type more admirable than another? The courage demanded depends on the circumstances. As Mark Twain said, "It's not the size of the dog in the fight, it's the size of the fight in the dog." All courage, regardless of the nature of the contest, is worthy of honor, and this book praises all those who doggedly persevere.

Live the courageous life, and you will live a full life.

George M. Spencer
Hanover, New Hampshire
July 2018

Chapter 1

Epictetus

Free to Choose

His master deliberately broke his leg.
But lameness only made this slave stronger.

*"Make the best of what is in our power.
Take the rest as it occurs."*

His name means "Newly acquired." In Greek, it is Epictetus (*Epic-tea-tus*). One way to translate the word might be "Slave." That is what Epictetus was, the property of his wealthy master Epaphroditus in present day Turkey. Born around 50 A.D., his real name is unknown.

Little is known about his life. He had few possessions. He had no wife and no children, although when he was elderly he adopted a child. When Epictetus was about 35, his master freed him. He then moved to Rome where he taught philosophy, and later he went to Greece. He became so well-known and respected that the Emperor Hadrian sought his counsel. He lived to be about 80, quite a long life for those times.

He owed his erudition to his owner who allowed him to be educated. Epictetus used this opportunity to become a master of a Greek school of thought which today is called Stoic philosophy. None of his writings have survived. One of his students wrote down his observations and published them under the title *Enchiridion* which means "Guidebook."

"Only Within Ourselves"

Although we think of a 'stoic' as someone who endures pain without emotion or has no feelings, that is not what it means to be a Stoic. The best way to sum up Stoicism might be the first lines of the Serenity Prayer: "God grant me the serenity to accept the things I cannot change, the courage to change the things I can, and the wisdom to know the difference."

Here is how Epictetus put it: "We have no power over external things. The good we should earnestly pursue is found only within ourselves....Don't demand that events should happen as you would like them to. If you are content to allow them to come to pass as they do, your life will be serene."

One fact is key to understanding Epictetus and his teachings—He was lame, a cripple. Some accounts say he was born that way. Other histories report he had rheumatism.

Early Christian theologian Origen tells a different tale. He wrote that Epictetus was tortured by his master. No matter how hard he twisted Epictetus' leg, he remained silent, refusing to cry in pain. He warned Epaphroditus that his leg was about to break. Then it did. "There," said Epictetus, "Didn't I tell you it would break?"

Another man might have given in to hopelessness. To be lame in the ancient world would have been a death sentence for many or a short and miserable life in the gutter begging.

Not Epictetus. He adapted his mind to his circumstances —and that may be the quintessence of his teachings. Virtue—the accumulation of good habits and beliefs (moral excellence)—is all one needs to be happy. Happiness, Epictetus believed, is not found in striving for wealth, glory, possessions, or gluttony of any form.

"Sickness impedes the body, not the will," he taught. "Lameness impedes the leg, not the will. Tell yourself this concerning all that comes to pass. If you do, you will find such things get in the way of other things, not to your *self*....

"Remember—you are an actor in a play, one that its author, not you, has written. If your role is brief, so be it. If your role is great, so be it. If it pleases the author that you play the role of a poor man, a cripple, a king, or a commoner, play that part gracefully."

MORAL: Free your *self*.

Chapter 2

Louis Armstrong

Looking So Lonesome

He played his first solo in a town run by the Klan.

"What we play is life."

Louis 'Satchmo' Armstrong was music. He was a larger than life figure so full of joy, rhythm, and melody his recordings seem barely able to contain his personality.

Armstrong must have been born happy and strong because his childhood would have broken anyone else. All his life he believed he was born on July 4, 1900, as though he was a symbol of America and a new era. (After his death, scholars learned that he was born on August 4, 1901.)

An illegitimate child, he grew up in the aptly named Battlefield district of New Orleans. He barely attended school. He made money singing in the streets and working for a junk-hauling company. He would walk alongside its wagon tooting on a tin horn to attract customers.

When he was 11, he fired a gun in the air. A judge sentenced him to a term of indefinite length at the New Orleans Home for Colored Waifs. During his three years there, he played in its orchestra. "Am always proud to tell the world of the place [that] started me out as a first-class musician," Armstrong would later say.

Returning to a rough life in the streets, he hauled coal in a wagon and even worked as a pimp, while also playing gigs at night until he was able to break into performing full time.

It's fair to say that Louis Armstrong personally created jazz. Before Armstrong, a New Orleans Dixieland group would play as a group. Lively, yes, but also restrained, even conventional to the modern ear. Armstrong used the group setting as a launching pad for his trumpet solos. They were loose yet tight, wild yet tasteful, and always fresh and always tasty. When other musicians heard his recordings, he became the man to imitate. Everyone wanted to be as free as the free-spirited Armstrong.

It's no surprise that a man as fearless as Louis Armstrong wanted to record his sound. Many jazz musicians in the early 1920s saw no point in doing so. The technology was so primitive it couldn't capture their sound, and they'd only be paid a pittance compared to what the record company would earn. Plus, musicians then were afraid competitors would steal their stuff.

Armstrong sensed though that being on records would bring new ears to his music. He didn't care where he recorded— even if it meant going into a stronghold of the Ku Klux Klan.

In April 1923, Armstrong played in King Oliver's Creole Jazz Band. Oliver told his musicians they were heading for Richmond, Indiana, a five-hour train ride from Chicago. There in early April they would cut tracks at the Gennett Record Division of the Starr Piano Company. At that time it may have been the world's largest manufacturer of pianos, making about 15,000 a year.

Its recording business was a way for the company to bring in extra revenue. The studio was as ramshackle as could be. It was a one-room wooden shack. Soundproofing consisted of sawdust on the floor and heavy drapes blanketing the walls.

The studio needed all the muffling it could get—The Whitewater River ran nearby. It's said that its rushing sound could sometimes be heard on recordings. Worse, train tracks were three feet away. Sessions often had to be halted when freight trains roared past.

All manner of now legendary musicians recorded there— band leader and composer Duke Ellington, pianists Jelly Roll Morton and Hoagy Carmichael, trumpet player Bix Beiderbecke, country music pioneers Gene Autry and Charlie Patton, and bluesman Blind Lemon Jefferson.

(In those days, jazz records were deemed so degenerate that whites-only stores sold them under the counter, and the word 'jazz' itself rarely, if ever, appeared on record sleeves. Gennett marketed its 'race' music under the heading of "Snappy

Dance Hits on Gennett Records by Exclusive Gennett Colored Artists.")

Every time Gennett recorded a group it would typically pay $15 to $50 per session. After all, the studio would be gambling on whether shoppers would buy the resulting discs.

But it did have one sure thing—a local cash-paying customer...the Ku Klux Klan. More Klan members lived in Indiana than in any other state. Somewhere between 250,000 and 500,000 Hoosiers belonged to the Klan. As many as half of all adult men in Richmond, including its mayor, belonged to the KKK.

Its members considered themselves patriotic Protestants. While the Klan's focus in the South might have been terrorizing blacks, in the Midwest the group was also known for its fiery opposition to Jewish influence in America as well as immigration, particularly by Catholics from Europe.

Because they paid us

One of the few things the Klan did like was music, and it recorded under its own KKK label. Some of its songs included numbers like *Daddy Swiped Our Last Clean Sheet and Joined the Ku Klux Klan* by the Logansport Ku Klux Klan Quartette, *Johnny, Join the Klan, Wake Up America--Kluck Kluck Kluck* and, more ominously, *There'll Be a Hot Time*.

The family-owned Gennett company held its nose while taking the Klan's money. Owner Clarence Gennett once overhead a Klan record being played in the company's reception room and told an employee to destroy it. Ezra Wickemeyer, the recording engineer who ran the studio, was Catholic. He hated the KKK. (Of course, there were no black employees at Gennett.)

In the company's defense, the owner's son later said, "We put out the [KKK] records because they paid us. That was all. We did a lot of vanity records for all kinds of people." The Klan's recordings never appeared in the catalog Gennett distributed to retailers.

Whether Wickemeyer liked black people is unknown, but when King Oliver's group came to record, he wanted to get the best possible sound out of them for his company.

He instructed the musicians to all stand in front of a giant five-foot megaphone and play directly into it. The sound would then be funneled down to a steel needle which would vibrate as its tip skimmed the surface of a spinning wax disc. The resulting nearly microscopic grooved impressions would leap back to life when the resulting disc was played at 78 revolutions per minute.

Besides the roaring, rumbling noises from outside, being in the studio was unpleasant. Bands couldn't cut loose and play at length because discs could only hold three-minutes of sound. Musicians couldn't hear each other. Because the wax had to be soft to take impressions from the needle, the room had to be kept hot. It was like playing in a sauna.

The band played a few takes, but something was wrong. Wickemeyer looked at Armstrong and told him to get away from the megaphone. He told Armstrong to stand at the far corner of the room 12 feet away. Armstrong played his horn with such power and verve that he was overwhelming the sounds of the other instruments.

The effect on Armstrong was visible to everyone. His wife Lil played piano in the band, and she recalled that "Louis was standing over there looking so lonesome. He thought it was bad for him to have to be away from the band.... I was convinced, he really can play good, because if his tone overshadows Joe [Oliver] that much, he's gotta be better."

That day the group recorded the song *Chime's Blues*. This legendary moment marked the first occasion Armstrong recorded a solo. The jaunty tune percolates along for its first two minutes. It's a toe-tapper, but nothing special. Then Armstrong kicks in. The effect is startling. "What is *that*?" one thinks.

"Suddenly [the song] fast forwards into the twentieth century," writes Lawrence Bergreen in 'Louis Armstrong: An Extravagant Life.' "His bold, ascending, trilling, metallic notes streak over the creaky proceedings like a comet. Louis demonstrates great presence; as soon as you hear his horn—jarring, fresh, jagged, and sinuous—you know he has it."

After recording, the band trooped back to the train station where they rode five-hours back to Chicago. Because of the Klan's dominance of Richmond, they couldn't safely spend the night there.

The next morning, they caught the train back and laid down more tracks, including *Dippermouth Blues*. ('Dipper' was one of Armstrong's nicknames, referring to the size of his mouth. 'Satchmo' is a shortened version of 'Satchel Mouth.")

Of that song, Bergreen writes, "He tickles the phrases, then wails and stomps, and sends them." Scholars say these renowned recordings perfectly capture the sound of New Orleans music in the 1920s. But it is Armstrong's playing that stands as a signpost to the future.

The band boldly returned to Richmond for another recording session on October 5, 1923. One disc came of the session— *Alligator Hop* and *Krooked Blues*. The Klan often held parades in in the city. By coincidence, the one that day was a record breaker.

"The largest Ku Klux Klan demonstration ever given in Wayne County was viewed last night by approximately 30,000 people," reported *The Richmond Item* newspaper. "Fully 6,000 members of the Klan participated in the monster parade, which in magnitude and impressiveness has had few equals in the city."

How Armstrong and his band got in and out of town that day is lost to history. It is sweet and fitting that the powerful band that ruled the streets that day has withered to nearly nothing, while a small band of men in a shack changed the course of music, gladdening the hearts of millions of people.

MORAL: Play your solo, but also be a team player.

Chapter 3

Grandma Moses

Lively Sparrow

Life begins at 80.

*"Life is what we make it,
always has been, always will be."*

As a little girl, Anna Mary Robertson Moses squeezed lemons and grapes to get 'colors' to paint her paper dolls. She also used sawdust, flour paste, and grass to create what she called her "lamb-scapes."

Her father was supportive, but her mother was more practical, telling her she should "spend [her] time other ways."

Her mother was right. She did have to be more practical. She had to be. Born in 1860 in Greenwich, New York, she was the third of five daughters and five sons. She only briefly attended a one-room school house. She left school—and her home—when she was 12 to do housework for a family that was better off.

She met her future husband in Staunton, Virginia, when they were both working on the same farm. They married when she was 27, and they settled in the Shenandoah Valley and had 10 children, only five of whom survived infancy. She helped support her family by churning butter. Being frugal, they were able to scrimp and save enough to buy their own farm.

After 40 years of marriage, her husband died of a heart attack in 1927 at the age of 67. Moses continued to run her family farm with the help of her children. But in 1936 she retired. That's when her family started calling her "Grandma Moses."

She had made quilts and embroidered country scenes all her life, but she finally had to stop around that time due to arthritis in her fingers. Her daughter suggested she take up painting again.

"I couldn't stand the thought of being idle," she said. At first, she copied images from postcards, then as she got more practice, she found the courage to imagine her own scenes. They were always idyllic visions of rural and farm life in Virginia and New England—harvests, country weddings, maple sap being boiled into syrup, steam-engine trains barreling down the line, prancing ponies harnessed to carriages, and townsfolk dutifully going about their business.

She first exhibited her paintings at a county fair near Eagle Bridge, New York. (She was now living with her youngest son.) She sent them along with her strawberry preserves and raspberry jam which she had entered in a competition. The jam won a pretty ribbon. Fairgoers ignored her art.

"I'll get an inspiration and start painting. Then I'll forget everything, everything except how things used to be and how to paint it, so people will know how we used to live," she said.

She created visions of an unspoiled, joyous, idyllic rural New England. "A strange thing is memory, and hope: One looks backward and the other forward. One is of today, the other of tomorrow," she said. "Memory is history recorded in our brain. Memory is a painter. It paints pictures of the past and of the day."

The truth is slightly more complicated. Like modern artists of the time like Andy Warhol, she had volumes of what she called "art secrets"—photographs, children's books, and magazine ads that she copied and traced to help her along.

She had no formal training as an artist, and perspective in her paintings is flattened with backgrounds and foregrounds all seemingly mostly one-dimensional.

"I paint from the top down," she said. "From the sky, then the mountains, then the hills, then the houses, then the cattle, and then the people."

In all her work, one senses joy and wonderment at the world. "I look out the window sometimes to seek the color of the shadows and the different greens in the trees," she said. "But when I get ready to paint I just close my eyes and imagine a scene."

Hoping to pick up a few dollars, she allowed some of her paintings to be displayed in the front window of the drug store in nearby Hoosick Falls, New York. An art collector passing through spotted them. All were priced between $3 and $5, and they had all been gathering dust for years. Sensing something special in her work, he bought them all.

Upon returning to Manhattan, he took them to prominent galleries. A year later her work appeared in a Museum of Modern Art show of "contemporary unknown painters." Her work was exhibited with her name and the label "Housewife. New York."

She became a sensation. She was an elfin charmer, just slightly over five feet tall. "Like a lively sparrow" is how her friend Norman Rockwell described her. She had a merry gleam in her eyes and wore tiny black hats and demure dresses with fine white lace collars.

Lipstick to coffee

Her work appeared on Christmas cards—an estimated 48 million Hallmark cards, and she licensed her paintings to sell everything from lipstick to coffee, wallpaper, draperies, china, and even cigarettes.

President Truman invited her to the White House in 1949 and played the piano for her. She appeared on the cover of *Time* magazine in 1953.

Norman Rockwell lived a few miles away across the river in Vermont. They became friends, and he even included her in one of his paintings—"The Homecoming," which was published on the cover of *The Saturday Evening Post* in 1949. "Grandma Moses is the cleanest woman I have ever seen," he said. "Her skin is clear as a young girl's."

When Rockwell asked to see her studio, she teased him, saying that no proper gentleman would ask to visit a lady's bedroom. She granted him admittance, and he was shocked to find that that she imbibed black coffee "incessantly" while painting.

He sketched her while she was at work. Later, when the drawing was published, she was upset to see that he included her coffee pot in the picture. She didn't want people to know she was a coffee drinker.

She became wealthy, earning an estimated $500,000 a year from licensing and selling her originals for nearly $10,000 apiece. In 2018 dollars, that's about $4 million a year. (In 2006, her painting "Sugaring Off" sold at auction for $1.2 million.)

Even though her paintings sold for thousands, Rockwell observed that she used "the same cheap brushes and house paint" she used before she was famous.

She remained humble, never getting above her 'raisings.'

"If I hadn't started painting I would have raised chickens," she once said, adding that "If you know something well, you can always paint it, but people would be better off buying chickens."

She died at age 101 in 1961. Her doctor said she just "wore out." President Kennedy eulogized her, saying "Both her work and her life helped our nation renew its pioneer heritage and recall its roots in the countryside and on the frontier."

"I painted for pleasure," she said. "To keep busy and to pass the time away, but I thought no more of it than of doing fancy work."

"I look back on my life like a good day's work," she said. "It was done, and I feel satisfied with it. I was happy and contented. I knew nothing better and made the best out of what life offered.

"And life is what we make it, always has been, always will be."

MORAL: Push the paint around.

Chapter 4

John O'Leary

Carrying the Fire

Severe burns scarred his body. His mother asked,
"Do you want to die? It's your choice, not mine."

*"You can't always choose the path that you walk in life,
but you can always choose the manner in which you walk it."*

Doctors will tell you that the worst pain is the pain caused by a burn. Now close your eyes and for a moment remember yourself as you were when you were nine-years-old. Think of all the silly, not-so-bright things you did. And think of how lucky you are to be alive.

One summer day nine-year-old John O'Leary watched older boys in his Midwestern neighborhood pour gasoline on the sidewalk and set it ablaze. 'It was amazing!' he thought. So John got some matches, and he went in his family's garage. He set a scrap of cardboard on fire. Then he went to a five-gallon can of gasoline. He wanted to tilt it so the gas would pour onto the cardboard.

But the can was too heavy for him to tilt. So, he put the burning cardboard on the garage floor. Then he knelt to the can and put his arms around it. Now he could tilt the spout towards the fire.

Everything exploded. A human torch, John tore into his home. His older brother tackled him and wrapped him in a rug, extinguishing the flames.

The Damage Was Done

Too late. The damage was done. One-hundred percent of John's body was burned, and 87 percent of those burns were third degree.

This is supposed to kill anyone, especially a child, but John was not just anyone. Nor was his mother. In the hospital—on the day he was burned—she told him, "John, do you want to die? It's your choice, not mine."

That is tough love.

He spent the next five months in the hospital, mostly strapped helpless to a bed to help his skin heal properly. His tiny fingers became infected. They were all amputated.

Many surgeries and much physical therapy and many years later, John became a hospital chaplain. Today he is an inspirational speaker and author. He's married, and he has four children. And he can play a dandy version of "Amazing Grace" on the piano. Without fingers.

He thrives—being "on fire" is what he calls it—because in his mind, he used his courage to make a choice, the choice his mother set before him. He could have had a bad attitude which might have made death more likely. Or he could be grateful for the gift of life itself. He could be grateful that being alive means he has the ability to choose what attitude he will wake up with.

"Take a Good Look"

One day in the hospital a doctor at his bedside asked a janitor named Lavelle to come over. "Take a good look at this little boy," the doctor said. "Lavelle, you are keeping him alive."

John couldn't understand what the doctor meant—How could a janitor be saving his life? It turns out that in hospitals, infection kills more burn patients than anything else. Keeping the room clean kept John healthy. More important, having a good attitude in what might seem a lowly job saves lives.

Have the courage to care about even the simplest, smallest thing in your life. It may be the biggest, greatest thing to someone else. So, what's at the end of your broom?

MORAL: Be in the moment.

Chapter 5

Werner Forssmann

Push for Success

The human heart is tougher than we think.

"There is a measure of justice."

In 1879, surprising as it may seem, doctors had yet to fully understand how the heart worked as a pump. In that year three French physiologists conducted what was then a most peculiar experiment. They threaded a catheter into a horse's jugular vein and then into the animal's heart. Once there, they inflated the balloon's tip. Why? To see if the horse's ventricle was contracting. It was. They published the result of this experiment in their book *Lecons de Physiogie Operatoire.*

Fifty years later a German surgical resident Werner Forssmann, 25, found a dusty copy of the book in the cupboard of the house he was renting. He became obsessed with the description of the experiment and its accompanying pictures. He tore the drawings out of the book and carried them everywhere.

At this time there no such thing as open-heart surgery. Doctors regarded the heart as a type of sacred chamber, one so fragile that they rarely, if ever, performed experiments on it, much less procedures on patients.

Forssmann was not like his peers. He likely asked himself, "What could doctors do if they could see inside a beating heart? Could you insert a catheter into a heart, inject dye, and then X-ray the organ—all without harming a patient? In what unimaginable ways might patients' lives be saved?"

Only on rabbits

He asked a senior physician, a Dr. Schneider, if he could explore this notion. Yes, he was told, but you may only experiment on rabbits. When he asked his supervisor if he could perform this experiment on humans, namely himself, his boss replied, "Drop this suicidal idea. What could I tell your mother if one day we should find you dead?" After all, the senior physician believed such catheters might become tangled in patients' hearts and kill them.

Undeterred, Forssmann practiced on cadavers and then enlisted (or perhaps seduced) an accomplice, an operating room nurse named Gerda Ditzen. "[I] prowl[ed] around her like a sweet-toothed cat around the cream jug," he later wrote. He told her that he would perform the procedure on her and that it would be absolutely harmless.

Whether Ditzen was seduced by the notion of furthering science or was otherwise seduced, she agreed, and the two of them went to a procedure room. Once there, she obtained the necessary equipment, especially a urethral catheter. (Of course, at that time cardiac catheterization equipment had yet to be invented.)

 Forssmann then strapped her arms and legs to the exam table. This is not as lurid as it sounds. Forssmann needed her help because only she had the keys to unlock the surgical supplies he needed. As a lowly resident, he wasn't trusted with such access.

He pretended to ready her for the experiment. Once she was unable to stop him, he numbed his own arm and inserted the tubing deep into his body—but not quite into his heart. Once she realized what was going on, she struggled to free herself and yelled for him to stop.

Now Forssmann had another problem. In his enthusiasm to perform the experiment, he realized they were in a room that had no X-ray machine. Thus, there would be no proof he had catheterized himself. So, as soon as he freed the nurse, the two of them walked down to the hospital's basement—with the tube stuck near his heart.

Once there, one of Forssmann's colleagues tried to rip out the catheter. Instead, Forssmann overcame him. He pushed the catheter into his heart, and X-rays were taken.

At first, Dr. Schneider was furious. But then he relented and took the young doctor out to celebrate at a "low-ceiling wine tavern" where waiters were impeccably attired.

Forssmann published the results of this and follow-up experiments. The resulting publicity got him fired from a new job as a surgeon in a different hospital. The chief of surgery resented his showboating.

And that ended Forssmann's career as a surgeon. "The time was not yet ripe for this discovery," he wrote, and in the early 1930s Forssmann became a urologist.

"A more critical distance"

After Hitler came to power, Forssmann also joined the Nazi Physicians League. While working in a Berlin prison in 1943, he tried but failed to convince the warden to allow him to sedate political prisoners before they were executed.

Perhaps more chilling, in 1937 Forssmann met Karl Gebhardt, the personal doctor of SS chief Heinrich Himmler. Along with Hitler, Himmler was the mastermind behind the Holocaust, and Gebhardt was later convicted of crimes against humanity at the Nuremberg Trials and executed. Gebhardt knew of Forssmann's cardiac research and offered to supply with him with subjects for human experimentation. Forssmann refused.

According to Forssmann's personal correspondence during the war (and with Jewish colleagues in the 1960s), while he was infatuated with Nazism in the early 1930s, he "developed a more critical distance to Nazi ideology," according to a paper in *Urologia Internationalis*.

Forssmann "will be remembered as the man who saved many innocent victims from the Nazis," according to a review of his autobiography in the British Medical Journal.

After being captured at the end of the war and put in a POW camp, Forssmann became a lumberjack and then a country doctor.

On October 11, 1956, while having a drink in a beer hall after work, his wife called to tell him to rush home. Someone with a foreign accent had called. He continued drinking and arrived home late at night. Someone else called. He refused to take the phone call.

The next day he performed two operations. He heard that two Americans had received the Nobel Prize for their work in the field of cardiac catheterization. Accounts vary, but Forssmann felt either crestfallen or numb. All his life his groundbreaking research had been ignored.

Then the head of the hospital burst into the operating room. There was good news—Forssmann had also won a Nobel Prize.

"I feel like a village parson who has just learned that he has been made bishop," Forssmann said. "It seems that sometimes there is a measure of justice in our world."

MORAL: Get to the heart of the matter.

Chapter 6

Dolly Shepherd

Aw, Chute!

She jumped in a big way.

"Good and proper!"

Buffalo Bill Cody's wife was no fool. She was part of his act in his Wild West show. When they were touring London in 1903, one of his trick shots went awry. Mrs. Buffalo Bill was supposed to stand still with a plaster egg on top of her head while Buffalo shot it off. Except this time, his bullet put a crease in her scalp.

She wisely decided to depart the stage with her hair neatly and newly parted. Now a volunteer was needed. Fearless sixteen-year-old Elizabeth Shepherd came forward. She took Mrs. Cody's spot, but legend has it she became a little disconcerted when she saw Cody's daughter blindfolding her father.

Nonetheless, with a bang, she became part of his act and changed her name to Dolly Shepherd.

(At least this is what one legend says. Another account says she wanted to see John Philip Sousa's band perform but had no money for a ticket. She got work as a waitress at the exhibition grounds. Its location gave her a view of the stage, and she overheard a pair of diners saying the job of human target was available. There could not have been too many candidates for the position.)

For whatever reasons, Dolly, like Mrs. Cody, also decided that she did not want him shooting a plaster egg on her head. It turned out that Cody was also an inventor. This was the year 1903. Everyone had aviation fever. Cody was working on building giant kites, especially one that would be large enough to take a person aloft, and he wanted this contraption to become part of his show.

While doing research, Cody took her to the workshop of a French balloon maker. Months later, he asked her to return. He asked to feel her grip. Finding that it was strong, he asked her to hang from a trapeze, but not the sort of trapeze one might imagine.

Soon enough, Dolly chose a different and possibly safer way to thrill crowds—She did parachute jumps from smoke balloons.

Here is how it worked: A pit would be dug, and a fire would be started in it. Then the sack of a balloon would be suspended above the blaze so the rising hot smoky air would inflate it. A parachute would be attached to the bottom of the balloon.

A daredevil, preferably a lovely maiden, would grab hold of a trapeze bar suspended below the balloon. The balloon would rise to a height of 1,000 to 4,000 feet with the girl dangling below it.

When she let go, the balloon was designed in such a way so that when her weight was gone, it would naturally deflate.

"When you pulled the rip cord that pulls the balloon almost in half, a sandbag pulls the balloon down, and you come down," she recalled years later.

"You couldn't say you were coming down in a particular spot," said Dolly. "You had to go where the wind took you. I've been on top of a chimney, over trees." One time she nearly landed on top of an express train. "That driver—he had some forethought and blew the steam and just blew me off into the canal at Bantham. Ah, yes, that was quite a nice time," said Dolly.

She saw one girl fall to her death when she landed on top of the roof of a factory but was dragged over its edge by her parachute.

Why did Dolly like parachuting? She is said to have once remarked that if she had to die, she wanted it to be from a high altitude. "I'd like to be killed completely—good and proper!" she said.

Not surprisingly, she herself was nearly killed on at least two occasions. One time, the balloon rose out of control. To make matters worse, she could not get her parachute to detach. The air grew colder and the oxygen thinner, until finally at 15,000 or even 18,000 feet she leapt to safety.

A massive electric shock

In 1908 she was doing a dual jump. The other girl's parachute tangled and would not detach from the balloon. Dolly wrenched the girl out of her harness and commanded her to wrap herself around her.

That became the world's first tandem parachute jump. Because Dolly's parachute was only designed for one person, they fell far too fast. When they hit the ground, Dolly hit first, and the other girl landed on top of her. The result? She was paralyzed. To cure her, a doctor thought giving her a massive electric shock would be just the thing. It worked.

For this amazing rescue, Dolly won a place in the Guinness Book of World Records.

While she recuperated, it's said that her mother did the jumps for her—pretending to be her. Her aerial adventures ended one day when an eerie voice in her head said, "Don't come up again, or you'll be killed." Consequently, she took up a safer occupation. She went to France during World War I and became a truck mechanic and driver. She died peacefully at the age of 96.

Thrill seeking runs in the Shepherd family. To honor her mother, her daughter Molly Sedgwick did a parachute jump on her 83rd birthday. It was her fifth. "I thoroughly enjoyed it before, and each time it has been a thrill and a wonderful experience," she said.

MORAL: Take a flying leap.

Chapter 7

Henri Matisse

Wild Beast

He made beautiful pictures—
despite the pain.

"When you can or not, you hold on."

Painter and sculptor Henri Matisse was a wild beast and a frail one, too.

He had a strong constitution—in matters both large and small—that served him well. He kept a fastidious schedule. He would typically rise with the sun so he could paint all morning. After lunch, he would return to his easel. Afterwards, he practiced playing his violin. Following a light dinner, he would retire early.

Matisse's willpower served him well throughout his life's many trials, especially chronic health problems that might have crushed a lesser man. After all, this was a man who was born in a cottage that had a dirt floor and a leaky roof. All through his life, he said that rain dripped through the roof onto the bed he was born in.

He was never able to please his father, a grain wholesaler who also owned a hardware store. He thought his son was a failure. Because he was sickly, his father did not think he was man enough to go into the family business. Another son took that role, and Henri was sent to law school. He hated it.

When Henry was a 21-year-old law clerk in 1889, he was hospitalized for an ailment. Historians disagree about what it might have been. Some say it was colitis, an ulcer, or appendicitis. Another theory is that he got a hernia lifting heavy sacks of his father's grain.

While he was in the hospital recuperating, the patient in the bed next to him suggested that he try 'chromos' to while away the hours. Chromos were a sort of 19th-century paint-by-number activity.

A beast that plunges

"The moment I had this box of colors in my hands, I knew this was my life," Matisse recalled. "I threw myself into it like a beast that plunges towards the thing it loves." (This was actually not his first exposure to painting. His father's store sold house paint. Henri's mother mixed them before they were sold, and he often observed her at work and helped her.)

When he returned to the law offices, he felt aimless. But now he rose before the sun to attend an art class. Then he rushed home from work to paint before dinner, and he painted in the evening, too.

Finally, he screwed up his courage and asked his parents if they would consent to his studying art in Paris. His father was livid. When Matisse left on the train, his father stood on the platform, shaking his fists at his son, yelling, "You'll starve!" He was now an utter embarrassment to his family.

Of his early years in Paris, Matisse recalled that he felt like an animal stumbling around in a dark forest. He was lucky enough to have a stern teacher who told him "No amount of willpower, perseverance, or doggedness in later years can ever make up for lack of technique."

He married a well-to-do woman and started a family. He achieved some minor success, but soon his father-in-law suffered a financial disaster (An employee had defrauded his company, and he was blamed.)

Thanks to his legal training, Matisse was able to help defend his father-in-law. But the experience left him so exhausted he was ordered to rest for two months. He became so depressed he considered putting down his paint brushes forever.

Fortune smiled on him. He had visited the south of France, and the quality of the light there—plus his growing maturity and self-assurance as an artist—brought a bold, dynamic, bright quality to his work.

In 1905, he proclaimed himself to the world as a Fauvist. (*Fauves* means 'wild beast' in French.) Such works have an Impressionist feel, but their colors are more vivid and unreal. His exhibition with Georges Braque and Raoul Dufy was received with great hostility. But because intellectual Gertrude Stein bought one of his works, he felt that he had finally arrived. The next year he would meet Picasso. He was on his way.

Soon his health plagued him again. When he was in his 40s, he lived a village best by constant winds. He came down with bronchitis. In 1917, he felt his health would improve if he moved to Nice where the weather was better.

But when he arrived there, it commenced to rain for a solid month. Weary, Matisse was about to pull up stakes again, but the next day, sunshine ruled the skies, and he decided to make Nice his home, and he lived there for the next 37 years.

Call on stubbornness

In 1940, the year the Nazis invaded and conquered France, Matisse was 70. He had outlived many of his peers, and he faced his greatest crisis. The next year he was diagnosed with intestinal cancer. Surgery successfully dealt with the tumor, but the complications were severe—a prolapsed stomach and two pulmonary embolisms.

He faced down this trial. "When you're out of will power, you call on stubbornness," he said.

For the rest of his life, Matisse was an invalid. He could only stand for brief periods. From then on, he painted while sitting up in bed or from his wheelchair. He even drew on the ceiling and walls, using charcoal fastened to the tip of a bamboo fishing pole. He also began doing paper cut-outs. "I call this drawing with scissors," he said.

Not long after the surgery, gallstones tormented him. They caused terrible pain, fever, and jaundice. His doctors again advised surgery to remove his gall bladder. But the complications from the first surgery had been so horrendous, Matisse chose to soldier through his agonies. He would spend six months in bed until the episode passed.

Matisse was grateful for his trials. They opened new doors to greater creativity. He called the years following his cancer *Un seconde vie*— A second life.

"I have needed all that time to reach the stage where I can say what I want to say," Matisse said. "Only what I created after the illness constitutes my real self: Free, liberated."

But that's not all. Matisse struggled with horrendous eye problems in the final decades of his life. In 1908, he was diagnosed with cataracts in both eyes. "Reds had begun to look muddy," he said. "My painting was getting more and more darkened."

His eyesight deteriorated so badly that he could only paint by memorizing where he had squeezed out colors onto his palette. By 1918 he had to read the labels on tubes of paint to know what colors he was applying to the canvas.

"I am almost blind," he said in 1922. By then he had gone blind in his left eye.

Following eye surgery in 1923, he could now see how wretched his recent work was. He threw away most of the canvases he had painted for the past 10 years.

His perception of color became distorted in his remaining good eye. A rare disorder, xantopsia, gave everything he saw a yellow tint. (It was partially corrected through special eyeglasses.) He told friends it took two years before he could again see colors as they truly were.

Matisse lived for 13 years after his cancer surgery and for more than 30 years after his eye surgery. He created some of his most acclaimed works during that period.

He saw more clearly now than ever. Said Matisse: "The time you live from now on is a gift from life itself—each year, each month, each day."

MORAL: See better.

Chapter 8

Robert Garrett

Spun Gold

Was his success beginner's luck
or supreme confidence?

"I wanted as much action as I could since it meant fun."

Imagine winning an Olympic gold medal for an event you've never competed in—and have barely practiced for. That's what happened when the captain of the Princeton track team Robert Garrett decided to enter the discus competition in the first modern Olympics held in Athens in 1896.

Hardly anyone in America had heard of the event much less ever held a discus. In fact, before coming to Greece, Garrett had never even put his hands on a real discus.

Having no idea how big or heavy ancient discuses were, he and a Princeton classics professor found a description of one in the writings of Lucian, a second-century Greek satirist. "A lump of brass, circular and not unlike a small shield," wrote Lucian.

That was all Garrett knew, and that was all he knew to tell the blacksmith he went to. The result? A 30-pound, 12-inch diameter beast that Garrett could barely lift much less throw. ("I guess he miscalculated a bit," his grandson would later say.) But he did try whirling this manhole-cover sized thing a few times, including on the ship while crossing the Atlantic. He wasn't worried about not entering the discus event—his sports were shot put, high jump, long jump, and standing triple jump.

Garrett thought he might have more time to practice after arriving in Europe. But planning for the Olympics in 1896 was not quite what it is today. The American contingent of 13 athletes thought the games were going to start on April 18. Instead, upon disembarking in Naples to their horror they learned the Greeks used the archaic Julian calendar, and the games were actually opening far sooner—on April 6.

With only days to spare, they crossed Italy overland, caught a ship to Greece, and took a 10-hour train ride to Athens. Garrett and his fellow athletes then immediately went to Panathenaic Stadium to familiarize themselves with area. Lo and behold, he found a discus lying on the ground. To his amazement, it only weighed about five pounds and had an eight-inch diameter. He tossed it a few times. Having won another athlete's permission to practice with his discus, then and there he decided to enter the event.

This took courage, especially because the favorite in the event was local hero Panagiotis Paraskevopoulos. His nickname? "Discus demigod." The correspondent for *The New York Herald* wrote, "Garrett entered the arena unknown and unheralded ....The Athenians gazed with pity."

The event took place on opening day. Garrett's first throw went awry and barely went anywhere. His second hurl was equally pathetic.

American competitor Thomas Custis described the competition this way: "His first two attempts... were laughable, as the discus, instead of sailing parallel to the ground, turned over and over and narrowly missed hitting some of the audience. Both foreigners and Americans laughed at his efforts, and he himself joined in the merriment.

"On his third and last throw, however, he succeeded in getting the discus away perfectly and, to the chagrin of the Greek champion who had made three perfect throws in the most graceful manner possible, it was found that Garrett's throw exceeded by some two feet the best throw of any other man. I think no one was more surprised than Robert Garrett himself."

A true Princeton tiger, Garrett had whipped his discus 95 feet and eight inches. That was seven-and-a-half inches further than the best the 'demigod' could do, and to everyone's amazement, Garrett had won the gold, one of four he would take home. His spin job set a new world's record.

The Greeks "were overwhelmed by the superior skill and daring of the Americans to whom they ascribed a supernatural invincibility enabling them to dispense with training and to win at games they had never before seen," wrote travelogue writer Burton Holmes.

Sixty years later, Garrett told a newspaper reporter, "I wanted as much action as I could, since it meant fun. I got into the discus thing never figuring I'd do anything but finish an absolute last."

MORAL: Take a spin.

Chapter 9

Betsy Ross

Thimble Pleasures

She eloped to a New Jersey bar. But when a man in uniform
came calling, this gutsy gal found her guy.

She eloped to New Jersey and married her first husband
John Ross in a bar. Her church then promptly excommunicated
her. He belonged to a different denomination, and he may have
been mentally ill. When Ross died shortly thereafter, she wasted
no time marrying again. And when that man died in a foreign
prison, she married the man who had told her the bad news.

She was Betsy Ross of Philadelphia, and she her own
woman. She ran her own business—a rarity for the time. In her
final years, she loved nothing more than dipping snuff while
sitting with the Bible in her lap.

Did she invent the design of the first American flag?
Probably not. Did she sew the first American flag? Maybe. But as
an exemplar of a courageous woman ahead of her time, she did a
banner job.

In the early days of the American Revolution, the
colonials dreamed up different flags. Some showed a British
Union Jack on a red field. Others had a Union Jack with stripes. A
coiled rattlesnake appeared on one flag above the words "Don't
Tread on Me."

General Washington loathed all American flags containing
the Union Jack. Said the future President: "I presume [the British
soldiers] begin to think it strange [upon seeing those flags] that
we have not made a formal surrender of our lines."

In June 1777, the Continental Congress passed a law
mandating that the new nation's flag consist of 13 alternating
red and white stripes with a blue field containing 13 stars.
Lawyers being lawyers, the law said nothing about how the
design would be arranged.

"Modesty and Self-Reliance"

Nearly 100 years later in 1870, William Canby, Ross's grandson, told a Pennsylvania historical society a story that was remarkable, all the more so because he was only 11 when his grandmother died.

"Sitting sewing in her shop one day with her girls around her, several gentlemen entered. She recognized one of these as the uncle of her deceased husband, Col. George Ross, a delegate from Pennsylvania to Congress. She also knew the handsome form and features of the dignified, yet graceful and polite Commander-in-Chief, who, while he was yet Colonel Washington had visited her shop both professionally and socially many times (a friendship caused by her connection with the Ross family) they announced themselves as a committee of congress, and stated that they had been appointed to prepare a flag, and asked her if she thought she could make one, to which she replied, with her usual modesty and self-reliance, that "she did not know but she could try; she had never made one but if the pattern were shown to her she had not doubt of her ability to do it."

At the time, Ross was an upholsterer. It was a different profession than the one we know today. She would have been sewing blankets and tents, repairing uniforms, and making cartridges colonial soldiers used in their muskets. (These were paper tubes in which musket balls were wrapped.) Upholsterers also made flags.

Historians agree that it is likely the visitors, whoever they were, showed her a design. Her family's account says that she liked the design except that the proposed flag had six-pointed stars. Ross said they were too much trouble to sew. The gentlemen disagreed, but by swiftly folding a piece of paper and making a few deft cuts, she showed them how easy it would be for her to manufacture stars with five points. Apparently, they agreed, the resulting evidence being on every American flag.

(Recent research has determined that Francis Hopkinson, a signer of the Declaration of Independence who represented

New Jersey at the Continental Congress, created the design that she saw.)

Born Elizabeth Griscom on January 1, 1752, she was the eighth of 17 children. Her family liked to say she was "born on the first day of the month, the first day of the year, the first day of the new style," because the new Gregorian calendar had just been adopted. It kept better track of leap years.

She was a Quaker. Her first husband was an Episcopal. They had apprenticed together in the same upholstery shop for five years. For whatever reasons, they made their away across the Delaware River and were married in Hugg's Tavern in New Jersey, and their marriage license was signed by Ben Franklin's son.

As a Quaker, she was forbidden to marry outside of her church. When the elders asked her to meet with them, she refused to admit she had done anything wrong by marrying an Episcopalian. What's more, she told them she would attend his church from then on. Her parents were censured for their inability to control her, and they apologized. The local Quaker records describe Ross as being "undutiful" and "Disorderly."

Changing churches proved auspicious for Ross. One account has it that she met Washington during Episcopal church services and thereafter embroidered ruffles for his shirt fronts and cuffs. No one knows whether this is true or not, just as there is no independent record of Ross and Washington ever meeting. This particular tale comes from Ross' daughter who also said he "had often been in her house in friendly visits, as well as on business," though she had not been born then.

Two years later in 1775, John Ross was dead. Some say he died in a gunpowder explosion while guarding a munitions at a wharf. Unfortunately, there is no record of any such disaster. When Betsy was elderly, she made cryptic references to her late husband's questionable sanity; his mother had spent years in an asylum.

After a year and a half, Ross married ship captain Joseph Ashburn in 1777. While he was at sea, the British surrendered to Washington at Yorktown in 1781. Then in April 1782, she picked up a newspaper which contained a list of the names of men captured at sea by the British during the winter of 1780. Her husband's name was on that list.

One Common Thread

How he died no one knows, though an account says he "bore with amazing fortitude retaining his senses till the last moment of his life."

Strangely, John Claypoole, the man who would become her third husband, informed Ross of her spouse's death. He, too, had also gone to sea and had also been imprisoned with Ashburn. She married Claypoole in 1783 after being a widow for only 14 months. He was Quaker, and together they ran an upholstery shop.

One common thread, so to speak, in Ross' life was her work as an upholsterer. She sewed for six decades. Her shop did more than make clothes. In those days establishments such as hers sold fine furniture, wallpaper, textiles, mattresses, and curtains. It was a stable—and lucrative—profession. After her husband had a stroke, she became the family's sole breadwinner and did so with four daughters at home under the age of 16.

She now began to regularly attend Quaker meetings, though towards the end of her life, these had so few attendees—only her and one other person—that the congregation disbanded.

The last three years of her life she was blind. The cause is unknown. Perhaps the demands of detailed sewing ruined her vision. She died in her sleep at the age of 84.

**MORAL: Keep people in stitches,
and they'll always remember you.**

Chapter 10

Franz Kafka

Heart of My Burrow

Had anyone else ever shared such
dark secrets?

"For writing means revealing oneself to excess..."

Management expert Peter Drucker believed that Franz Kafka invented the hard hat construction workers wear. How ironic it would be if that were true (and there is no evidence to prove that it is), because if anyone in human history would have had a safe or a steel girder fall on him, it would have been Kafka, and, of course, the hat would have done him no good.

It should surprise no one that Kafka's work as an insurance claims analyst in Prague often involved investigating claims by workers whose fingers had been scissored off or legs mangled into jelly by industrial accidents.

During his short and exceedingly unhappy life, Kafka, who died of tuberculosis at age 40 in 1924, wrote stories and novels that are the quintessence of dread. Misery, shame, claustrophobia, self-loathing, disgust, horror, anguish, fear, anxiety—all describe what one feels when reading his tales of existential meaninglessness.

In some respects, Kafka was a coward. He lived most of his life under the same roof as his overbearing, selfish father, suffering in silence in their cramped apartment.

His love life might best be described as excruciatingly excruciating. Engaged to marry three times, he had low self-esteem and feared sexual encounters, once writing that he perceived of "coitus as punishment for the happiness of being together." He also said that "the idea of a honeymoon trip fills me with horror." No wonder that a character in the movie 'Annie

Hall' says to Woody Allen's character "Sex with you is really a Kafkaesque experience."

Kafka could not even find joy in his own creativity, once telling his diary, "The story came out of me like a real birth, covered with filth and slime."

"Be quiet, still, and solitary"

He wanted only to be left alone to write—"You do not need to leave your room. Remain sitting at your table and listen. Do not even listen, simply wait, be quiet, still and solitary. The world will freely offer itself to you to be unmasked, it has no choice, it will roll in ecstasy at your feet."

The greatness of Kafka's work comes thanks to his courage—the bravery with which he revealed his tortured soul on paper. One of his friends praised him for his "absolute truthfulness."

As Kafka wrote in his diary "For writing means revealing oneself to excess; that utmost of self-revelation and surrender, in which a human being, when involved with others, would feel he was losing himself, and from which, therefore, he will always shrink as long as he is in his right mind."

Writing was what his lived for, he yet felt that writing itself was akin to dying. "My talent for portraying my dreamlike inner life has thrust all other matters into the background," he wrote. "My life has dwindled dreadfully, nor will it cease to dwindle...I waver on the heights; it is not death, alas, but the eternal torments of dying." Yet Kafka also called the hours he spent writing "a form of prayer."

Guilt and punishment obsessed him. The central theme of his works is that individuals, through no fault of their own, must suddenly pay for crimes whose nature is never known. To Kafka, it was as if life itself was a punishment and that brutal chastisement served no purpose and had no meaning.

In *Der Process* (The Trial), Josef K. is arrested by unknown authorities. Neither he or the reader is ever told what crime he has committed. When the story ends, he is stabbed to death. His last words are "Like a dog!"

Die Verwandlung (Metamorphosis) begins with the sentence: "When Gregor Samsa woke up one morning from unsettling dreams, he found himself changed in his bed into a monstrous vermin." Not necessarily a beetle as is commonly believed but something worse —"a vermin."

Trapped in his room, he either disgusts his relatives or is ignored by them, until his father attacks him. "No plea of Gregor's availed, indeed none was understood; however meekly he twisted his head his father only stamped the harder." Finally, the father kills him by hurling apples at him, one of which becomes embedded in his flesh.

In *der Strafkolonie* (In the Penal Colony) an explorer is shown 'the harrow,' an instrument which embroiders into a prisoner's flesh the text of the rule he has disobeyed.

"My guiding principle is this: guilt is never to be doubted. The prisoner is never told the nature of his crime," says the officer who runs the machine and who decides to submit himself to it. "There would be no point in announcing it to him. You see, he gets to know it in the flesh."

Although Kafka wrote this story between 1914 and 1919, one sees in it and in many of his other works a foreboding of what was to come in Europe in the following decades. In *Der Bau* (The Burrow), he writes of a mole-like creature who dwells in a sealed-off underground labyrinth of tunnels and chambers. "I live in peace in the heart of my burrow, and meanwhile from somewhere or other the enemy is boring his way slowly towards me."

His three sisters Ottla, Valli, and Elli were murdered by the Nazis. All were deported from Czechoslovakia to Poland. Elli and Valli died in the Lodz Ghetto, the second largest ghetto the Nazis created in Poland. His favorite sister Ottla was taken to Theresienstadt concentration camp. She volunteered to accompany 1,260 children as part of a "special transport" to Auschwitz where she was killed.

"Man cannot live without a permanent trust in something indestructible within himself," Kafka wrote. "Though both that indestructible something and his own trust in it may remain permanently concealed from him. One of the ways in which this hiddenness can express itself is through faith in a personal god."

**MOTTO: If you think you are vermin,
you're having a bad dream.
In reality, you are a tiger, a butterfly, or a rose.**

Chapter 11

James Havens

Safe Havens

A father wouldn't give up.
If he did, his son would die.

"I can do it!"

When Jim Havens was 14, he wanted to grow up to be an artist, but now he was too ill to sit up, much less hold a paintbrush. It was May 1922, and he was dying as he lay on the family sofa in Rochester, New York. He was skin-and-bones, gripped with pains in his legs, terribly hungry, and subsisting on a near starvation diet ordered by his doctor.

Eight years had passed since Jim had received his death sentence—diabetes. In 1914 when he was diagnosed, most people died within weeks or months of learning their fate. Few survived more than a year or two. Yet the strong-willed Jim had managed to finish school and three years of college.

His family's doctor had given up. Nothing else could be done. Perhaps Jim was ready to go, too. But his father James was a battler. A former congressman, he was the chief attorney at the Eastman Kodak company, the manufacturer of film and incredibly popular and inexpensive "Brownie" cameras. Ever since his son had fallen ill, James had researched the disease and communicated with anyone and everyone to try to save his son's life.

Diabetes has afflicted mankind since ancient times and was known to physicians in India, China, and Egypt as early as 1500 B.C. Its symptoms include excessive thirst and frequent urination. In fact, the word 'diabetes' comes from a Greek term meaning to "pass through."

It was the sugar killer. Doctors noticed that ants were attracted to the urine of those with diabetes due to its high sugar content. The technical name of the disease is *diabetes mellitus*, the latter word being a derivation of the Latin word for honey.

"The patient is short-lived…The melting is rapid, the death speedy," wrote the 2nd century A.D. Greek physician Aretaeus of Cappadocia. Thomas Willis, a British physician in the 1700s, called diabetes "the pissing evil." But like so many physicians before him, he had no idea "why the urine [of those afflicted] is wonderfully sweet like sugar or honey."

It was not until 1889 when experiments with dogs led doctors to understand that the disease had something to do with the pancreas. In 1920 Frederick Banting, a young Toronto surgeon, became curious about the relationship between the pancreas and how the body processes carbohydrates and sugar.

He and fellow physician Charles Best extracted material from an area in the pancreases of dogs called the islets of Langerhans. They named the resulting processed liquid 'insulin' meaning "of the islands" in Latin.

It so happened that George Snowball, the manager of a Kodak store in Toronto, visited Havens one day in his Rochester office. Desperate, Havens asked Snowball if he could help. He said he would ask a fellow golfer who was a doctor at the University of Toronto's medical school.

He gave Snowball no hope—not a chance in Hell, perhaps—but the manager was persistent. He met other physicians at the med school. It turned out that one of them— Frederick Banting—was experimenting with dogs and had isolated the newly named insulin.

When Snowball and Havens learned that it was being used experimentally in Canada on humans, Havens went into high gear, and the Havens' family doctor cajoled a few doses from Banting to give to young Jim.

Even when there were no positive results, Snowball wouldn't give up. He told Banting he would personally pay his air fare if he would fly to Rochester. Upon arriving, he began injecting Jim with larger doses every two hours. After many hours and many injections, Jim's test results showed there was no sugar in his blood.

"How do you feel?" Banting asked the young man. "Try sitting up."

At first, Jim didn't think he could. At last, he lifted himself off the sofa. "I can do it!" he exclaimed. "I do feel better!"

That day for lunch he ate a normal meal, and the pains in his legs had vanished.

Jim achieved his goal of becoming an artist and lived to be 60. He became a painter, illustrator, and sculptor renowned for his wildlife scenes, and today his work is in the collections of the Metropolitan Museum in New York and the Library of Congress.

Banting and Best won the Nobel Prize in 1923. By that year, insulin was being produced in massive quantities and saving thousands of lives. Today, largely due to modern dietary woes, more than 25 percent of Americans over the age of 65 have diabetes, according to the Centers for Disease Control, and if current trends continue within 30 years as many as one in three people in the U.S. may have the disease.

MORAL: Keep searching.
There may be a Snowball's chance.

Chapter 12

John Cage

He Pulled Strings

It takes a bold man to play a piano
with a fish.

"I only learn what to do when I have failures."

If anyone was ever born with the wrong name, it was the composer John Cage. His art was uncaged. No other 20th century composer did as many things in as many radical ways that overthrew so many ways in which people thought about music.

His most famous—or notorious—composition is *4'33"*. In it, a "performer" sits at a piano (or stands by a piano) and does not play for four minutes and 33 seconds (or for some indeterminate length of time).

The composition is divided into three movements. Their parts are divided by the opening and closing of the keyboard lid. The music of the "performance" is the sounds the audience hears in the absence of "music."

At its 1952 premiere, a critic wrote, "You could hear the wind stirring outside during the first movement. During the second, raindrops began pattering the roof, and during the third, people themselves made all kinds of interesting sounds as they talked or walked out."

"Let sounds be just sounds," Cage believed. He was a student of Zen Buddhism and the I Ching which divines the future through random interactions. Cage devoted his life to exploring the principle that "the purpose of music is to sober and quiet the mind, thus making it susceptible to divine influences."

He inherited his zest for the unconventional from his father, an eccentric inventor who, among other things, wanted to find a way to "travel in space without the use of fuel." His father told him, "If someone says *can't*, that shows you what to do."

In grade school, other children called him a sissy. "People would lie and wait for me and beat me up," he said. (After a brief marriage, Cage acknowledged his true self, and he and choreographer Merce Cunningham, with whom he collaborated artistically, became life-long partners.)

Cage's high school yearbook contains the inscription: "Noted for: being radical."

As one might imagine, he quickly dropped out of college. "I was shocked...to see one hundred of my classmates in the library all reading copies of the same book," Cage wrote. "Instead of doing as they did, I went into the stacks and read the first book written by an author whose name began with Z. I received the highest grade in the class. That convinced me that the institution was not being run correctly. I left."

Instead of sitting in a regimented classroom, he traveled to Europe. On a street corner in Spain, he noticed "the multiplicity of simultaneous visual and audible events all going together in one's experience and producing enjoyment." Said Cage: "It was the beginning for me of theater and circus."

After returning home, Cage studied for two years under avant-garde composer Arnold Schoenberg. After two years, they both realized Cage had no sense of harmony. Schoenberg told him he would be a failure as a composer.

"Why?" Cage asked.

"You'll come to a wall and won't be able to get through," Schoenberg replied.

Cage shot back: "Then I'll spend my life knocking my head against that wall."

True to his art, he spent many years in near poverty. From the mid-1950s to the late 1960s, he lived in a two-room cabin in rural New York. He received no income from *4'33"* and earned little or nothing from his music during that period. He didn't even have a music publisher. He supplemented what little income he had by supplying restaurants with mushrooms. (He was an amateur mycologist, co-founded the New York Mycological Society, and even won $8,000 on a quiz show by answering arcane questions about fungus.)

"Music as weather"

Cage thought of "music as weather" telling an interviewer near the end of his life that "I think it is true that sounds are, of their nature, harmonious, and I would extend that to noise. There is no noise, only sound. I haven't heard any sounds that I consider something I don't want to hear again, with the exception of sounds that frighten us or make us aware of pain. I don't like meaningful sound. If sound is meaningless, I'm all for it."

He took to heart something he once heard inventor Buckminster Fuller say— "I only learn what to do when I have failures."

His earliest explorations used "prepared" pianos in which objects, such as nails, were inserted between the strings or attached to their hammers. One of his most Dada pieces involved slapping the strings of a piano with a fish. (It was dead.)

In 1951, his *Imaginary Landscape No. 4* involved 12 radios playing simultaneously. Two "performers" operated each device constantly altering the volume and shifting between stations.

A year later, Cage's *Water Music* recreated everyday sounds, and its instruments included cards being shuffled, water poured from one container to another, a radio being turned on and off, a whistle blown into a bowl of water, and a piano keyboard lid slammed at random moments.

As a guest on the "I've Got a Secret" TV game show, his performance involved a bathtub, a rubber duck, and an electric mixer. It also included radios, but not the way Cage intended. Union rules forbid him from playing them, so he created sounds with them by dropping them on the floor.

Not surprisingly, the Soviet Union banned Cage's music.

"My favorite music is the music I haven't yet heard," he once said. "I don't hear the music I write. I write in order to hear the music I haven't yet heard."

MORAL: "   !   "

Chapter 13

Kevin Cosgrove

Not Ready to Die

Prosecutors used the dying man's phone call to convict his killer.

"Tell God to blow the wind from the west."

Kevin Cosgrove was an executive at Aon Corporation, an insurance company. He worked on the 105th floor of Two World Trade Center. On the morning of September 11, 2001, he made this phone call at 9:54 a.m.:

911: What's the telephone number I can tell FD to push up? What's the telephone number you're calling from?
    Kevin Cosgrove: I can barely see.
911: You can barely see?
    Kevin Cosgrove: 4-4-1
911: 4-4-1
    Kevin Cosgrove: 2-6-2-3
9-11: That's on the 105th floor of the Northwest corner, right?
    Kevin Cosgrove: Right.
911: At number Two World Trade Center?
    Kevin Cosgrove: Right. Lady, there's two of us in this office. We're not ready to die, but it's getting bad.
911: I understand, sir. We're trying to get all the apparatuses there. I am trying to let them know where you are. Stay on the line.
    Kevin Cosgrove: Oh, please, hurry.
Fire Department: Let me talk to the caller, please. Let me talk to the caller. Where is he?
911: He's on the line.
Fire Department: Let me talk to him. Where is the fire, sir?
    Kevin Cosgrove: Smoke really bad. 105 Two Tower.

Fire Department: Alright. Sit tight. We'll get to you as soon as we can.

Kevin Cosgrove: They keep saying that, but the smoke's really bad now.

Fire Department: That's all we can do now.

Kevin Cosgrove: What floor are you guys up to?

Fire Department: We're getting there. We're getting there.

Kevin Cosgrove: Doesn't feel like it, man. I got young kids.

Fire Department: I understand that, sir. We're on the way.

911: He's on the 105th floor in the Northwest corner.

Kevin Cosgrove: He hung up on me. Hello, operator?

911: Yes?

Kevin Cosgrove: Come on, man.

911: We have everything we need, sir.

Kevin Cosgrove: I know you do, but doesn't seem like it … You got lots of people up here.

911: I understand.

Kevin Cosgrove: I know you got a lot in the building, but we are on the top. Smoke rises, too. We are on the floor. We're in the window. I can barely breathe now. I can't see.

911: Okay, just try to hang in there. I'm going to stay with you.

Kevin Cosgrove: You can say that, you're in an air-conditioned building. What the hell happened?

911: Okay. I'm still here, still trying. The Fire Department is trying to get to you.

Kevin Cosgrove: Doesn't feel like it.

911: Okay, try to calm down so you can conserve your oxygen, okay? Try to…

Kevin Cosgrove: Tell God to blow the wind from the West. It's really bad. It's black. It's arid. Does anyone else wanna chime in here? We're young men. We're not ready to die.

911: I understand.

Kevin Cosgrove: How are you going to get my ass down? I need oxygen.

911: They're coming. They're getting you. They have a lot of apparatuses on the scene.

Kevin Cosgrove: It doesn't feel like it, lady. You get them in from all over. You get 'em in from Jersey. I don't give a shit— Ohio.

911: Okay, sir. What's your last name?

Kevin Cosgrove: Name's Cosgrove. I must have told you about a dozen times already. C-O-S-G-R-O-V-E. My wife thinks I'm alright. I called and said I was leaving the building and that I was fine and then — *bang*! Cherry. Doug Cherry. Doug Cherry's next to me. 105. Whose office? John Ostaru's office?

911: That's where he said? That's the office?

Kevin Cosgrove: We're in John Ostaru's office. O-S-T-A-R-U.

911: -A-R-U.

Kevin Cosgrove: Right. That's the office we're in. There are three of us in here.

911: Ostaru. Hello?

Kevin Cosgrove: Hello. We're looking in…. We're overlooking the Financial Center. Three of us. Two broken windows. Oh, God. Oh…

(The tower collapses.)

Kevin Cosgrove's remains were found in the rubble. He was buried on September 22, 2001.

He is survived by his wife and three children.

Federal prosecutors used the recording of his phone call to help convict 911 conspirator Zacarias Moussaoui.

MORAL: Try your best. That is all God expects.

Chapter 14

Walt Disney

He Was No Mouse

He never had a childhood. So he made
sure every child did.

"I never had any real play time."

When Walt Disney was in his 50s and a millionaire many times over, sometimes he would wake up in the middle of the night. He'd be in a cold sweat from a nightmare about his childhood job.

His father owned a newspaper delivery route. That was his job. That was the family's source of income. Its sole source of income.

His father had put the business was in his older brother's name, perhaps because he was embarrassed to have such a demeaning job.

Walt was nine years old when his father started getting him up early to deliver papers. Early as in 3:30 a.m. The little boy and his brother and father would get the newspapers. He would get 50. At first, he walked his route on foot, then he rode his bike.

He was home by six a.m., and after such a rousing morning's work, he went back to sleep and arose again for breakfast.

His pay? Usually nothing. After all, it was his father's business.

He did make a few cents by also delivering medicine (at the same time as he delivered the newspapers) for a neighborhood druggist.

Finally, he got his dad to give him another 50 papers. He tried selling them at a trolley stop. Kids hawking competing papers there bullied him away, so he sold papers onboard the trolley—and all this was in the morning.

Then Walt went to school. Of course, he had to leave school early—to get the afternoon papers.

There wasn't much time for fun on the weekends either. He collected subscription money on Saturdays. Of course, Sundays were the worst day—because the papers were so thick and heavy.

Snow up to his neck

Winters? They were the worst time to deliver papers. In later years, he boasted that he somehow walked in snow drifts up to his neck. He recalled that sometimes he was so exhausted he fell asleep on the floor of apartment building lobbies and then got up to finish his route.

How long did he do this? He did this for six years. During that time, he only took off three weeks, and two of those were because he was sick.

"I was working all the time," Walt Disney recalled. "I never had any real play time." The experience made him appreciate what little free time he had. As he got older and got serious about his hobby, drawing, he knew he didn't have a moment to waste. No wonder that his first mega-success was *Snow White and the Seven Dwarfs*, a story about a girl trapped by cruel adults in a life of misery and thankless toil.

From as far back as he could remember, he always liked to draw. When his only aunt came to visit, she always brought him pencils and pads of paper. An elderly doctor took a liking to him. One day he asked little Walt to use his crayons to draw his horse which was a fine stallion.

The old man gave him a nickel in exchange for his finished work. Then he framed it and hung it on his wall. That was one of the shining moments of his childhood. He remembered it the rest of his life.

"Don't be afraid to admit your ignorance," the doctor told him.

He may have remembered that wise advice, but as a young entrepreneur he forgot it. The young Disney, having incorporated with his brother Roy as Disney Brothers, went to work for movie producer Charles Mintz.

Mintz apparently looked like a villain in Disney movie. He chain-smoked. He obsessed over his favorite thing—his collection of police badges. His eyes were cold, his features grim. He rarely stooped to speak with his employees. Disney had a contract with Mintz (and his wife Margaret Winkler). Disney would make the cartoons with his own staff, and Mintz would bankroll his work and distribute the films to movie houses.

It wasn't such a bad deal. After all, Disney got a share of the ticket revenues. Now Mintz wanted more—more cartoons and more jokes in every cartoon. Disney and his team could hardly keep up. Soon Mintz wanted even more movies.

The hare was a hit

The two men vied for creative control, but Mintz held the whip hand and wouldn't give in. The financial pressures drove Disney to distraction. No matter what he did he couldn't make ends meet working for Mintz. He so badly needed extra money to meet his payroll that he sunk to making a short film called *Clara Cleans Her Teeth*, a movie about proper dental care.

Then in early 1927 Mintz told Disney the good news— he'd struck a new deal with Universal. There was one condition—Disney would make no cartoons about cats. Apparently, there was a glut of cat cartoons on the market, thanks to the popular Felix the Cat series.

So Walt drew what seemed to be the next best animal— rabbits, and they agreed to produce a series of 26 cartoons about Oswald the Lucky Rabbit. Of the resulting short films, Motion Picture News raved, "This series is destined to win much popular favor."

The hare was a hit, but Disney was about to be dumped. Mintz and his partners decided they no longer needed him. Behind Disney's back, Mintz hired away most of his animators.

Disney struggled to negotiate his own deal with studios to produce the Oswald series. But Walt, still a babe in the Hollywood woods, didn't know what he didn't know. Disney was ignorant and didn't know he was ignorant. He learned the sickening truth—Mintz owned all the intellectual property rights to the character of Oswald.

He could have kept working for Mintz, but by now far too much ill will had arisen between the two men. In later years he told friends, "it was just like the plot of one of [my] stories where good will win and the villain will be defeated."

In reality, Disney's disastrous comeuppance with Mintz was the best thing that ever could have happened to him. He learned the legal ropes, albeit the hard way, and he got strong experience supervising staff, managing production, and running a studio—except that he didn't have the final say.

Seething with anger and humiliation, he vowed that he would never again work for anyone—but himself. He would be his own boss, and he would create—and own—the characters he created.

Disney's courage led to a real Mickey Mouse achievement. Now his own man again, Disney got the idea for the renegade rodent when he saw a mouse at his windowsill. On the other hand, his wife said Mickey's genesis came from brainstorming at work. Film historians have pointed out that mice had played second banana roles in earlier Disney cartoons. Others contend Mickey was merely Oswald drawn differently and that cartoons in humor magazines were the inspiration for Mickey.

Why was Mickey a hit? Yes, he was cute—and sassy, but his first film *Steamboat Willie* wasn't even the first cartoon with sound. But it was the first cartoon with sound that was *good*. It had that Disney magic.

"Laughs galore," raved Variety. Almost instantly, Disney had offers galore. The man who had been too busy to play as a child now found it child's play to make children's dreams come true.

MORAL: Low points lead to high points.

Chapter 15

Enrique Granados

Until Death Do Us Part

His finest performance was at
the moment of his death.

"All my present happiness is more for what is to come."

Spanish composer Enrique Granados missed the boat. His greatest success forced him to rebook his passage across the Atlantic, and his shining moment cost him his life and that of his wife.

He won fame in his homeland in the late 1890s with his first opera *Maria Del Carmen*. His piano compositions were regarded as among the world's best. An English critic called them "the finest piano music of the day."

International acclaim came in 1911 with his *Goyescas*, a suite for piano consisting of six compositions based on the paintings of fellow Spaniard Francisco Goya. The Paris Opera then commissioned him to write an opera based on the suite. It was to have premiered in 1914; however, the onset of the First World War forced the cancellation of its first performances.

There was, nonetheless, good news. New York's Metropolitan Opera told Granados it wanted to stage his new opera, setting it on its calendar for late January 1916. Thrilled yet also apprehensive, he and his wife Amparo traveled to New York City from Barcelona. Granados had a morbid fear of dying a watery death and often had nightmares on that theme.

The financial successes he achieved in America delighted him. The Met handsomely paid him, and he was well compensated for piano-roll recordings and private recitals during his time in New York. In a review of one of his solo piano performances a *New York Times* critic wrote, "Mr. Granados....played with brilliance and power: there were also the languor, the smoldering fire, the tenderness and passion which belong in this music, by which it is marked with Spanish character."

Until this time, Granados, 50, had been a struggling artist. Now he was out of debt, and his financial future looked promising.

"I am only now beginning my work," he wrote a friend from Manhattan. "But I am full of confidence and enthusiasm about working more and more.... I am a survivor of fruitless struggle [due] to the ignorance and indifference of [my] country. All my present happiness is more for what is to come than for what I have done up to now."

Critical reaction to the performances at the Met was mixed, yet word of the premiere reached the White House. Out of the blue, Granados received an invitation to perform for President Wilson. He had said that music was "a national need" in time of war. His daughter was a semi-professional singer and may have arranged the invitation.

The resulting delay meant that Enrique and Amparo missed the departure of their ship to Spain. Instead, they booked passage to England on the ocean liner *S.S. Rotterdam*. They night before they embarked, terror gripped Granados. "Never again will I see my children," he wept to a friend on the telephone. "This is the end."

Yet a week later the *Rotterdam* arrived safely in England. From there they boarded the ferry and mail boat *S.S. Sussex*. At one p.m. on March 24, 1916, the *Sussex* carrying 378 passengers and crew left Dover for the four-hour trip across the English Channel to Calais. At the time, German U-Boats had orders to conduct "unrestricted submarine warfare" on any target. The ferry, however, had no military escort. No U-Boat had ever attacked a cross-Channel ferry.

It was a lovely day. The sky was clear, the sea calm. Two hours into the voyage, Granados was playing the piano in the ferry's smoking room, according to an eyewitness.

The captain of the *Sussex* spotted a German torpedo, and he ordered his ship hard to starboard. Had he seen torpedo a few seconds earlier, his evasive action would have caused it to miss the ship. Instead, it hit near the bow, exploding with devastating force.

"A moment of silence, then Hell let loose," wrote an American survivor.

Terrified passengers leapt into the water, whether or not they were wearing life jackets. Because the threat from U-Boats was not taken seriously, the ferry did not have enough life vests onboard, and many that it did have were so old they were rotten.

"The scenes around us were harrowing," the survivor wrote. "The water was full of men and women, swimming, sinking, drowning, clinging to spars, boards, and other bits of wreckage, crying out in the agony of the last hold on life."

In the panic and confusion, the *Sussex's* radio operator sent out the wrong location for his ship, causing French destroyers to search 20 miles away. The first rescue vessel did not reach the *Sussex* until midnight, seven hours after the attack.

In a bizarre twist, the *Sussex* broke in half. The forward part of the ship sank, while the stern remained afloat and was later towed to shore. As a result, no more than 100 passengers and crew died. The Granados' cabin was in the stern, and had they been there at the time of the attack, they might have survived.

The captain had also begged passengers not to abandon ship. A friend of Enrique and Amparo also implored them not to go into the water. Both husband and wife considered their chances and leapt into the sea.

Passengers still onboard the *Sussex* watched in horror as Enrique became separated from Amparo, who was a better swimmer. Accounts differ. Some eyewitnesses saw Amparo struggling to keep Enrique afloat. Others saw both floating on a raft in the frigid water. Amparo slipped over the side. Seeing her fighting to stay afloat, Enrique jumped in to rescue her, and both went under the waves, leaving their six children orphans.

In Europe and America, musical organizations held fund-raising concerts to benefit the six children. In May 1916 at a benefit at the Met, Ignace Paderewski performed Chopin's *Funeral March*. The audience stood in silence. At the end of his performance, all the lights in the theatre were extinguished, except for a lone candle on his piano.

MORAL: To have and to hold.

Chapter 16

Mary, Queen of Scots

Chin Up

She faced the ax man
with dignity rarely seen.

*"I think it were well, my dears, that I should eat something
and then retire, that on the morrow I may do
nothing undignified, or lack courage."*

The queen rose before dawn at Fotheringay Castle on February 8, 1587. She wanted to look her best. All eyes would be on her. She would be the center of attention at the momentous event.

Her ladies-in-waiting helped her into a vivid crimson petticoat and then into a black velvet gown. The final touch? A black veil and headdress.

Today Mary, the Queen of Scotland, would be beheaded. Her cousin Queen Elizabeth I of England had signed her death warrant a week earlier. It would be the first legal execution of a European head of state.

Mary had been held prisoner for a score of years. Elizabeth came to her decision after great deliberation. She and Mary had long been rivals for the throne of England. They were cousins, both descended from Henry VIII.

Elizabeth was the daughter of Henry's second wife Anne Boleyn who, incidentally, had lost her head, as well. When the bed-hopping Henry ended his first marriage to Catherine of Aragon, the resulting furor with the Catholic Church was so calamitous that Henry left the flock. As a result, Catholics never regarded Elizabeth, a Protestant, as a legitimate heir to the throne.

Instead, they contended that Mary, the Queen of Scotland, should rightfully rule England. (In those days Scotland and

England were separate realms.) After all, Mary was the granddaughter of Henry's sister.

Mary had ascended to the Scottish throne after her father's death when she was only six days old. When she was five, her mother sent her to France to be raised. She married the son of the French king. When her father-in-law died, she also became queen of France.

Now queen of two countries, Mary's claim to the English throne as Henry VIII's grand-niece would ultimately prove her undoing, literally.

Soon after Elizabeth became queen in 1558, one of her ministers correctly saw that so long as Mary lived "this quarrel [between Protestant and Catholics over rival queens] is undoubtedly like to be a perpetual incumbrance of this kingdom."

Mary was still living in France in 1560 when Scottish rebels (with English military assistance) overthrew their Catholic rulers backed by French troops stationed in Scotland. When they sailed home, France's king formally recognized Elizabeth's authority over England.

With Protestants now ruling Scotland, a humiliated Mary returned home. She attempted to make amends with Elizabeth, writing her that they were "both in one isle, both of one language, the nearest kinswoman that each other hand, and both queens."

Unfortunately, she gravely complicated matters by asking Elizabeth to make her heir to the English throne. This Elizabeth would not do.

Mary made her situation much worse in 1565 when she wed Lord Darnley. This Catholic nobleman, like Mary, also claimed direct lineage to Elizabeth's crown, thus threatening Elizabeth's status further. Two years later they had a son, further strengthening their presumed title.

In a bizarre turn of events, Darnley died in a mysterious explosion. Three months later, Mary married the Earl of Bothwell, the prime suspect in the murder. Mary's allies in Scotland had had enough. They renounced her, forced her to abdicate, and imprisoned her. She escaped and fled to England where Elizabeth held her in custody.

Elizabeth put Mary on trial to determine whether she had abetted in the murder and, more important, to determine her loyalty to England. Eight scandalous—and unsigned—letters were put into evidence. Supposedly from Mary to Bothwell, they proved her adultery and complicity in Darnley's murder.

Elizabeth thought the letters were forgeries. While still feeling some sympathy for her cousin, she also feared that if she accepted the correspondence as legitimate, some might regard them as proof that no woman, including Elizabeth, was fit to rule.

Over the next few years, Elizabeth uncovered several new Catholic plots swirling around Mary, all designed to remove her from power. She beseeched Mary to admit her involvement in treasonous acts. Mary refused, saying that because she was queen of a foreign land, she could not be guilty of treason.

At her trial in August 1586, Mary told the court, "Look to your consciences and remember that the theatre of the whole world is wider than the kingdom of England."

Though the court found Mary guilty, Elizabeth hesitated to put her to death. After all, if she ordered the execution of one queen, it would legitimize the deed, thus weakening her standing if she were later dethroned. At last, however, Elizabeth authorized Mary's death, saying her acts had "compassed and imagined the hurt, death and destruction of the royal person."

Elizabeth's men arrived at the castle the day before Mary's execution. When they read the death warrant to her, she seemed unsurprised and "thanked them for their good news." After years of imprisonment, she had wearied of its accompanying sorrows and sufferings.

The night before her execution there being no priest available, Mary wrote out her confession and farewell letters to various nobles. She invited her ladies-in-waiting into her chambers, and upon opening her chests of jewelry and riches, distributed them to her court, saying that she was sorry she had so little to share with them, according to French historian Pierre deBrantome. He heard the story of her execution from two of Mary's "trustworthy serving-women, who were faithful to the promise they made their mistress to bear witness of her constancy."

They said that on her last night Mary prayed for two hours. Before going to bed, she told her servants, "I think it were well, my dears, that I should eat something and then retire, that on the morrow I may do nothing undignified, or lack courage."

After a fitful night's sleep, Mary arose and was dressed. A loud knocking came at the door. Her final escort had arrived. She told Queen Elizabeth's men, "I am ready to meet my death. I feel that the Queen, my sister, is doing me a great favor."

An account by Robert Wynkfielde, a witness of the day's events, reported that Mary also said "All this world is but vanity, and full of troubles and sorrows; carry this message from me, and tell my friends that I die a true woman to my religion, and like a true Scottish woman and a true Frenchwoman.

"But God forgive them that have long desired my end; and He that is the true Judge of all secret thoughts knoweth my mind, how that it ever hath been my desire to have Scotland and England united together."

She walked with her escorts to a large room in the castle where more than 100 witnesses had gathered. A two-foot high scaffold had been erected in the middle of the chamber, and a black cloth had been thrown over it.

To everyone's amazement, she had such dignity and beauty, she looked as though she were making a grand entrance to a formal ball. When one of her ladies broke down crying, Queen Mary put her finger over her lips, signaling her to be quiet.

Upon mounting the scaffold, the executioner grabbed her. With the aid of two of her servants, he pulled down her dress to her waist. Everyone now saw her petticoat, its brilliant red the traditional color of a Catholic martyr. She told those assembled that "she never had such grooms to make her unready, and that she never put off her clothes before such a company."

When one of Elizabeth's noblemen asked her if she would repent, according to Wynkfielde, she replied, "I am settled in the ancient Catholic Roman religion, and mind to spend my blood in defense of it."

"Madam, change your opinion," he implored her. "Repent you of your former wickedness, and settle your faith only in Jesus Christ, by Him to be saved."

"Trouble not yourself any more, for I am settled and resolved in this my religion, and am purposed therein to die," she replied.

Other nobles followed suit saying, "We will pray for your Grace, that it stand with God's will you may have your heart lightened, even at the last hour, with the true knowledge of God, and so die therein."

"If you will pray for me, my Lords, I will thank you," she said. "But to join in prayer with you I will not, for that you and I are not of one religion."

Now the executioner knelt at her feet, as was the custom, and begged her for forgiveness.

"I forgive you with all my heart, for now," she said "I hope you shall make an end of all of my troubles."

Mary laid down her Catholic prayer book and crucifix. She took out a gold-embroidered white veil and gave it to her servant, instructing her to fasten it as blindfold.

She began praying aloud in Latin. Kneeling on a black cushion that had been provided for her, she lay her head on the chopping block. As she said *In manus tuas, Domine, commendo spiritum meum* ("Into Thy hands, Lord, I commend my spirit."), the ax slammed down.

But it barely grazed her head.

"Sweet Jesus," Mary moaned.

Down thundered the ax again. It left the head dangling "saving one little gristle."

A third stroke took it off, and the head rolled free.

Standing before the scaffold, the Earl of Kent cried, "Such end of all the Queen's and the Gospel's enemies."

"God save Queen Elizabeth!" the executioner cried, holding up Mary's head. "May all enemies of the true Evangel perish thus!"

To everyone's horror, when he picked up her head by her red hair, the head fell. Mary had been wearing a wig. She had cut off all almost all her hair. Everyone saw that what hair she had left had turned white due to the grief and stresses of her long imprisonment.

"Her lips stirred up and down a quarter of an hour after her head was cut off," Wynkfielde reported.

The executioner lifted the hem of Mary's floor-length dress to take her garters, as was then the custom of executioners. (Women in those days tied garters at their knees to hold up their socks.) There under her skirts came another shock. He found Mary's pet dog Geddon, a white skye terrier, cowering under her hems.

At the sight of his bloody, lifeless mistress, the dog howled and lay between her head and shoulders. One of the noblemen grabbed the dog and pressed its face into the bloody mess. The dog bit his hand.

So that none of her effects would be treasured as relics, her crucifix, prayer book, and clothes were burned.

History does not record the fate of her dog.

MORAL: Hold your head up.

Chapter 17

Theodor Geisel

"A Book No One Will Publish"

Here is a man who pulled
a cat out of a hat.

"Be who you are and say what you feel, because those who mind
don't matter and those who matter don't mind."

Theodor Geisel made a comfortable living drawing illustrations for Vico Motor Oil, Standard Oil, Narragansett Beer, and, most notably, the household insecticide Flit. In fact, the advertising tagline he dreamed up—"Quick, Henry, the Flit!"— became a popular catchphrase all over the country.

But Geisel wanted more, and he wasn't afraid to try. He wrote a book which he titled "A Story No One Can Beat." It tells the tale of a little boy named Marco who, while walking home from school, recounts all the preposterous things he dreams of seeing.

Twenty-seven publishers rejected Geisel's manuscript in the winter of 1936. Some said it was too fantastic. How outlandish to think a child would see an old man with a 20-foot-long white beard, a Chinese boy with chopsticks, a rajah riding a blue elephant, giraffes, or a blue plane dropping confetti.

Other publishers said that children's stories in verse form were too old fashioned. After all, the book was written in the galloping anapestic tetrameter rhyme scheme. Worse, some editors chastised Geisel because his book offered children no strong moral message. It was just silly.

In the end, all the rejections came down to just one thing. "Too different from other juveniles on the market to warrant selling," sniffed one publishing house.

Deeply dejected, the 33-year-old Geisel trudged home carrying under his arm a portfolio that contained his manuscript and its accompanying drawings. Suddenly, coming down the sidewalk was one of his Dartmouth college friends. He asked Geisel what he was toting. "That's a book no one will publish," he said, "I'm lugging it home to burn."

It so happened that Geisel's friend had just been hired as an editor in the children's book division at Vanguard Press. He asked Geisel to come straightaway to his office. Once there, he took Geisel to Vanguard's president. He bought the book on the spot, and 20 minutes later, Geisel had a contract.

Geisel did have to agree to one change—His title had to go. The book appeared as *And to Think That I Saw It on Mulberry Street!* and was published under the pen name Dr. Seuss, a name dreamed up when he was at Dartmouth.

The book did modestly well. After six years, Geisel (and his whimsical alter-ego) had earned royalties of only about $3,500 (about $48,000 in 2018 dollars).

Leading critics lavished him with praise. The head of the children's department in the New York City Public Library called the book "true to the imagination of a small boy." She was so impressed she sent a copy to Beatrix Potter, the creator of Peter Rabbit. She replied saying that it was "the cleverest book I have met with for many years."

To date, more than 650 million books Dr. Seuss books have been sold in 95 nations in 20 languages. His works seem to grow more popular every year. In 2013, Americans bought 4.8 million Dr. Seuss books, 50 percent more than in 2010.

But *Mulberry Street* alone didn't make Geisel a legend. He had to keep at it for years before his name became a household world. The turning point came in 1957.

Sly Smile

That's when *The Cat in the Hat* appeared. It contains only 236 different words. Why? A top Houghton Mifflin editor challenged him write an entertaining book for first-graders.

Both he and Seuss thought children's reading would improve, if only they had books that were more fun than fun could be. Geisel worked from a list of 348 words that research had shown were words all first-graders needed to be able to read.

(Geisel modeled the Cat's sly smile and white gloves after an elegant elderly African-American woman who was an elevator operator in Houghton Mifflin's offices.)

Geisel wrote books that lit fires under the consciences of millions of children—and adults. His Yertle the Turtle was Hitler. Sneeches is about anti-Semitism. (Some wear stars, just as the Nazis forced Jews to wear the Star of David on their clothes.) Horton the elephant cares for the individual, no matter how small. The Lorax protects nature. The greedy Grinch repents the evils of consumerism.

His young heroes learn to stand up for themselves—as all children must. Young Bartholomew Cubbins saves the world from drowning in oobleck by teaching the king to say, "I'm sorry." Mack the Turtle overthrows King Yertle, a reptilian fuhrer, because he can no longer abide his lowly position. "And the turtles, of course...all the turtles are free," the story ends. "As turtles, and maybe, all creatures should be."

Live life to its fullest, Geisel believed. "You're off to great places. Today is your day!" he wrote in *Oh, the Places You'll Go!* "Your mountain is waiting. So...get on your way!"

Of course, he wanted everyone's life journey to be funner than fun, too. In *Fox in Socks*, Luke Luck licked lakes while tweetle beetles battled with paddles in puddles. *Hop on Pop* encouraged doing just that while it taught phonics. And if a cat in white gloves and a red bow tie knocks on your door, enjoy yourself—just make sure no one gets hurt and your house is in order, before mother gets home.

In all his works, he invited his readers to join the parade on Mulberry Street, so that soon they'd be thinking "Now my troubles are going to have trouble with me!"

**MORAL: Work hard and luck will walk
down the street towards you.**

Chapter 18

Eddie Rickenbacker

A Six-Word Formula

On a secret mission, his B-17 ditched in the Pacific. Eight men, two rafts, four oranges—24 days adrift.

"Courage is doing what you're afraid of doing."

Daredevil. Defier of death. That was Eddie Rickenbacker. He raced cars before World War I, competing in the Indianapolis 500 four times. Never mind that he started as a lowly mechanic with only a sixth-grade education, this man set a world record of 134 miles an hour in 1916.

His childhood? It was tough. He sold newspapers on street corners when he was five. To heat the family home, Rickenbacker's parents sent him out to the railroad tracks to hunt for coal that had fallen off trains.

During the Great War, he became America's "Ace of Aces," shooting down 22 German planes. Never mind that he entered the war as a chauffeur for General Pershing.

He wasn't a college grad like the other pilots, and at 22 he was two years over the age limit to be a pilot. Other fliers loathed him for his vulgarity, fame, and insistence on personally checking out his plane and its guns before every combat mission. Gentlemen didn't do such things.

Fight Like a Wildcat

How did he get 22 kills? (Actually, he had 26, when including shoot-downs of four German balloons.) He called his strategy "planned recklessness."

"I've cheated the Grim Reaper more times than anyone I know," Rickenbacker said, "And I'll fight like a wildcat until they nail the lid of my pine box down on me."

Truer words were never spoken. This was a man who was in two horrendous air crashes in two consecutive years.

In February 1941, he was flying on Eastern Airlines. He happened to be the company's president and ran it well from 1935 to 1960, except on this particular day when he was a passenger on a DC-3 that crashed on its approach to the Atlanta airport. Rickenbacker's injuries? A shattered pelvis, a fractured skull, a broken knee, a shattered left elbow, six broken ribs, a broken leg, and one of his eyelids was nearly ripped off.

Nonetheless, he not only remained conscious but comforted injured passengers, telling them not to give up hope, though he was trapped in the wreckage.

"Courage is doing what you're afraid of doing," Rickenbacker was fond of saying. "There can be no courage unless you are scared."

The ambulance crews ignored him, thinking he was dead. When he was finally taken to the hospital, the doctors thought he was dead, too, and they did the same thing. They ignored him.

Nearly a year and a half later, he had a limp, but otherwise he so fit that President Roosevelt sent him on a secret mission to meet with General MacArthur. (The purpose? To rip MacArthur a new one because of his criticisms of FDR's wartime leadership.)

His B-17 went hundreds of miles off course due to a faulty navigation system. It crashed deep in the Pacific far from shipping lanes.

Snapped Its Neck

Rickenbacker was one of eight men on two tiny rafts. Their food? They had to make four oranges last for days. No water. Rickenbacker, of course, put himself in charge of distributing the segments of the oranges. On the eighth day, when a seagull made the unfortunate mistake of landing on his head, he grabbed it, snapped its neck, plucked its feathers, tore out its guts, and divvied up its meat.

The other men hated him. He literally would not let them die. He said cruel things to them to make them ashamed of wanting death to come

One night, he heard a man praying aloud, wishing that God would let him die. Rickenbacker snapped, "He answers *men's* prayers. Not that stuff." And when someone moaned in agony, he said, "When we get out of this, you better crawl home to the women where you belong!"

Seven survived. The one who did not drunk sea water. When they were rescued, some of the men never even thanked him. He was cruel, but he wouldn't let anyone quit, even in a seemingly hopeless situation.

Rickenbacker was an incredible lifelong optimist. "If you think about disaster, you will get it," he said. "Think positively and masterfully with confidence and faith, and life becomes more secure, more fraught with action, richer in achievement and experience. This is the sure way to win victories over inner defeat."

He was meticulous in every aspect of his life—except in the wild fearlessness of his combat flying. Said Rickenbacker: "I can give you a six-word formula for success: Think things through—then follow through."

MORAL: Eat your oranges wisely.

Chapter 19

Isaac Newton

A Bodkin to the Eye

To see better, his risked
losing his sight.

"This most beautiful system of the sun, planets and comets,
could only proceed from the counsel and
dominion of an intelligent and powerful Being."

What is a 'bare bodkin,' and would you put one in your eye socket?

In Hamlet's meditation on whether life is worth living, he asks, "Who would bear the whips and scorns of time, the oppressor's wrong, the proud man's contumely [taunts], the pangs of disprized love, the law's delay, the insolence of office and the spurns that patient merit of the unworthy takes [the insults that the worthy bear], when he himself might his quietus [relief] take with a bare bodkin?" In other words, why suffer life's trials when an unsheathed dagger will end it all?

Consider now the master mathematician and scientist Sir Isaac Newton. Why should he suffer the displeasures of remaining ignorant when he can end his dissatisfaction and find enlightenment by putting a "bodkine" in his eye?

And that is what he did. He did not stab himself in the eye with a stiletto. A 'bodkine' in the parlance of the 1600s was also a large sewing needle. And he did not poke himself in the eye with it. He inserted it between his eyeball and the bone of the eye socket as far to the rear of the eye as he could possibly make it go. Then he pressed it against his eyeball.

As one of his notebooks recounts, "I tooke a bodkine...& put it betwixt my eye & [the] bone as neare to [the] backside of my eye as I could: & pressing my eye [with the] end of it (soe as to make [the] curvature...in my eye) there appeared severall white darke & coloured circles.... Which circles were plainest when I continued to rub my eye [with the] point of [the] bodkine, but if I held my eye & [the] bodkin still, though I continued to presse my eye [with] it yet [the] circles would grow faint & often disappeare untill I removed [them] by moving my eye or [the] bodkin."

When he wasn't obsessively creating revolutionary theories about gravity and bodies in motion, Newton was also fascinated by the nature of light and color. The purpose of the experiment? To determine whether or not colors were produced within the eye or something outside the eye. The French philosopher Descartes had postulated that light was a kind of "pressure" pulsating through the ether, a mysterious substance which scientists then thought was necessary for the transmission of light. The results? Inconclusive. All Newton saw were gray spots.

On another occasion, he went into a dark room and stared at the sun's reflection in a mirror with one eye, injuring it to such a degree that he had to spend the next three days in darkness and saw after-images for weeks and months afterwards.

At the time people thought clear white light (daylight) was a unified thing. Newton conducted other experiments with a prism and a mirror in a darkened room and found that light was a combination of seven colors, the visible spectrum of light. Newton revealed that these colors are red, orange, yellow, green, blue, indigo, and violet.

"Light is a confused aggregate of Rays indued with all sorts of Colours," he wrote. He further believed that light was made of "corpuscles," writing "Are not the rays of light very small particles emitted from shining substances?" In other words, a color is a property of the light that is reflected from an object—a color is not a property of the object in and of itself.

"What is hee good for?"

Born on Christmas day, Newton was so tiny that he said that his mother once told him "he was so little they could put him into a quart pot."

Like other geniuses, he was a misfit, especially as a child. In his first year at school he ranked 78th of out 80 students. He was "very negligent" at his studies, according to one biographer.

Instead he got saws and hammers and made a sundial, a four-foot tall water-powered wooden clock, and a mouse-powered wooden mill. A woman who knew him as a childhood playmate said he was "always a sober, silent, thinking lad," and instead of playing with other boys, he preferred to make little tables, cupboards, and utensils for girls.

His teenage years were peculiar as well. He was an incompetent shepherd who was once fined for "suffering his swine to trespass in the corn fields." On another occasion while leading a horse home, its bridle slipped off. So lost in thought was young Isaac that he arrived dragging the bridle in the dirt, unaware that the horse was long gone.

When he was 16 he kept a notebook in which he translated English phrases into Latin. Among them were "What imployment is he fit for? What is hee good for?"

It turns out that what Newton was good for was conceiving a comprehensive scheme for understanding the nature of the universe.

"I derive from the celestial phenomena the forces of gravity with which bodies tend to the sun and the several planets," he wrote. "Then, from these forces, by other propositions which are also mathematical, I deduce the motions of the planets, the comets, the moon and the sea."

This is the key concept in his magnum opus *Philosophiae Naturalis Principia Mathematica* (The Mathematical Principles of Natural Philosophy), a 511-page leather-bound book whose first edition was 300 to 400 copies. Newton was a professor at Cambridge, and it is said that a student who was there at the quipped, "There goes the man that writ a book that neither he nor anyone else understands."

Thanks to Newton, we know that all things in the universe are in relation to each other under the guidance of fixed mathematical laws. The wilderness is not wild. It is not chaotic. It is ruled by a universal force which he called gravity. "To every action there is always opposed an equal reaction," he wrote, or put another way, the Moon exerts a gravitational force on the Earth just as the Earth exerts a force on the Moon, and the two are bound in each other's gravity until and unless another force intervenes.

"The cause of gravity is what I do not pretend to know," Newton once wrote. Yet he also wrote a friend that he believed that when the universe was created, God endowed every bit of matter "with an innate gravity towards the rest."

Did his theory of gravity suddenly come to him when an apple bonked him on the head while sitting under a tree? Newton told friends and relatives that is exactly what happened, though, in truth, he developed his theory over many years. While the apple tree story is, on some level, false, it does have a peel.

MORAL: Think hard enough, and the fruit of your labor will fall in your lap.

Chapter 20

Van Cliburn

The Czar from Texas

One man took on
the Soviet Union—and won.

"Your responsibility is to solve your problems."

"The Texan Who Conquered Russia." That's how *Time* magazine described Van Cliburn. Its 1958 cover story raved that he was Elvis, Liberace, and violinist Vladimir Horowitz all rolled into one. Not to be outdone *Variety* dubbed him "a musical Lindbergh."

This lone eagle of the keyboard competed against 49 other pianists from 19 nations, flying away with first-place honors at Moscow's immensely prestigious quadrennial International Tchaikovsky Competition. This gawky, baby faced pianist was all of 23 years old—and terribly shy. His only weapon? The intense—and romantic—way he attacked the keyboard.

His mother Rildia began teaching him when he was about three or four. (She had studied under a teacher who had been taught by Lizst.) Why so young? She found him at the keyboard rendering a splendid imitation one of her students.

His talent quickly became so evident that his parents built a practice studio for him attached to the garage of their Kilgore, Texas, home.

At the age of nine or 10, his mother wanted him to play the *Transcendental Etudes* of Liszt. He balked, saying, "I can't play this because I don't have perfect hands like you."

He always remembered his mother's stern reply: "No one has perfect hands! Everyone has problems. Your responsibility is to solve your problems."

Cliburn first performed with the Houston Symphony when he was 12. When he was 13, he placed first a statewide competition.

Right place, right time

The legendary Julliard School offered him a scholarship, but he was too much of a mama's boy to attend. He would only take lessons from Rildia. Only after graduating from high school when he was 17 did he make the leap to study there.

In 1954 he won the prestigious Leventritt Award. It had gone un-awarded for the three preceding years, as none of the contestants had sufficiently impressed the judges. Cliburn did, and his victory won him debut performances with five top U.S. orchestras. His signature piece—Tchaikovsky's *Piano Concerto No. 1.*

So, when the Moscow competition rolled around in 1958, "Cliburn was the right man, at the right place, in the right moment," said one writer.

The amazing thing was that the fix was definitely in. The grand prize was supposed to have gone to a Russian. After all, this was a Tchaikovsky competition. The Ministry of Culture had told the Kremlin's new boss Nikita Khrushchev that a son of the motherland would obviously capture the honor.

It would be yet another inspiring victory for communism. Months earlier the Soviet Union had sorely bruised America's self-confidence by successfully orbiting Sputnik, the world's first artificial satellite.

But when the competition left outer space and hit the concert stage, things didn't go quite as the commissars had hoped. Russian music lovers were agog. And teenage Russian girls adored Cliburn and his bouffant hairdo the way American teens would later go gaga for John, Paul, George, and Ringo. They fainted and wept when he performed.

As the young gentleman from Texas advanced from round to round of the competition, he found himself besieged by bouquets of flowers and stacks of fan mail from admirers. At six-foot four, Cliburn towered over his competitors in more ways than one.

Russian girls called him "Cleeburn." Strangers stopped him on the sidewalk to hug him. *The New York Times'* Moscow correspondent Max Frankel covered the competition and wrote that "Especially the young girls were going absolutely crazy about Van's performances, heaping flowers on him....And there were long lines to get in [when he played], even longer than usual."

When he finished performing the night of the first round of competition, the Russian audience was so overwhelmed it chanting, "First! First prize!" The night of the finals his standing ovation lasted eight minutes. The vote of the judges— unanimous.

Clearly, Muscovites wanted the American to win, but would the Kremlin permit that. Fearful of the Soviet regime's response if Cliburn took first prize, the judges asked Khrushchev for permission to give the honor to the American.

"Is the American really the best?" Khrushchev asked. When told that he was, Khrushchev replied, "So you have to give him the prize!"

At a Kremlin reception at few days later, Khrushchev threw his arms around Cliburn and after giving him a hearty Russian bearhug asked him, "Why are you so tall?"

"Because I am from Texas," he replied. "I guess because my father gave me so many vitamins."

A transcendental force

On his return, New York City feted him with a ticker-tape parade. More than 100,000 people lined Broadway to welcome home the conquering keyboard king, the only time the city has given a musician such an honor.

When he went on tour around the U.S., the sight of him caused riots. Fans in Philadelphia ripped the door handles off his limo. The local branch of the Elvis Fan Club changed its name to the Van Cliburn Fan Club. His album showcasing his award-winning piano concerto vied with Elvis and the soundtrack from

My Fair Lady for the top spot on the charts. It became the first classical album to sell more than a million copies.

"In 1958, he proved to the world that music is a transcendental force that goes beyond political boundaries and cultural boundaries and unifies mankind. He was a very concrete example of that," said Veda Kaplinsky, the head of Julliard's piano department.

Besides having the courage to go into the heart of mother Russia to represent America, Cliburn, as a grateful artist, also said nice things about America's foe, when it was unthinkable to do so.

"The only thing that the Russians want from the Americans," Cliburn remarked, "is to meet them in an atmosphere of friendship, sincerity and mutual understanding."

That was enough to for FBI director J. Edgar Hoover to start a file on Cliburn. It also didn't help that Cliburn also said, "You can't love music enough to want to play it without other kids thinking you're queer or something."

In later years, Cliburn and his partner led a quiet life out of the spotlight.

Though he became wealthy from his performances and recordings, his career never ascended higher than it did at its outset.

A lifelong Christian, he was devoted to his Baptist church and would typically slip into services just before they began, taking a seat in the back row. Towards the end of his life, he told his minister that "one of the most profound truths that has characterized my life is St. Paul's advice to 'pray without ceasing.'

"That's how I have lived my life," he said.

MORAL: Stay keyed up.

Chapter 21

John James Powers

Hoping He Is Worthy

He was an American,
and he was a kamikaze.

"I am going to get a direct hit."

His classmates at George Washington High School voted him "the typical American boy."

Navy Lieutenant John James Powers "never thought of himself as any sort of hero," said *Life* magazine. But Powers was a great hero. In the Battle of the Coral Sea in early May 1942, his superhuman actions decisively turned the battle in the Allies favor—at the cost of his own life. For his heroism and sacrifice, he won the Medal of Honor, America's highest military honor.

Powers grew up "in the big city wilderness," according to *Life*. To be precise, he called the Washington Heights section of Manhattan home. "He shot immies [glass marbles with swirls], played cops and robbers, had fist fights, joined the Boy Scouts, went hiking, fishing, and sailing." In high school he was "a good but not an exceptional student."

He must have been better than good, because he won a hard-to-get appointment to the U.S. Naval Academy at Annapolis. Cadets nicknamed him Jo-Jo. His roommate wrote his senior profile in the yearbook. It read: "Sure we know him, who doesn't? That 'certain something' that makes everybody his friend on sight is Jo's most noticeable trait.

"Entirely unencumbered with any peculiarities, hobbies, or diversions, Jo is a markedly positive character, keen, caustically cynical about most of his life of ours, yet with a sense of humor always in charge of the most stable temperament you've ever seen. Never trust him to respect conventionalities.

He's a hilarious rebel, and his own man. You'll like him for it all the more when you meet him."

Punch in the face

He must have been a tough guy among tough guys—he made the boxing team. Double tough, he could take a punch in the face and give one back.

After graduating in 1935, he did a tour in China and in 1942 was serving as a squadron commander aboard the *U.S.S. Yorktown*, flying a Douglas Dauntless dive bomber.

A Japanese armada planned to invade the strategic port of Port Moresby in New Guinea. Thus far in World War II, the Japanese had been unstoppable. Had their strategy succeeded, their next target would have been Australia. That's why Australians call the Battle of the Coral Sea "The Battle That Saved Australia."

(This battle in early May 1942 was historic for two other reasons. First, it was the first battle in which aircraft carriers engaged each other. Second, it was the first naval battle fought at a distance. Neither side saw each other or directly fired on each other.)

The Allies went into battle outnumbered. Besides the *Yorktown*, they had only one other carrier in the fight, the *U.S.S. Lexington*. The Japanese had three carriers—the *Shoho*, *Shokaku*, and *Zuikaku*.

During the first day of the battle, Powers sank the *Shoho*. He "scored a direct hit on [the] carrier which burst into flames and sank soon after," according to his Medal of Honor citation.

"Scratch one flattop," radioed Lt. Robert E. Dixon, a pilot from the *Lexington*.

That wasn't enough to satisfy Powers. On that day and the next, according to his citation, "in the face of blasting enemy anti-aircraft fire" he "demolished one large enemy gunboat, put another gunboat out of commission, [and] severely damaged an aircraft tender and a 20,000-ton transport."

The next morning, immediately before takeoff, Powers gave a pep talk to the men in his squadron. "Remember—the folks back home are counting on us," he told them. "I am going to get a direct hit if I have to lay it on the flight deck."

That is what he did. To make good on his promise, he led his squadron to the *Shokaku*. Once there, he dove his plane from 18,000 feet through a barrage of fierce anti-aircraft fire directly down towards the carrier's deck. He released his bomb which weighed between 500 and 1,000 pounds at the last possible second.

Awed by his valor

Whether Powers intended to crash onto its deck is unclear. He was last seen through smoke and debris 200 feet above the carrier. The Douglass Dauntless was known to be difficult to fly when laden with heavy munitions.

Though the *Shokaku* stayed afloat, it required such extensive repairs it was unavailable to the Japanese one month later in June 1942 at the Battle of Midway, the decisive battle of the Pacific war in which the Japanese lost four carriers.

Awed by Powers' valor, President Roosevelt devoted a Fireside Address to him in September 1942. He repeated what Powers told his fellow fliers— "The folks back home are counting on us."

Then FDR drove his message home: "You and I are the folks back home," and he went on, asking his listeners, are we "playing our part 'back home' in winning the war?" Then he answered his own question, saying, "We are not doing enough."

A year or so earlier on Father's Day, Powers sent a telegram to his father who had served in the Navy and fought in the Spanish-American War. The message read: "Dear Dad one thousand miles away doesn't make any difference and your bad son is thinking of you hoping that he is worthy of being called a chip off the old block."

He was worthy.

**MORAL: Do what needs doing
for your folks back home.**

Chapter 22

Satchel Paige

Don't Look Back

He threw "bloopers," but his every pitch
was a strike in the history book.

*"If they don't know how smart you are,
you've got an upper hand on them."*

In February 1936, Joe DiMaggio, 21, played for the San Francisco Seals, a Yankee farm team. He'd been MVP the year before, hitting .398 with 34 homers.

The Yankees were thinking about bringing him to the big leagues. First, they needed to test him—to see if he was as good as all that. A phone call went out not to a major league pitcher but to a Negro League pitcher who had been playing for a southern California team in the off-season. His name—Satchel Paige. Some say he was the greatest pitcher in baseball history.

The two faced off, and the game was tied 1-1 in the tenth. Paige had 14 strike-outs. After three at bats, DiMaggio hadn't gotten a hit. Now with two outs and a runner on third. Joltin' Joe chopped one to Satchel's right. He nabbed it, but his only throw was to second. The throw to first came an instant too late. DiMaggio was safe. The runner scored. The game was over. The telegram from the Yankee's scout to the Bronx read: "DiMaggio all we hoped he'd be."

Later, DiMaggio would say that Paige was the best pitcher he had ever gone up against.

Paige's reaction? "I got more notice for losing that game that I did winning most of my other games."

Paige played professional baseball for 41 years in a career that sounds like something only Hollywood could create. Just as Babe Ruth learned to play ball in an orphanage, Paige mastered the game during five years in a reformatory. "Those years there did something to me," he said. "They made a man out of me…. You might say I traded five years of freedom to learn how to pitch."

He kept an almanac

The lanky six-foot-three right hander became the oldest major league rookie in 1948 at the age of 42. He'd been playing ball since 1926 in the Negro Leagues on teams everywhere from Mobile, Alabama, to Bismarck, North Dakota, often in dismal conditions and living in third-class accommodations.

He kept an almanac of his performances. The accounts indicate he played in 2,500 games for 250 teams and won 2,000 of those games. It also says he had 21 wins in a row, 50 no-hitters, and pitched for 62 consecutive scoreless innings. If the numbers sound outrageous, consider that Paige played year-round for 41 years as a barnstormer, in the Negro League, in Latin America, and in the majors.

After six years in the integrated majors, he coached and played minor league ball. At the age of 62 he struck out Hank Aaron when the future home run king he was a minor-leaguer. Paige played his last pro game in 1966 when Lyndon Johnson was president, four decades after taking the field as a pro during the Coolidge administration.

How good was he? On more than a few occasions he felt so confident of his ability to strike out the opposition that he told all the fielders to come in. On occasion, he even told them all to sit down. The stunt didn't always work, but it worked often enough. His eye was so good that from the pitcher's mound he could knock a matchbook off the top of a stick.

Jackie Robinson won lasting fame when he broke baseball's color barrier in 1945. He was 13 years younger than Paige, and Paige, long a star, would have commanded a higher salary. Perhaps more important, Robinson's taciturn temperament enabled him to endure slurs from fans that Paige would have struggled with.

"Jackie didn't have to go through half the back doors as me, nor be insulted by trying to get a sandwich as me, nor be run out of places as me," Paige said years later. "I couldn't have took what Jackie took."

Later, Robinson said Paige was "the greatest Negro pitcher in the history of the game, a compliment Paige took as a back-handed insult.

"If they don't know how smart you are…"

But Paige was far a sour character. He was a master showman. He played hundreds of exhibition games in which a black team would take on a white team. He had a lazy gait that made him look unthreatening to white fans, yet when the time came he could turn on the heat to please black fans—and white ones, too. Paige once told his friend Harlem Globetrotter Meadowlark Lemon "If they don't know how smart you are, you've got an upper hand on them."

By the late 1930s he'd become such a star that he could assemble barnstorming teams of black players and demand the best accommodations.

In 1937, he had the moxie to tell the press he had devised a test for determining whether black players should be in the major leagues. It had three parts: First, the World Series winner would play a team of black all-stars, and the blacks would not get paid unless they won. Second, he would play for any major league team and defer his salary unless he did a good job. Third, ultimately, the fans would decide—they would vote to determine whether blacks could play.

To whom did he give this interview? Unfortunately, to the Communist *Daily Worker* newspaper. His notions went nowhere, except to the FBI, which started a file on him.

Fans didn't care. He sold out major league stadiums in the late 1940s and early 1950s. Once after a game while sitting in a whirlpool, he was surprised to see a funny-looking man with a big bushy moustache and eyebrows kneeling beside him asking for an autograph. It was the movie star Groucho Marx.

Perhaps the fast-talking comedian envied Paige's way with words. Here is how the pitcher once described his art on the mound: "I got bloopers, loopers, and droopers. I got a jump ball, a be ball, a screw ball, a wobbly ball, a whipsy-dipsy-do, a hurry-up ball, a nothin' ball and a bat dodger. My be ball is a be ball 'cause it 'be' right there where I want it, high and inside."

Today Paige is best known not for his blazing fastball, longevity, or sufferance of years playing without the recognition he deserved. He's remembered for his rules for staying young. They are:

* Avoid fried meats which angry up the blood.

* Go very light on the vices, such as carrying on in society. The social ramble ain't restful.

* If your stomach disputes you, lie down and pacify it with cool thoughts.

* Avoid running at all times.

* Keep the juices flowing by jangling around gently as you move.

* Don't look back. Something might be gaining on you.

Did Paige actually live up to his maxims? Well, maybe. He loved fried foods and had legendary stomach upsets. He trained by going on runs as long as 10 miles. Did he look back? No one knows. He kept going.

MORAL: Broil that catfish.

Chapter 23

George Washington

Strictly Charge and Command

Barely out of his teens, the young man
led a 1,000-mile mission.

"I have been particularly cautious not to augment."

King George II himself signed the orders. He sent them to
Robert Dinwiddie, the lieutenant governor of the Colony of
Virginia. Their tenor was as follows—Determine if the enemy is
building forts on our land. If so, bid the enemy to withdraw. If
the enemy fails to do so "we do hereby strictly charge and
command you to drive them off by force of arms."

The ultimate goal? To build an array of British forts
throughout the region to defend settlers and drive out the
French and their hostile Indian allies.

In the early 1750s, investors, such as Dinwiddie, had
beseeched the king to defend their interests in the Ohio
Company. By royal decree, it had won the right to speculate on a
massive stretch of land extending from present-day West
Virginia to Indiana. Meanwhile, the French claimed everything
from New Orleans to the Great Lakes. Both empires knew that
whoever controlled the Ohio region would control the continent.

On October 31, 1753, Dinwiddie met with a 21-year-old
man who hoped to win the honor and privilege of carrying out
the King's orders. A few months before in February he had been
appointed district adjutant to the colony's militia. That role
bestowed on him the rank of major.

That said, however, this young man—George
Washington—had no military experience.

There were good reasons why Dinwiddie chose him to
deliver the King's ultimatum. He was a surveyor who had
travelled the western frontier. He was young and had a hardy

constitution, making him fit for an arduous winter odyssey. He had no blemishes of youthful misbehavior.

There was another reason. Washington later wrote, "I believe few or none [other than myself] would have undertaken it." Many years later he would marvel "that so young and inexperienced a person [such as myself] should have been employed on a negotiation with which subjects of the greatest importance were involved."

Washington also had a certain self-interest—his two half-brothers, like Dinwiddie, were investors in the Ohio Company. They stood to make massive profits if settlers could live safely in the new country.

"A vast quantity of snow"

Immediately, Washington set forth upon receiving his orders. He rode to Fredericksburg 100 miles to the northwest. There he hired a French-speaking Dutchman who was a renowned sword fighter. Together they journeyed 150 miles further northwest to the western edge of the colony—Mills Creek, Maryland (present day Cumberland, Maryland). Washington then hired the accomplished backwoods guide and Ohio Company trader Christopher Gist, as well as four other men, two of whom had traded goods with Indians many times.

Now in mid-November they set forth "thro an uninhabited wilderness country," as Washington would describe it. As they wound their way on barely passable trails, they faced "a vast quantity of snow" as they struggled through the Allegheny Mountains.

Their destination? Fort La Boeuf, a French outpost in present day Waterford, Pennsylvania, 15 miles south of Erie, Pennsylvania, on the shores of Lake Erie. They would make this 230-mile trip, Washington would write, "when the whole face of the earth was covered with snow and the waters covered with ice."

First, Washington took his expedition 110 miles north of Mills Creek to the Forks of the Ohio. This is strategic military site where the Monongahela, Allegheny, and Ohio Rivers meet. This three-river junction also makes it a natural hub for commerce, and it is where Pittsburgh, Pennsylvania, is located. "I spent some time in viewing the rivers and the land in the Fork, which I think extremely well situated for a fort, as it has the absolute command of both rivers," Washington wrote.

Here the young commander demonstrated his steely leadership skills. His party blanched at the thought of crossing the freezing, fast-rushing Allegheny River on horseback. Fearless, Washington drove his horse forward and made the crossing sternly mounted in his saddle.

The others crossed by canoe.

Having mastered this "very rapid swift-running water," Washington's orders instructed him to determine the intentions of the French by meeting with Indian leaders. On November 22, three-and-a-half weeks after leaving Williamsburg, Washington met with the Seneca chief Tanacharison, whom the English called the Half-King. He represented the powerful Iroquois Confederation, the Six Nations.

The Half-King knew Washington by reputation, or so Washington said. The future president claimed the Indian leader gave the him the Indian name Conotocarius— 'devourer of villages.' Through Indian oral histories, the Half-King knew that name had been bestowed on Washington's great-grandfather John Washington. He won it not because of his skill as a warrior but because he had adroitly used the white man's law to take Indian land. The young Washington, it is believed, was proud to be honored with his ancestor's title.

The Half King was predisposed to like the colonists. He had signed a treaty with the British the year before. Thinking they were only interested in trade, he preferred them to the French who he knew were there to steal his land.

The colonists and Indians continued north. After five days, they came to a French trading post named Venango. The French officers there received the travelers gracefully. After dinner, they became drunk on their own wine. Washington had the fortitude to remain sober. They freely told him that "it was their absolute Design to take Possession of the Ohio, & by G they wou'd do it." What's more, they let slip where they planned to build their forts.

Seeking further intelligence, Washington pressed another 120 miles further north in bitterly cold weather to Ft. Le Boeuf. On arriving he saw at least 120 canoes arrayed nearby, ready to be put to military use. He counted more than 100 French soldiers stationed at the fort.

Washington was received warmly by the French commanding officer, a one-eyed veteran of the frontier. Washington told him that "the Lands upon the river Ohio, in the Western Parts of the Colony of Virginia, are so notoriously known to be the Property of the Crown of Great Britain, that it is a Matter of equal Concern & Surprize to me, to hear that a Body of French Forces are erecting Fortresses, & making Settlements upon that River within his Majesty's Dominions." He conveyed King George's decree—Leave peaceably or be removed.

"As to the summons you send me to retire, I do not think myself obliged to obey it," the French officer replied.

During this parley, the Half-King's allegiance to the British pleased Washington.

"If you had come in a peaceable Manner like our Brethren the English," the Seneca chief told the fort's commander, "We shou'd not have been against your trading with us as they do, but to come, Fathers, & build great houses upon our Land, & to take it by Force, is what we cannot submit to."

The Half-King also hedged his bet, telling both men that nothing is permanent. "Both you & the English are White. We live in a Country between, therefore the Land does not belong either to one or the other; but the GREAT BEING above allow'd it to be a Place of Residence for us."

Upon departing, Washington was furious to learn the French had promised the Indians liquor and guns, if they remained at the fort. Eager to return to Virginia with news of the French intransigence, Washington made haste in the cruel weather. His party's horses were so exhausted, they collapsed.

Washington and Gist had to proceed on foot through the wilderness. At the ominously named Indian village of Murdering

Town, they hired several natives to guide them to the Forks of the Ohio.

Although Washington trusted one of them to carry his backpack, Gist was suspicious. Rightly so. When they reached a clearing, the Indian dashed forward, spun around, and fired his musket at close range, somehow missing both men.

Gist tackled the Indian and was about to shoot him dead when Washington told him to let him go. They kept the Indian until nightfall and then released him.

Gist was furious. "As you will not have him killed," he told Washington, "We must get him away and then we must travel all night."

To put distance between themselves and the inevitable war party, they marched until dawn.

When sunrise came, they found their planned path of escape blocked. They thought a nearby river would be frozen over. Instead it was only covered with patches of ice. The two men had only "one poor hatchet" to use to construct a raft. They worked furiously for an entire day before being able to push off.

Then—disaster. Their pitiful craft got caught in the ice. Washington tried to push it free.

"I put out my setting pole to try to stop the raft that the ice might pass by, when the rapidity of the stream threw it with so much violence against the pole that it jerked me into ten feet water," he wrote.

Struggling in the deadly cold water, Washington caught hold of the raft and pulled himself back aboard. Unable to make the crossing, they spent the night on an island. By morning, the river had completely frozen over, and they dashed to safety.

Washington returned to Williamsburg on January 16, 1754, completing his nearly 1,000-mile mission. He dashed off a 7,000-word account of his expedition.

He immediately made his report to Dinwiddie who was justly alarmed at its contents. The French did indeed have plans to militarize the region. Worse, they were actively doing so.

He told Washington to write his observations in publishable form. Within weeks, newspapers throughout the colonies printed *The Journal of Major George Washington*. It appeared as a booklet in London.

"I have been particularly cautious not to augment [my account]," wrote the young man. His readers understood. They knew that this young man's courage—without embellishments—marked him as someone to watch.

MORAL: Seize opportunity.

Chapter 24

Rufus Porter

The Power Balloon Man

He dreamed of transcontinental air travel
long before its time.

"Look at the facts..."

"A flying ship, an air blower, punching press, trip hammer, pocket lamp, pocket chair, fog whistle, wire cutter, engine lathe, clothes drier, grain weigher, camera obscura, spring pistol, engine cut off, balanced valve, revolvidal boat, rotary plow, reaction wind wheel, portable house, paint mill, water lifter, odometer, thermo engine, rotary engine, and scores of other inventions."

Such was the list of creations that *Scientific American* credited to the genius of Rufus L. Porter upon his death at the age of 92 in 1884. In fact, the magazine itself was his invention! He founded it in 1845.

This most ingenuous man also invented a machine that would make ropes, a gristmill powered by the wind, a device for pressing cheese, a portable home, a fog whistle, a gizmo for shelling corn, and a revolving rifle (a rifle whose bullets rotated in the weapon's stock). He sold the rights to his 'revolver' for $100 to Samuel Colt who then created...the revolver.

In his early years he was an itinerant mural painter who traveled throughout New England painting scenes of villages and seacoasts in dwellings. "A painter of democracy," *The New York Times* called him, and his works may still be seen today in some of the region's older inns.

Porter may have even been the inspiration for Mark Twain's novel about an ingenious time-traveling inventor *A Connecticut Yankee in King Arthur's Court*. (Both men lived in Hartford at the same time.)

Depending on one's point of view, Porter was either a visionary or a crackpot. Though most of his ideas were down to earth, he spent years trying to raise money to build a massive dirigible that would have been what he called an "Air Line to California."

The first manned balloon flight had taken place in Europe in 1784. The trouble with balloons was that they went where the air pushed them. Porter made his first model dirigible in 1833.

Tinkerer's Imagination

His tinkerer's imagination went into overdrive in 1848 when gold was discovered in the territory of California. People couldn't get there quickly enough. Ultimately, the Gold Rush lured a half million people west.

The problem was getting there. The shortest but perhaps most arduous route was overland by wagon train from Ft. Joseph in western Missouri, a bone-jarring trip that might take seven months.

The safest, but probably most expensive way, was to go around Cape Horn at the tip of South America. That 15,000-mile voyage took four to eight months.

The speediest way? Sail to the Isthmus of Panama, go overland, and catch a northbound ship on the Pacific side. That 7,000-mile journey would only take two to three months, but travelers risked contracting yellow fever or other deadly diseases in Panama. Not until July 4, 1876, would the transcontinental railroad permit travelers to make the journey in four or five days.)

Porter had a better idea. He wanted to build an 800-foot-long 50-foot diameter hydrogen-filled dirigible that could carry as many as 300 people in a wooden passenger 'saloon' outfitted with 26 windows. It could cross the continent (or cruise to Europe) in a week or less, possibly in even two days, staying aloft for 12 hours at a time and traveling at the then outrageous speed of 100 miles per hour.

Steam engines would drive twin propellers that would be 20 feet in diameter. The zeppelin's construction would require

20,000 feet of spruce rods for the frame and 8,000 yards of cloth coated with India rubber. In case of emergency, the craft's engines and boilers could be swiftly dropped.

He dubbed his airship "the aeroport." Other names for it included the aerial locomotive, the aero-locomotive, and the power balloon. Porter's thinking was in line with his day's emerging technology. The first steam-powered dirigible had flown in 1852 in Paris.

Porter had business savvy. He founded the Aerial Navigation Company, and in early 1849 he laid out his plans in a booklet titled—*Aerial Navigation: The Practicality of Traveling Pleasantly and Safely from New York to California in Three Days.*

His first indoor 'test drive' of a model airship went well. "On a succession of wintry Wednesday nights early in the year 1849, audiences in the cavernous amphitheaters of New York City's Tabernacle Church at Broadway and Worth Street witnessed a curious demonstration," a New York City newspaper reported.

"A toy-sized model airship, shaped like a long cigar and driven by two small propellers with clockwork motors, rose lightly from the pulpit and to the accompaniment of cheers from the watchers began a wide circle in the air. Following the tilt of its rudder, it made the round of the great chandelier that hung from the center of the dome, then returned obediently to the platform from which it was launched."

A year later he demonstrated a model at the Merchant's Exchange in Manhattan. It circled the building's rotunda 11 times. A New York City newspaper raved that "Mr. Porter's 'flying machine did all that it promised on Wednesday evening. It rose above the audience and went around the hall exactly as he said it would, and the spectators gave three cheers for the successful experiment."

Investors lent him the money to build his first aeroport. But this 240-foot-long dirigible never left the ground and may not have even neared completion. A tornado ripped it to shreds. Porter then began building a 700-foot-long airship. When he let the public view it on Thanksgiving Day, a mob ripped its gasbag to bits.

To give a sense of the gargantuan and ambitious nature of Porter's project. consider that Count Ferdinand von Zeppelin's first dirigible, the gas-engine powered 420-foot-long LZ 1, would not fly until 1900. The largest zeppelin ever constructed, the *Hindenburg*, was 776 feet long and could only carry as many as 133 passengers and crew at a maximum speed of 85 mph.

In 1852 Porter sought funding via a newspaper announcement that read: The "safe and durable aerial ship.... will be patronized with abundance of business (more than 50,000 persons are now ready to engage passages) at $200 per passage, which will amount to $30,000 per trip, each way; or $60,000 per week, besides $4,000 for carrying mails. If this aeroport is owned in shares of $5 each, a single share will produce an income of $20 per week."

His imagination glowing, Porter added a P.S.: "It is confidently believed that by this invention unexplored regions may be examined, and the light of civilization and Christianity may be disseminated through benighted lands with facility; and that the world will honor the names of those who now subscribe to aid the introduction of an invention calculated to confer immense benefits upon the entire human race."

Porter had his critics. "It would seem as if the gullibility of human nature kept even pace with the wit of knaves, and that nothing could be proposed for an exhibition too preposterous to find believers," said an editorial in a Philadelphia newspaper. "Now, a flying machine... can never be steered. Yet, as in the analogous instance of perpetual motion, there will be found dolts to believe in it, we suppose, to the end of time.'

Things soon started to fall apart for Porter. In May 1853, he wrote a newspaper "What a world of fools; or rather, what a nation of skeptics and moral cowards.

"Look at the facts. More than ten years ago I published , described, illustrated, and demonstrated the practicability of a convenient mode of traveling safely and rapidly through the air, in any required direction; and subsequently have not only refuted all arguments against it, but demonstrated its practicability by the frequently repeated exhibition of an operating aerial steamer...on a small scale, and proved...that this mode of traveling would be incomparatively more safe, as well as more pleasant and expeditious, than nay mode in present use; and that the cost of an aeroport of such size and proportions as to be capable of carrying 200 passengers safely, at a good speed of 100 miles per hour, would be less than that of an ordinary steam ferry boat; and that the earnings of this aeroport would pay more than 200 percent per week on its cost; and that no accident or emergency could possibly occur to subject the passengers to more danger than that of a hotel residence.

"Yet with these facts before them, and while people are being burned, drowned, smashed and ground up by hundreds, by collisions, overturning and plunging railroad trains, and the burning of steamboats; and while thousands are exposing their lives by land journeys across the thousand miles of desert and wilderness, or submitting to the hardship and dangers of a six months voyage around Cape Horn, such a total apathy, or mental disease of skepticism, and the fear of vulgar sneers pervades the community that not one man of wealth can be found in these United States, willing to furnish the requisite funds for introducing this incomparable and greatly needed improvement."

In 1854 Porter again tried to persuade investors to back him, but for whatever reasons, perhaps including Porter's visible frustration and anger, he had to abandon the project. He had the right idea—and the courage, but he lived too early to realize his dream.

MORAL: Float the idea but stay grounded.

Chapter 25

The Sentinelese

Respect Sentinels

Do the world's most primitive people
have the strongest will?

"I'd give my right arm to know what they're thinking."

If a flying saucer wanted to land in your front yard, would you greet it with a shotgun? What if a Jeep crammed with armed soldiers came barreling down your street, would you blast it? Most people probably wouldn't.

But what if you thought that doing so would be the only way to prevent your relatives from being kidnapped? What if you thought that doing nothing would mean certain death? After all, if you fired the first shot, maybe you would at least have a chance.

The Sentinelese people are violent. At least that is how outsiders see them. They are a Stone Age hunter-gatherer tribe who live on the utterly remote North Sentinel Island. It is one of 572 islands in the archipelago of the Andaman Islands in the Bay of Bengal between India and Myanmar (Burma).

The Sentinelese, whose island unbeknownst to them belongs to India, have lived in solitude possibly for as long as 60,000 years. Experts on ancient human migration believe that they may be a lost remnant of a great movement of people who ventured eastward from Africa and then to Asia and ultimately to the New World.

No natural harbor

No one knows how many Sentinelese there are. Estimates range from as few as 50 to as many as 500. Their 23-square-mile island is heavily forested with mangrove trees.

Its narrow white beaches may be alluring, but the island is not an easy place to get to or to leave. Though there are other populated islands within a reasonable distance, North Sentinel Island has no natural harbor. Worse, it is encircled by treacherous submerged coral reefs that make landing there nearly impossible and leaving equally arduous.

Perhaps the Sentinelese are lucky. Native tribes on other islands, such as the Onge who once numbered as many as 8,000 have seen their populations severely reduced by disease and due to contact with outsiders. Today there are fewer than 100 Onge.

No one can speak the language of the Sentinelese. Even one of the Onge who was brought to North Sentinel Island could not understand what the Sentinelese were saying.

Sentinelese homes are lean-tos. They have raised floors and no walls. Three to four families live in one structure. The Sentinelese typically keep a small fire burning near the corner of each home, possibly to ward off snakes and insects.

They use harpoons to catch fish and sea turtles, and they hunt monitor lizards and wild pigs with longbows. Shrews, bats, and rats live on the island, though whether the Sentinelese feast on them is not known. The islanders' diet also includes coconuts, wild honey, and nuts. They husk the coconuts with their teeth which is to say they tear off the nuts' fibrous outer shells with their teeth, a feat that is actually not so difficult.

It is believed that they have no chief or any sort of leader.

They do not farm.

Their music has only two notes.

They only know the numbers one and two. Anything above that is apparently just 'many.'

They weave baskets, use adzes (small ax-like cutting tools), and know how to make outrigger canoes, though these vessels lack the wherewithal for trips outside the shallows near the island. Their arrowheads are made of metal they have scavenged from shipwrecks and hammered.

Ancient Persian and Arab voyagers who first contacted them thought they were cannibals. This is apparently not true, but the Sentinelese have been known to wear jawbones of deceased relatives as necklaces.

Contact with the Sentinelese has been limited. This is due not only to the remoteness of their island but also to the difficulties involved in going ashore. Plus, the Sentinelese have a well-known reputation for wanting to be left alone. They are not shy about firing barrages of arrows and javelins at outsiders.

Consider why this might be. In 1880, the British kidnapped six islanders. It was British policy to do this when they met new tribes. After abducting some of a tribe's members, they would be returned bearing with lavish gifts to show that the British wanted to be their friends.

However, in the case of the abducted Sentinelese, several died before returning. One might surmise that among the islanders this terrible tale has been passed from generation to generation. Present-day Sentinelese would naturally fear the same evil fate might befall them or their loved ones.

However, when the British ship the *Nineveh* ran aground on the island's reef in 1867, naked Sentinelese attacked the 86 survivors who made it ashore. They waited three days before going after them with iron-tipped spears.

In 1974, a *National Geographic* film crew hoped to film a documentary on the island. It retreated and left after the Sentinelese attacked and struck the director in the thigh with an arrow.

Three years later the freighter *Primrose* wrecked on the island's reefs. Its captain radioed for help. When he saw armed islanders building canoes on the beach, he frantically radioed again, asking that firearms be air-lifted to him and his crew.

A person on Reddit purporting to be the son of *Primrose's* captain, recounts what he says his father told him when he was 12-years-old:

"Their weapons were primitive; arrows and spears. Certainly not the most intimidating weapons by today's standards. But put these primitive weapons in the hands of 30-40 primitive people that have exclusively hunted with them for centuries against a group of 20 civilized men armed with only a flare gun, and you wind up with a fairly uneven fight.

"They tried to board our ship, but the surrounding coral reef preventing them from getting on board. They got close enough for me to see the anger...pure hatred on the faces of the warriors."

"I watch[ed] as my father [told] the story, his body visibly shaking and his voice trembling as he recall[ed] the moment in his life that brought him the closest to his own demise.

"Once they were within range they unleashed their weaponry on the ship. Most of us were below deck and we heard the pings of a volley of arrows hitting the side. The few men on deck weren't afforded the luxury of a steel barrier. They had been trying to communicate and ease tension with the Sentinelese.

"They threw them some food, made friendly gestures. It did nothing to ease their hostility towards us." He grew silent for a moment, reliving the next moments before he finally spoke. "Two of our guys...two were hit. One was struck in the leg. The other...they got him in the head."

Volleys of arrows

A Sikorsky helicopter sent by the Indonesian company P.T. Airfast Services rescued the crew. Its daring pilot Bob Fore made multiple landings on the freighter's deck. There were only two feet of extra space between the tips of his spinning rotors and the vessel's superstructure.

More recently, in 2006, islanders killed two fisherman who went to the island to illegally hunt crabs. When the Indian government dispatched a helicopter to retrieve their bodies, Sentinelese emerged from the underbrush and loosed volleys of arrows at the great metal bird.

Not every Sentinelese interaction with the outside world has been violent. Between the late 1960s and early 1990s, the Indian government sent the islanders "contact missions" whose members were anthropologists.

"I'd give my right arm to know what they're thinking, but we just haven't learned enough about them yet," said Trilokinath Pandit, the Director of Tribal Welfare of the Anthropological Survey of India.

The islanders were most wary of the outsiders and baffled by them. "Clothing doesn't make much sense to them," said Pandit. "They're curious about what we were trying to hide underneath."

Female anthropologist Dr. Madhumala Chattopadhyay had many experiences with the Sentinelese. "Never ever in my six years of doing research alone with the tribes of Andamans did any man ever misbehave with me," she said. "The tribes might be primitive in their technological achievements but socially they are far ahead of us."

Her encounters suddenly ended when the Indian government imposed a three-mile protective zone around the island. Too much harm had been done to other tribes in the islands, either inadvertently through exposure to disease or because modern ways destroyed their cultures. Today the Sentinelese are left in peace as they have been for most of their 60,000 years.

MORAL: Respect your ancestors.

Chapter 26

Estella Pyfrom

Driven Woman

She wouldn't take a back seat on anyone's bus.
She took the wheel.

"I knew it was going to work."

Estella in Spanish means star. Former Palm Beach County, Florida, educator Estella Pyfrom shines brightly indeed. When Pyfrom, 78, retired after 50 years serving in roles such as teacher, guidance counselor, and summer school principal, she wasn't ready for a rocking chair.

Instead, she bought a bus she dubbed "Estella's Brilliant Bus," remodeled it, and loaded it with computers. Then she sat in its driver's seat and started steering it to local neighborhoods where children didn't have computers for math, reading, or social studies at home or transportation to get to them.

"Kids call me 'the gadget lady,' " said Pyfrom. She now has two buses, which she takes on educational field trips to the midwest. "Estella's Brilliant Bus is a big gadget with a mission on a movement," she says.

Pyfrom's not alone in her odyssey. Microsoft, Wells Fargo, Comcast, Office Depot, and dozens of Florida organizations support her efforts. CNN named her a Top 10 Hero in 2013, calling her a "community crusader."

Her goal? "To be able to connect with bus companies that in some way can assist me with this mission." There's more: "My destination," she said, "is to have a bus not just in every city in the U.S. but also across the world."

Pyfrom knows all about beating the odds. Her parents were migrant farm workers. She began picking beans alongside them when she was six years old as her family moved from farm to farm, from Florida to New York. Later, her father became a contractor, operating trucks and buses, and that's how Pyfrom as a youngster learned to handle a big vehicle.

"I paid for that bus with all my pennies," she said. "To get the first bus on the road and to continue to move forward, I've spent more than a million dollars." Cost has never deterred her.

"I knew it was going to work," she explained. "Otherwise, I wouldn't have taken the risk. You have to start out knowing that God is on your side and realize that you're going to have some temporary setbacks because with God on your side and your own determination, failure is not an option. You are going to make it."

MORAL: Accelerate.

Chapter 27

Viktor Frankl

All is Lost, All is Found

In the death camp, he found life.

"We had to learn ourselves and, furthermore,
we had to teach the despairing men
that it did not really matter what we
expected from life, but rather what life expected from us."

Shortly after Pearl Harbor, the American consulate in Vienna issued a visa to the Jewish psychotherapist Viktor Frankl. But it was only for him and not for his parents. He was torn. He knew it not be long before the Nazis would transport all the Jews to the death camps.

He went for a walk, hoping for "a hint from heaven." Upon returning home, his father told him he had brought home part of a marble slab from a synagogue that had been burned to the ground. Frankl studied it. A portion of one of the Ten Commandments was inscribed on it. He could make out enough to see that the complete sentence was "Honor thy father and thy mother."

Frankl decided to stay with his parents.

They then spent nearly two years in Theresienstadt, which was both a ghetto and a concentration camp. Frankl received news he was to be shipped to Auschwitz. His wife worked in a munitions factory. She got no such orders. She was too valuable to be taken from her post. Frankl told her to stay. Instead, without his knowledge, she volunteered to go on the same train with him to the death camp.

Before leaving, she sewed the manuscript of his new book on psychotherapy into the lining of his jacket. That way the Nazis at Auschwitz wouldn't get it.

Frankl recalled thinking as he approached its gates, "No one could yet grasp the fact that everything would be taken away."

He confided to an older prisoner, "I must keep [this manuscript] at all costs,"

"*Scheisse*," the prisoner replied.

The guards took everything from Frankl—his clothes and, of course, the hidden manuscript and even his hair which was shorn off to prevent the spread of disease.

Guards did let Frankl keep his belt and his shoes.

"I struck out my whole former life," he recalled. "All we possessed, literally, was our naked existence."

He became #119,104

There was one thing that Frankl realized the guards and the horrors of the death camp could not take from him—his spiritual freedom—his attitude towards the reality confronting him.

Frankl became #119,014. He lost his parents, his wife, and his brother in the camps. He slaved as a laborer at Auschwitz and Dachau and worked as a physician at Turkheim.

After being liberated, in nine days he wrote the book *Man's Search for Meaning*. It has since been translated into 24 languages. More than 12 million copies have been printed. It is regarded as one of the greatest written works of the 20th century.

Frankl came to believe that the purpose of life is not about the pursuit of pleasure, power, or glory. The purpose of life is the pursuit of meaning. He writes that even when a person is subjected to the most brutal degradation, no one can rob him of his spiritual power to transform seemingly meaningless suffering into a noble achievement.

"When a man finds that it is his destiny to suffer, he will have to accept his suffering as his task; his single and unique task," Frankl writes. "He will have to acknowledge the fact that even in suffering he is unique and alone in the universe. No one can relieve him of his suffering or suffer in his place. His unique opportunity lies in the way in which he bears his burden."

Everyone, regardless of the plight they find themselves in, must "face up to the full amount of suffering, trying to keep moments of weakness and furtive tears to a minimum." In the camps, Frankl said there "was no need to be ashamed of tears, for tears bore witness that a man had the greatest of courage, the courage to suffer. Only very few realized that."

If you were alive, you could have hope. "Health, family, happiness, professional abilities, fortune, position in society—all these were things that could be achieved again or restored," he wrote. He understood that if one is resilient enough the suffering one endures can be turned into an asset—something that strengthens the soul.

Often it was only hope—and hope alone—that kept inmates alive. Many made the mistake of thinking they would be freed by a certain date, perhaps Christmas. When that date came and went, so did their will to live. Wrote Frankl: "The prisoner who had lost faith in the future—his future—was doomed."

"Fate was one's master"

In retrospect, Frankl estimated that he had only a one-in-20 chance of surviving. What kept him Frankl alive?

He says he had an "inborn optimism."

His training as a psychiatrist made him a good listener. On at least one occasion he says a guard took a liking to him "because [I] listened to his love stories and matrimonial troubles."

He believed that those with sensitive natures had a better chance of survival, even though they might have been less physically robust. "Sensitive people who were used to a rich intellectual life may have suffered much pain (they were often of a delicate constitution), but the damage to their inner selves was less," he writes. "They were able to retreat from their terrible surroundings to a life of inner riches and spiritual freedom."

He accepted the reality of his situation. "I just waited for things to take their course....Fate was one's master, and [I learned] that one must not try to influence it in any way," he said.

Frankl watched other prisoners try to outwit fate by guessing which work details might offer a chance for freedom. For example, on one occasion his "friends who had thought they were traveling to freedom that night had been taken in the trucks to [such-and-such] camp, and there they were locked in the huts and burned to death."

Frankl even put his sense of humor to work. Grim laughter was also a survival tool, "another of the soul's weapons in the fight for self-preservation."

But, most of all, what kept Frankl and others alive was love. He believed that if anyone in a survival situation can focus their imagination on a beloved, that awareness gives the strength to live another day.

"Nothing could touch the strength of my love, my thoughts, and the image of my beloved," he writes. "Had I known then that my wife was dead, I think that I would still have given myself, undisturbed by that knowledge, to the contemplation of her image, and that my mental conversation with her would have been just as vivid and just as satisfying....

"The truth—that love is the ultimate and the highest goal to which man can aspire. Then I grasped the meaning of the greatest secret that human poetry and human thought and belief have to impart: *the salvation of man is through love and in love*."

Those who survived conquered fear forever, according to Frankl. For the rest of their lives they would fear nothing— except God.

MORAL: Be worthy.

Chapter 28

Alfred Ely Beach

He Dug Deep

Life underground was a day
at the beach for this bold businessman.

"A hurricane of frightful power"

If you were a businessman in Manhattan in the 1860s and 1870s, you wanted William 'Boss' Tweed as a friend. He ran the Democratic Party's political machine. It controlled the city. What's more, Tweed was the Big Apple's third-biggest landholder. Nothing happened without Tweed's permission—at least until 1877 when he went to prison for stealing tens of millions of dollars from taxpayers.

Even in those days, traffic was horrid in New York City, especially Manhattan. Alfred Ely Beach had a dream—a subterranean dream—and he defied Tweed. Beach wanted to build a subway. Tweed didn't.

Beach was no eccentric. He knew how to make an underground train system work. He had the scientific, legal, and business savvy, and the money to make it happen. What he didn't have was Tweed in his back pocket.

Born into a wealthy New York City family, Beach had in 1849 proposed the construction of an underground horse-powered tram system. That idea went nowhere. Around the same time, he designed and patented a typewriter for the blind. It embossed letters on paper. That notion fizzled, too.

He then became publisher of *The New York Sun* newspaper. It was the city's first daily paper that cost only a penny. It was also the first paper to publish lurid crime stories. The result? A huge success.

Then a new publication called *Scientific American* came to his attention. Oddly, though, it published poetry and essays.

Beach had big plans for it. As its co-owner, he turned it into a publication about scientific progress.

Experts on the history of American patents think Beach's vision for the magazine caused such excitement in the scientific community that it was at least partly responsible for the vast jump in the number of patent applications during the mid-1800s—from 600 in 1846 to 20,000 in 1886.

Ambitions ran low

But Beach's ambitions ran low, much lower than patents and papers. His underground urgings led him to establish the Beach Pneumatic Power Company. In 1867 his *Scientific American* proclaimed: "It is probable that a pneumatic railway of considerable length for regular traffic will soon be laid down near New-York, under the auspices of the Pneumatic Dispatch Company of New Jersey, of which Mr. Beach has lately been elected President."

His subway would run on air-power. A giant fan would propel underground carriages. It would push them with air, and when the fan's direction was reversed, it would suck them backwards.

Beach's problem was political, not technological. He went before New York City's government and proposed the following: He would build not a "railway of considerable length" but a test line consisting of one stop with one car. It would run 312-feet underneath Broadway connecting Murray Street and Warren Street. (This is near the Wall Street area in the southern tip of Manhattan.)

Unfortunately, local—and powerful—landowners felt threatened by digging near or under their properties. The millionaire John Jacob Astor came out against the project. He was one of the city's biggest landlords. Alexander T. Stewart wanted no mechanical moles burrowing anywhere near his buildings, threatening their stability. He owned the Marble Palace (otherwise known by its lower Manhattan address 280 Broadway). It was the city's first department store and had a well-heeled clientele. And, unfortunately for Beach, the swank store stood on Broadway one block north of Warren Street.

What's more, there were also discussions in New York City about building an 'el' system, a network of 'el'-evated trains that would run on trestles above the city's crowded streets. Property owners preferred that plan. And "Boss" Tweed liked it, too. He especially fancied the thought of the millions of dollars he would surreptitiously make in bribes from its construction.

In the end, Beach could only get the city fathers to approve tunneling to build much smaller postal tubes. A system of shooting air-powered underground mail had already proven successful in London.

He wasn't going to give up on his dream. "I won't pay political blackmail," Beach told his brother, who was the co-publisher of *The Sun*. "I say, let's build this subway furtively."

After getting his permit, Beach quietly went back to the city. He had the permit amended so he could dig a tunnel with a greater diameter. No one noticed the change, and Beach had his day in the sun—or in the dark, as the case may be.

His men dug secretly in the day using a hydraulic tunneling bore. To help keep the project hush-hush, the resulting great heaps of dirt were brought to the surface and hauled away by teams of horse-drawn wagons only at night. Beach went to such lengths that the wagons had muffled wheels.

When the mayor wanted to visit this stygian construction site, Beach refused to let him descend. After all, Beach was footing the bill. It's estimated he sunk somewhere between $70,000 and $350,000 of his own funds into the project ($1.2 million to $6.1 million in 2018 dollars).

In February 1870 Beach opened his subway to acclaim. Passengers entered through air-tight doors in Devlin's, a men's clothing store. Then they descended into a 112-foot-long waiting room. *The New York Times* reported that instead of a "dismal, cavernous retreat," travelers found a "light, airy tunnel" complete with an "elegant reception room."

Here passengers waited in style amid Greek-style statues. Gas lamps burning in chandeliers kept the hall brightly lit. Those waiting enjoyed gazing at frescoes and at goldfish swimming in a fountain. There was even a baby grand piano.

Adjacent to the hall was the Great Aeolor. This steam-powered air pump got its name from Aeolus, the god the ancient Greeks believed controlled the winds. But most people called the grand gizmo The Western Tornado.

Its enormous throat

Wrote one passenger: "As we went in, we felt a gentle breeze; but after we arrived at the mouth of the great blower, and while we were gazing in wonder at the motions of the gigantic blowing-wings, the engineer put on more steam and increased the speed, so that the blast instantly became a hurricane of frightful power.

"Hats, bonnets, shawls, handkerchiefs, and every loose thing, were snatched away from our hands and swept into the tunnel; while all of us, unable to stand against the tornado, hastily retreated from the machine to a corner of the air-box, where we were slightly sheltered. At this juncture the speed of the Aeolor was reduced, the storm was over, and only a gentle summer's breeze issued from its enormous throat."

The train did indeed have one car which held 22 passengers. It ran 312 feet in a tunnel that was nine feet in diameter. It went 10 miles per hour. The fare was 25 cents. All proceeds benefited a home for orphaned children of men who fought for the Union Army in the Civil War.

The *Times* raved that Beach's conveyance was "the most novel, if not the most successful, enterprise that New York has seen in many a day." The public agreed. Beach sold 400,000 tickets.

He wanted to dramatically extend his subway. "We propose to operate a subway all the way to Central Park, about five miles in all," said Beach. "When it's finished we should be able to carry 20,000 passengers a day at speeds up to a mile a minute."

That, however, was not to be. Tweed was furious and shut him down after a year. Nonetheless, Beach fought back. Bills supporting an expanded subway line passed in the state legislature in 1871 and 1872, but the governor, who was conveniently in Tweed's employ, vetoed them, saying the project lacked adequate state and city supervision.

Finally, in 1873 when it looked like Beach would get political approval and financial backing, the U.S. fell into a severe depression, and his financial backers had to withdraw their proposed funding.

For a time, Beach rented out his underground world as a rifle range and then as a wine cellar. Ultimately, those ventures failed, and when Devlin's burned to the ground, the entrances to the subway were sealed and not opened again until 1912 when the city built the BMT subway line. His subway car was donated to Cornell. Its whereabouts is now unknown.

**MORAL: Get down if you want
get up in the world.**

Chapter 29

Gene Simmons

Dressed to Kill

He went around the world kissing people
to get the respect he deserved.

"Go big, or go home."

Israeli-born Chaim Witz came to America at the age of
eight. When he first saw Santa Claus, he thought he was a Russian
rabbi. His mother was a Holocaust survivor. He grew up in
poverty. No indoor plumbing. No toys. No phone. No toothpaste.
"You actually don't need much," he now says. "But that doesn't
mean you shouldn't have it all."

When he emigrated to America, he'd never watched
television or been inside a grocery store. To him, jam on Wonder
Bread was a fantastic luxury. "America taught me no one has the
right to make you feel less than what you are," he says. "The
uniquely American spirit of individuality and pride allowed me to
embrace the idea of entrepreneurship; that not only can you do
anything—you can do everything."

As a teen in Queens, N.Y., he sought out any job. He took
typing lessons and worked as a secretary (partly to meet girls)
and even worked at *Glamour* and *Vogue*. Obsessed with virile
comic book heroes, he resold old comics often for big money.

When Gene Simmons and his partner Paul Stanley started
their business (which reflected their flair for fashion and
machismo), neither knew anything about marketing, law, or had
any education in their field.

Named "The Demon"

Today, thanks to the massive success of that business
venture—the rock band KISS, he is one of the most famous people

in the world. And what a presence he is—a black-and-white faced kabuki actor meets a Nazi SS officer meets a blood-spitting Godzilla meets a hairy-chested leather drag queen in massive platform heels. Or something like that. His bass-playing 'character' is named "The Demon." (The band's logo is banned in Germany and Israel where such iconography is banned.)

When the band started, his philosophy was "Go big, or go home." That's attitude from someone who never had music lessons and doesn't know how to read music." His attitude wasn't so much that he was a musician but that he was a business man in the music business.

Most prominent rock musicians appear to be left-of-center politically. Not Simmons. "I will forever be grateful to American for going into World War II, when it had nothing to gain…and rescued my mother from the Nazi German concentration camps," he said. "She is alive, and I am alive because of America, and if you have a problem with America, you have a problem with me."

He owns racetracks, restaurants, gives speeches for $100,000, and on and on. His charitable efforts support hundreds of children in Africa. "Sink or swim," he says. "You have to jump into the deep end. If you wait until you are ready, you will wait forever."

MORAL: Lick it up.

Chapter 30

Dick O'Kane

Surfacing to Life

His own torpedo sank him, but not even a
POW camp could sink his hope.

"It was hot territory, but where else would we want to go?"

Only nine.

Of its crew of 87 men, only nine would survive the sinking of the submarine *U.S.S. Tang*. When they were rescued—by the Japanese—further horrors awaited them.

In October 1944, the *Tang* was on its fifth patrol. Its commander Dick O'Kane, known as the underwater ace of aces, had volunteered for the most dangerous assignment possible, cruising the Formosa Strait between Formosa (present day Taiwan) and China. These narrow waters were heavily trafficked with Japanese convoys, and he knew the hunting would be good there.

"We knew we were going into very dangerous waters," one crewman recalled. "It was hot territory, but where else would we want to go?"

During its first four patrols under O'Kane's aggressive command, the *Tang* had proven itself the deadliest U.S. submarine in the Pacific. It sank 33 enemy ships, more than any other sub in terms of numbers and tonnage.

On its last patrol, the *Tang* sent eight Japanese tankers and freighters to the bottom of the ocean. O'Kane also spotted a distinctive vessel. It had a white hull and a red cross emblazoned on it—A hospital ship. Another officer suggested he fire on it, noting that it might be transporting as many as 10,000 Japanese soldiers.

"We play by the rules," O'Kane replied.

While serving as the executive officer on another submarine, he was present on the bridge when it sank a Japanese transport, sending hundreds of Japanese troops into the water. His commanding officer gave orders to sink their lifeboats and then kill their survivors floating in the water. That wasn't O'Kane's kind of war.

Now, after successfully firing 23 of his sub's 24 torpedoes, O'Kane sent the last one hurtling towards a crippled transport ship. Instead, it malfunctioned, made a 'circular run,' and, despite frantic evasive maneuvers, struck the Tang 20 seconds after being fired.

The massive explosion killed half of the *Tang's* 87-member crew instantly. O'Kane and two other seamen scrambled to safety out of the bridge and into the water.

The sub went down by the stern, but instead of sinking to the bottom, air trapped in its forward ballast tanks kept it suspended nearly vertically in the water, its bow bobbing a few feet above the surface.

With the sub dangling, there was no way the survivors could use the escape trunk in the forward torpedo room. A sailor pulled a hydraulic lever flooding the tanks. Soon the sub settled 180 feet down on the sea bed.

As the survivors fought their way to the torpedo room, the Japanese hurled depth charges down, rattling the sub and causing a slow-burning fire. The air grew fouler by the minute.

Each crewman had three options—Suffocate, escape, or shoot himself in the head. "There was no panic," recalled motor machinist mate Clayton Decker. "Everyone was calm."

The escape trunk was the size of a phone booth. Here is how it worked: Several men would seal themselves inside and fill it with sea water until the water pressure in the trunk equaled the water pressure outside. The first man out would release a buoy which was connected by a rope to the sub.

Then each man would clamber out into the pitch-black darkness and rise slowly hand-by-hand along the rope but not so quickly that he would get the bends and die upon reaching the surface.

Every crewman had a special undersea rescue device—a Momsen Lung—and wore it strapped to his chest. When a sailor exhaled into it, the chemicals in the bag converted carbon dioxide into oxygen, allowing for a slow ascent.

The first man out panicked. He got lost inside the superstructure of the sub, unable to find the exit. Those inside heard him pound the hull again and again before drowning. Other men panicked inside the escape trunk, refused to leave, and crawled into bunks to die.

Of the 30 seamen still alive (many of whom were too injured to enter the escape trunk), only 13 left the sub. "You never let go [of the rope]," said Decker. "Many of the guys who didn't make it didn't get a hold of that line." Only five survived the ascent, one of whom reached the surface without using a Momsen Lung.

After floating in the water for several hours, a Japanese naval vessel picked up the nine survivors. At first, the Japanese thought they were German sailors. This ship happened to have picked up seamen from ships the *Tang* had sunk. The enraged survivors and the ship's crew tortured the Americans.

"They kept us on this hot steel deck under a blazing sun for five days and five nights," said Decker. "We were a mass of blisters. Those Jap survivors would grab us by the hair and stick lit cigarettes up our noses. They just beat the shit out of us. No water, no food. We thought, this is the end."

The Japanese sent the *Tang's* crew were sent to the Ofuna prison camp. Other POWs had nicknamed it the "Torture Farm." The Japanese said the Americans had killed civilians and refused to grant them POW status. They were given only half the usual food ration and were isolated from other prisoners.

Until they were liberated in August 1945, O'Kane and his men were starved and beaten and tortured regularly. "The guards would sneak in and whack you with a club when you were sound asleep," said Decker. "They didn't give a damn where they hit you. Sometimes they'd even hit you in the back of the head and knock you cold."

Of all the crew, O'Kane suffered the most. When he was liberated, he was near death. He weighed only 88 pounds and was suffering from jaundice, beriberi, and dysentery. Doctors only gave him a 50/50 chance of surviving. He lived to be 83 and died of pneumonia.

"He was without a doubt the finest submarine skipper in the entire Navy," said Decker. He received the Medal of Honor and was buried at Arlington National Cemetery.

**MOTTO: Sometimes you have to give
up the ship to sail again.**

Chapter 31

Roger Boisjoly

The Deadly Seal

Uncle Sam was in a hurry.
One man said, "Slow down."

"I fought like hell..."

Roger Boisjoly would not take "No" for an answer. An aerospace engineer at the Morton-Thiokol company, he was gravely concerned about the safety of Space Shuttle launches. His Utah-based employer built the Shuttle's external rockets. Even during their early testing, he feared that a design flaw in those rockets might cause a Shuttle to explode on launch.

Starting in the early 1980s, Boisjoly (pronounced like *Beaujolais* wine) served as his company's senior structural engineer (technically a fluid dynamacist and aerodynamicist) overseeing the development and construction of the rockets' casings. He also headed his company's efforts to redesign their seals and joints.

Sections of the rockets' massive cylinders were manufactured separately. When they were assembled one on top of each other, massive rubbery O-rings separated the giant metal cylinders, and the structures came together in a joint sealed with putty, a complex fabrication designed to prevent superheated gases from leaking, an event that would cause an explosion.

During the design process, however, the company altered the manner in which the cylinders were built (partly to cut costs), and their assembly also deviated from the original engineering plans.

Boisjoly inspected seals from earlier missions. He found that that the pressures and stresses of launch had severely eroded them. Boisjoly had worked in the space program since Apollo, and he knew that at low temperatures O-rings became brittle, and their loss of resiliency might cause fiery gases from inside the rockets to leak, causing a catastrophe.

When the Space Shuttle Challenger launched on the morning of January 28, 1986, the temperature was 36 degrees, 15 degrees colder than on the day of any previous launch. Seventy-three seconds after lift-off, what Boisjoly feared happened. The right solid-rocket booster suffered a catastrophic structural failure. The Challenger erupted into a fireball, killing all seven astronauts.

Six months before the disaster, Boisjoly had written a memo to his company's senior vice president, predicting the O-rings would fail causing a "result [that] would be catastrophic of the highest order—loss of human life."

Partly due to his concerns, the company formed a task force to study the effects of cold on the O-rings; sadly, however, the project became bogged down in paperwork and the feverish demands of keeping Shuttle launches on schedule.

The night before the launch Boisjoly and his colleagues argued for hours with their company's executives, pleading with them to tell NASA to postpone lift-off. Finally, Morton-Thiokol told NASA to delay the launch. In response, NASA's deputy director of science and engineering George Hardy told Morton-Thiokol: "I am appalled by your recommendation." Another NASA executive said, "God sake, Thiokol, when do you expect me to launch—next April?"

As a result of this phone conference, Morton Thiokol reversed its decision and gave NASA its blessing to proceed.

"I fought like hell to stop that launch," Boisjoly later said.

He mistakenly believed the Challenger would explode at the moment the rockets ignited. As it rose into the sky, he became increasingly relieved. The first minute after launch is the most dangerous. During that period, the spaceship passes through "maximum dynamic pressure" when the physical forces on the vehicle are greatest.

Time of greatest danger

Immediately after lift-off the rockets are actually throttled down to reduce stresses on the spacecraft. At 68 seconds into the flight, ground control told the Shuttle, "Go at throttle up," meaning that the time of greatest danger had passed and that the shuttle's mission commander could now rev up the rockets to use 100 percent of their power to propel the ship into orbit.

Boisjoly felt slightly relieved. A colleague turned to him, saying "Oh, God! We made it!"

"Roger, go at throttle up," replied mission commander Richard Scobee, sending the last transmission from the shuttle. Seconds later it disintegrated.

Some criticized Boisjoly for not verbally dissenting from his company's final decision when it was made on the conference call.

"I never [would] take [away] any management right to take the input of an engineer and then make a decision based upon that input, and I truly believe that," he later said. "There was no point in me doing anything any further than I had already attempted to do…[but] I left the room feeling badly defeated. I personally felt that management was under a lot of pressure to launch and that they made a very tough decision, but I didn't agree with it."

Boisjoly spent the next 24 years lecturing on business ethics. He received the Award for Scientific Freedom and Responsibility from the American Association for the Advancement of Science in 1988.

**MORAL: Stand your ground.
Speak up for what is right.**

Chapter 32

Chuck Close

Up, Close!

He found that life lay in the details.

"I never back up."

"In life," says Chuck Close, "you can be dealt a winning hand of cards, and you can find a way to lose, and you can be dealt a losing hand and find a way to win. True in art and true in life: You pretty much make your own destiny. If you are by nature an optimistic person, which I am, that puts you in a better position to be lucky in life."

Chuck Close is the world's most famous living portraitist, and he knows a thing or two about bad luck.

His paintings are unmistakable. He starts with a photograph of a face and then reconstructs it on grid that can be as large as eight by nine feet. Up close (so to speak), the face dissolves into blobs and dots of pointillist color, but at a distance, the likeness is precise, yet fragmented, pixelated, and distorted, almost like a stone mosaic made out of paint.

In his early years, his works were utterly merciless in their photorealism, showing every tiny hair and deformity.

"I deconstruct"

"In my paintings," says Close, "I deconstruct a photo image—breaking it into pieces—and create a whole new image. In fact, all artworks that interest me are constructed."

Why such a fascination with the minuscule? Says Close: As a child, "I would take my grandmother's magnifying glass, and I'd scan the covers of the magazines, which during that time were mostly hand-painted illustrations, to figure out how paintings got made; what different touch each of them had."

He starts by disassembling a photograph, dicing it into a grid containing hundreds, even thousands of three-inch squares. Then he painstakingly transfers by paintbrush the colors in each square onto his huge canvases.

He mostly paints self-portraits and faces of friends, but he has also done portraits of the Dalai Lama, Barack Obama, Brad Pitt, and composer Philip Glass.

"There's a real job in putting these little marks together," says Close. "They may look like hot dogs, but with them I build a painting."

A born artist, when he was 11, he saw a Jackson Pollock in a museum, and he remembers thinking, "I was absolutely outraged, disturbed. It was so far removed from what I thought art was. However, within two or three days, I was dripping paint all over my old paintings.

"In a way, I've been chasing that experience ever since. That's the reason I've been going to see shows in different galleries, trying to look at the work of emerging artists as much as I can, in an attempt to recreate or re-live that sensation of being shocked."

His work is all the more remarkable for two reasons. First, Close suffers from face blindness, whose technical name is prosopagnosia. As a result, he cannot remember people by their faces. It would be all too convenient an explanation if that was why Close paints faces, and some say he doesn't actually have the disorder at all—That it's just a legend that surrounds the artist and his works.

Close himself doesn't buy that. "I don't think it's a coincidence that having face blindness, I paint people's faces," he says. "It's my way of getting closer to people. When I paint someone, it's always a person's face I want to remember."

Completely paralyzed

Close has confronted even worse woes. In 1988, when he was 48, a spinal-artery collapse left him nearly completely paralyzed from the neck down.

He had already struggled with physical ailments as a child. The kidney disease nephritis kept him in bed at home for a year when he was a sixth-grader. (And at around the same time his father died, and his mother was diagnosed with breast cancer.) He also had a rare neuromuscular disorder that made it hard for him to pick up his feet. Plus, he was dyslexic.

After being reduced to quadriplegia, within eight months he was painting with a brush held between his teeth. "The worst possible thing in the world can happen to you, and you will overcome it," he says. "You will be happy again."

Now, after months of intensive physical therapy, he paints with a brush strapped to his wrist and has regained much more mobility, though he remains confined to a wheelchair. His motorized easel will rotate canvases and move them up and down to bring his works-in-progress within his reach.

"I never back up," says Close. "If I did, I'd never get the damn things [the paintings] done."

MORAL: Push around the paint of your life.

Chapter 33

Harry Markopolos

The $65 Billion Dollar Fraud Finder

The feds wouldn't listen, but one man wouldn't give up.

"We don't quit."

Harry Markopolos' father owned a chain of 12 Arthur Treacher's Fish 'n' Chips restaurants. As a child, he must have developed a nose for knowing when something smells fishy. When he grew up he became an investment advisor and portfolio manager at a Boston investment company.

In 1999 another money manager at his firm told him about a hedge fund that was earning its luxe clients a steady one to two percent net return on their money every month—month after month, with only a very few monthly exceptions. The question was—Should we get our clients in on this action?

To Markopolos, this smelled like week-old haddock in August. After all, when Markopolos was a young man he discovered fraud at his father's restaurant chain—An employee was stealing cases of frozen fish fingers, and Harry put his thumb down on the not-so-well breaded bandit.

It is impossible for any investment to always return a profit (unless it is something like a bank savings account that has a fixed return). Instantly, Markopolos knew he was looking at a Ponzi scheme.

This type of financial rip-off gets its name from con artist Charles Ponzi who promised investors fantastic returns. He was able to achieve this, for a while by taking money from latecomers and parceling it out to those who got in first on the deal. The only way it works is if the con man has a steady and growing stream of new money coming in.

What Markopolos had stumbled onto was Bernie Madoff's $65 billion con game serving some of the wealthiest people in the world, likely including the Russian mafia and international drug cartels.

Back in 1999, Markopolos calculated that based on how much money the secretive Madoff was taking in, he should have been running the world's largest hedge fund managing and actively trading as much as six billion dollars, and this was at a time when the best-known hedge funds had no more than two to three billion under management. No matter how hard Markopolos looked he couldn't find traces of Madoff's trading activity in the financial markets. That meant he really wasn't doing much trading at all.

Justly pleased with this insight, Markopolos in 2000 wrote an eight-page report and took it to the U.S. Security and Exchange Commission (SEC), the federal agency that regulates the American banking and financial industries.

"I had given them the case on a silver platter and gift-wrapped it, too," he said. The result? Nothing happened. Why? Markopolos guessed (correctly as it turned out) that the SEC was staffed with lawyers, not finance wizards. The SEC enforcement director he had met with simply didn't understand what he was saying.

Not one to give up, Markopolos went back in 2001 this time with an 11-page report, containing even more evidence and asserting that Madoff had now sucked in $12 billion from investors. Again, nothing happened.

The report got kicked up the ladder to the SEC's New York office, but its chief had ruled that since Madoff was not a registered investment advisor he, therefore, could not be conducting dishonest business as an investment advisor.

For the next four years, Markopolos and his small team of financial sleuths continued to investigate Madoff. In the interim, in 2001 the well-respected U.S. financial journal *Barron's* picked up a disquieting report on Madoff's business published by an obscure finance magazine. Yet nothing happened.

So, in 2005 Markopolos wrote yet another report, this one 21-pages long, and gave it to the SEC. Now he estimated that Madoff had nabbed as much as $50 billion from his pigeons.

For a year, the SEC did nothing. Then it sent agents to talk to Madoff. They suspected that he was lying to them but concluded that his misdeeds, whatever they were, simply "were not so serious as to warrant an enforcement action."

In 2008, Markopolos tried again, and again the SEC did nothing. But later that year the markets crashed, and Madoff, unable to pay investors demanding their money, was exposed. In December 2008, his two sons, who worked for him, asked their father why he seemed so distressed. Madoff confessed to them. The sons called an attorney. The attorney called the SEC, and the next day Madoff was arrested.

Around this time, Markopolos started packing a .38 revolver. After all, he had helped bring down a man who was managing money for Moscow mobsters and South American cocaine cartel leaders.

As much as $65 billion vanished. The hardest hit were hundreds of philanthropies, charities, museums, and foundations around the world, as well as the Royal Bank of Scotland, the Japanese investment firm Nomura, Massachusetts Pension Reserves and wealthy individuals such as Holocaust survivor and author Elie Wiesel, real estate magnate Mort Zuckerman, the family of former New York Governor Eliot Switzer, and movie actor Kevin Bacon.

Madoff was sentenced to a 150-year term in a federal penitentiary. His eldest son hanged himself on the second anniversary of his arrest. His younger son died of cancer four years later. His wife refuses to communicate with him.

Markopolos won acclaim for his dogged pursuit of Madoff, and he's become a global fraud investigator. Before going in finance, Markopolos served in the Army, and today he says, "I came from an Army background, and the one thing I can say about the Army is that we don't quit."

MORAL: Make sure things add up.

Chapter 34

John Wesley

Heart Strangely Warmed

He had a method, and it caused riots.

*"Catch on fire with enthusiasm,
and people will come for miles to watch you burn."*

"Knock his brains out! Down with him! Kill him at once!" shouted a mob of several hundred men surrounding John Wesley. Riots often accompanied Wesley, the mild-mannered founder of the Methodist Church. The worst violence he encountered probably came at the coal-mining town of Wednesbury in October 1743. The rioting went on for six days. Homes of Methodists were vandalized and wrecked, and Wesley's followers were beaten in the streets.

"It is no wonder that Satan should fight for his own kingdom, when such inroads are made upon it," Wesley remarked.

The mob marched him from place to place in the rain, either trying to muster the courage to lynch him or to find a magistrate willing to jail him. A 1903 biography of Wesley says the turning point came when Wesley "began to pray aloud. Then the ruffian who had headed the rabble, struck with awe, turned and said: "Sir, I will spend my life for you! Follow me, and not one soul here shall touch a hair of your head!' " One by one, members of the mob felt ashamed, and Wesley went free.

He had a remarkable ability to keep his head when people were throwing rocks at him or otherwise threatening to kill him. He believed that one must "always look a mob in the face."

Said one admirer, he had "an indescribable dignity in his bearing, a light in his eyes, and a spiritual influence pervading his whole personality that often overawed and captured the very leaders of the riots," said one admirer.

"Plucked out the fire"

He was the 15th child of an Anglican cleric and memorized much of New Testament while still a boy. From an early age, he believed God had a special purpose for him. When he was five, he was trapped in the home of a minister when it caught on fire.

Upstairs and with no way out, death looked certain until a parishioner (who was standing on another man's shoulders) reached in the window and lofted him to safety. Throughout his life, Wesley would quote Zechariah 3:3 saying he was "a brand plucked out of the fire" to burn an impression on the souls of men.

Unfortunately, however, as a young Anglican minister, Wesley got off to a poor start. He showed great courage in accepting an offer to be the minister of the church in the newly created town of Savannah in the Colony of Georgia. But while crossing the Atlantic, he fell in love with a young woman, Sophia Hopkey.

He ultimately concluded that his vows required him to be celibate. When she fell in love with another man and married him, Wesley humiliated her by refusing to offer her communion. It did not help that she was the niece of the local magistrate.

Wesley was reassigned to a smaller parish. That did no good for her reputation. The magistrate brought charges against Wesley calling him "a liar, villain, and so forth" for defaming her reputation. He said Wesley denied her communion out of revenge because she had spurned his repeated marriage proposals.

Wesley was commanded not to flee the colony, but he did exactly that. In December 1737, he fled Savannah at night, sailing down the river. He then walked to South Carolina and bought passage on the next ship home.

But his miserable experience in the New World contained the seeds of his spiritual rebirth. During the voyage to the colonies, a furious storm hurled his ship terrifically, snapping off its mast. Wesley was petrified. During the tumult, he noticed that some of his shipmates were calmly praying and singing hymns. They were Moravians, German Protestant settlers. The purity of their faith astonished him.

Humiliated and depressed, he felt adrift back in London. Then one day in May 1738, he came upon a group of Moravians holding an evening service in Aldersgate Street. "About a quarter before nine, while [the leader of the service] was describing the change which God works in the heart through faith in Christ, I felt my heart strangely warmed," Wesley recalled.

"I felt I did trust in Christ, Christ alone for salvation, and an assurance was given me that he had taken away my sins, even mine, and saved me from the law of sin and death."

A year later Wesley received an invitation to preach outdoors near the coal-mining town of Bristol. By the standards of the day, this was a strange thing to do, but it was an excellent way to reach some of England's most downtrodden people—coal miners, many of whom didn't go to church.

As an Anglican, Wesley, like the miners, had been raised and taught to believe in predestination. This concept contends that God determines before men are born whether or not they will go to Heaven or Hell.

"Going on to perfection"

Slowly, out of compassion for the poor and because he believed God loves everyone equally, Wesley developed what would become a primary tenant of the Methodist Church—prevenient grace. It holds that God loves all people before they are born, and that God's grant of free will gives everyone the possibility of "going on to perfection," the chance to live an increasingly better life whose reward will be eternity in heaven.

Wesley took a dim view of the Anglican Church which felt was corrupt and did too little to reach out to people in the greatest need of salvation.

Originally, the term "Methodist" was used to mock Wesley and his followers, because Wesley took great stock in his belief that one should have an organized approached to living a Godly life.

He also steadfastly opposed drinking and gambling. This did not endear him to ruffians who thought he should mind his own business and contributed to mob violence.

In the end, however, Wesley was a tireless promoter of his young denomination. He preached as many as 15 sermons a week, many outdoors and in places other than churches—wherever he could reach new souls.

In the course of his life, it is estimated that he rode his horse 250,000 miles to spread the gospel. By the time he died in 1791, he left a thriving movement which had 72,000 members in England and 60,000 in the United States.

Interestingly, his views on health and diet may have been equally influential (and ahead of their time). His book *Primitive Physick* was a best-seller. In it, he offered the following advice: Eat a light dinner and fast for several hours before going to bed; retire at 9 p.m. and rise at 4 or 5 a.m.; work standing if you are in an office; shun coffee and tea because they create anxiety; drink lots of water; exercise regularly, especially by walking; exercise on an empty stomach; and take cold baths to stimulate the blood.

MORAL: Have faith. Stare down the mob.

Chapter 35

Winston Churchill

Fight On

He saved Western Civilization.

"Victory—however how long and hard the road may be."

Two days after Churchill became Prime Minister, the Nazi lightning advance conquered Luxembourg in a day. It crushed Holland in less than a week. The Luftwaffe bombed Rotterdam to ashes, killing 1,000, destroying 30,000 buildings, and leaving 85,000 homeless.

The Germans would take France in six weeks. A few days after the Germans invaded France, a top French general told Churchill "We are beaten." Churchill said it was the most stunning thing he had ever heard in his life.

"Doom marches on," said Churchill. He said this not in May 1940 but in 1936 in the House of Commons where he was an MP, a 'backbencher' (a member who did not serve a role in the administration). "Virtuous motives, trammeled by inertia and timidity, are no match for armed and resolute wickedness," he told Parliament

Churchill believed that the natural state of affairs between nations was war, with periods of peace merely brief aberrations. He had opposed the Treaty of Versailles, recognizing that its punitive terms would cause Germany to fulminate against the victorious Allies. In 1931, he issued his first public warning of a coming war which he predicted would be fomented by revenge-seeking Germans.

As early as 1929, four years before Hitler seized power, Churchill's friends in the British government began leaking him secret documents showing that Germany was rearming, violating the Treaty. Throughout the 1930s, ministry officials, at great risk to themselves, routinely violated secrecy laws to give Churchill the latest secret reports on German militarization.

"I shoot him down…"

Churchill's vision was diamond clear, his resolve irrefragable. In 1930, after a German diplomat met Churchill at a party, he wrote a memo to Berlin saying that Churchill had told him that "Hitler…will seize the first available opportunity to resort to armed force."

Shortly after Hitler took power in 1933, Churchill told another German diplomat in London (who also wrote a memo to Berlin) that there was only one way to deal with Nazis. Comparing them to a mad dog, he said, "If a dog makes a dash for my trousers, I shoot him down before he can bite."

Hitler knew Churchill's views well. He often read translations of his speeches and articles. He knew Churchill was the one British leader who was unafraid of him. British foreign policy towards Germany in the 1930s often seemed designed not to offend Hitler, so great was the fear of another Great War.

The two men almost met in 1932 in a Munich hotel. A longtime friend of Hitler's offered to introduce Churchill to him, as he knew that Hitler came to the hotel every day at five. Everything was set.

Then, Churchill, an ardent Zionist since 1908, said to Hitler's friend, "Why is your chief so violent about the Jews?…What is the sense of being against a man simply because of his birth? How can any man help how he is born? Tell your boss for me that anti-Semitism may be a good starter, but it is a bad stayer." When the friend conveyed these sentiments to Hitler, he cancelled the meeting.

Four years earlier the British government had promised the British people it would keep up with—and surpass—German military rearmament. When it became clear in 1936 that the government had failed to live up to its promise, during a debate in Parliament, Churchill said British leaders had been "decided to be undecided, resolved to be irresolute, adamant for drift, solid for fluidity, all-powerful to be impotent.…We are entering a period of consequences....Germany may well reach the culminating point of her gigantic military preparations..." In his speeches before Parliament, he even warned that when war came again the Germans would plow through Holland and Belgium into France.

In that same year, in a series of lectures and newspaper articles, Churchill begged England to wake up: "It is worth a supreme effort—the laying aside of every impediment, the clear-eyed facing of fundamental facts, the noble acceptance of risk inseparable from heroic endeavor—to control the hideous drift of events and arrest calamity on the threshold. Stop it! Stop it! Stop it!!! NOW is the appointed time."

Yet when the time came for Prime Minister Baldwin to select a Minister of Defense he chose not Churchill but a lawyer whose greatest leadership role had been to oppose changes to the Anglican prayer book. Not only had Churchill first been elected to Parliament in 1900 at the age of 26, he was his government's civilian leader of the Royal Navy during World War I.

Churchill spent the 1930s in disgrace. The public wrongly blamed him for a terrible British defeat at Gallipoli, Turkey, when a naval landing he had planned went badly awry. He changed parties, leading people to think he was inconstant. Perhaps worst, he was a militarist at a time when few in Europe (except the Nazis) thought that war would ever come again in their lifetimes.

"What more can I do?"

At one of his lowest moments he told his fellow parliamentarian (and future prime minister) Harold Macmillan, "I have done my best. I have made all the speeches. Nobody has paid any attention. All my prophecies have turned out to be true. I have been publicly snubbed by the government. What more can I do?"

Now two days after becoming prime minister, Churchill spent the day drafting a radio address to the nation and a speech to Parliament, both to be delivered the next day. Everyone knew England might find its neck under the iron heel of fascism. (Indeed, in 44 days the aerial Battle of Britain would begin, a prelude to naval invasion.)

In a brief appearance before the House of Commons, Churchill told his nation: "....I would say to the House, as I said to those who've joined this government: "I have nothing to offer but blood, toil, tears and sweat."

"We have before us an ordeal of the most grievous kind. We have before us many, many long months of struggle and of suffering. You ask, what is our policy? I will say: It is to wage war, by sea, land and air, with all our might and with all the strength that God can give us; to wage war against a monstrous tyranny, never surpassed in the dark and lamentable catalogue of human crime. That is our policy. You ask, what is our aim? I can answer in one word: victory. Victory at all costs, victory in spite of all terror, victory, however long and hard the road may be; for without victory, there is no survival."

Astonishingly, two weeks later when the Nazi occupation of Western Europe was nearly complete, Churchill's foreign secretary Lord Halifax told the press he would like to "invite Chancellor Hitler to make a new and more generous peace offer."

Churchill saw things differently. He told his family to personally prepare to kill German invaders. When his new son-in-law asked what he could do, Churchill replied, "Get a carving knife from the kitchen and take [it] with you." And to the French he said, "Whatever you may do, we shall fight on forever and ever and ever."

MORAL: Never, never, never quit.

Chapter 36

Arturo Toscanini

The Stick Up Artist

The tune he played to was liberty.

"It is the duty of everyone to fight and help in this sort of cause according to one's means."

Conductor Arturo Toscanini had strong opinions. For example, he hated fish. He had no beef against fish minding their own business swimming in the ocean, but he loathed fish on the dinner table.

At the age of nine he won admission to a local music conservatory where he lived for the next eight years. It often served fish to its students, and often the fish was rank, thus leaving him with a lifelong loathing of finny foods.

His years at the conservatory were a blessing for his financially struggling parents. His elementary school teacher had marveled at young Arturo's ability to memorize poems and his singing voice, telling his father, "Have this boy study, because he has a great capacity for music!"

The school was not luxurious. Students lived a "regular and monotonous life" of lessons, lessons, and more lessons. The boys slept on bedbug infested straw-filled cots and shared one toilet. They were served wine, but it was such dreck, Arturo sold his allotment to other students, so he could buy sheet music.

"Fire to his baton"

Personal privations aside, he loved life there and thrived on his diet of musical studies. Given no choice of what instrument to play, he was assigned the cello. He mastered it so well that when he was 14 he played in the local opera company's orchestra. Other students crowned him with the nickname *Geni* ("Genius").

After graduation, he joined a traveling opera company and memorized the score of *Aida*. When the conductor suddenly quit, others asked Toscanini to fill in. He wowed the audience. He was only 19. "The beardless maestro is a prodigy who communicated the sacred artistic fire to his baton," read a review the next day.

Thus began an international career as a conductor which culminated in his serving as musical director of the NBC Symphony for 17 years.

As befits the stereotype of orchestra conductors, Toscanini had fits on the podium. In rehearsal, if he thought a musician was inattentive or lazy, he might snap his baton, shout at him, or even fling his baton at the transgressor.

Toscanini saved his strongest opinions for politics. He was well known for his long-standing hatred of Italian and Germany fascism. In the 1930s, Mussolini ordered musical groups to open each performance with a rendition of his Fascist Party's anthem. Toscanini refused. The result? In 1931, goons beat him outside of Bologna's opera house.

In the early 1930s, he was a fixture at the annual Wagner Festival in Bayreuth, Germany, but in 1933, the year the Nazis took power, he announced he would not return. He then led orchestras in the mid-1930s at Austria's annual Salzburg Festival, but with Nazi invasion looming, he announced in 1938 he would not go back.

"To breathe freedom"

As a result, Mussolini seized his passport. After an international outcry, il Duce returned it. That same day Toscanini and his family fled Italy for America. "To flee in order to breathe freedom—life!" he wrote.

When invited in 1936 to conduct the first ever performances of the Palestine Orchestra, Toscanini immediately accepted. Its founder asked him what his fee would be. Toscanini dismissed that notion out of hand and said he would travel to Palestine at his own expense.

(From 1920 to 1948, the British government administered the land that is present-day Israel. The League of Nations created this territory, which was known as British Palestine, following the collapse of the Ottoman Empire. The goal was to give Arabs who lived there and Jewish natives and immigrants support "until such time as they are able to stand alone.")

His involvement with what is today the Israeli Philharmonic meant a great deal to the fledging ensemble, most of whose members were Jewish musicians who had fled Nazi Germany and Eastern European nations where they were oppressed.

"I never before saw a country as small as this where there was so much culture as among the Jewish labor and farmer classes," wrote Toscanini.

No less a luminary than Albert Einstein wrote Toscanini to congratulate him, saying: "Honored Master! I feel the need to tell you for once how much I admire and honor you. You are not only the unmatchable interpreter of the world's musical literature, whose forms deserve the highest admiration. In the fight against the Fascist criminals, too, you have shown yourself to be a man of the greatest dignity."

The symphony's inaugural concert featured works by Rossini, Brahms, Schubert, Mendelssohn, and Weber. Many in attendance were so overcome with the grandeur of the event that they wept.

Said Toscanini: "It is the duty of everyone to fight and help in this sort of cause according to one's means."

MORAL: 'Stick' up for what you believe in.

Chapter 37

Mary Tyler Moore

A Beautiful Surface

She was America's sweetheart, but no one knew her
struggles with alcohol and illness.

*"Had I not been forced to confront myself, I might never
have come to know and admire the person I am."*

"Nothing is so deceiving as a beautiful surface," wrote
Leo Tolstoy. When dazzled by a beautiful TV star (or handsome
movie actor), who among us does not think, "How perfect that
person looks. How wonderful it must be to live that person's
carefree life."

The gorgeous Mary Tyler Moore won fame for her comedic
gifts, starring in two hit TV programs, yet she faced severe trials
in her personal life—divorce, alcoholism, diabetes, and the tragic
death of her only child.

In the early 1960s for five years she played a suburban
housewife on *The Dick Van Dyke Show*, and she did it so well
people actually thought that she and her co-star were married.
Daring for her day, she wore tight-fitting capris at a time when
other TV moms vacuumed in pearls and pumps. And given the
quaint customs of the day she had to tone down the tight fit of
her pants to make herself less alluring.

A few years later in *The Mary Tyler Moore Show* she
played a single career woman. It was a groundbreaking role
because single career women were mostly nowhere to be seen
on television, especially those who dated, as she did on the show.
Even before the show premiered, the producers had to tone
down her character. Originally, she was to have been a divorcee,
and that was too much for those times.

The women she portrayed on television were unceasingly
cheerful and good-hearted. Their problems were resolved in 30

minutes. Their woes either involved enduring a nitwit work colleague or keeping dinner warm for a husband on a late train out of Penn Station.

In reality, Moore was married three times. Her first marriage to an Ocean Spray cranberry salesman ended shortly after her first series went on the air. "During the first year of the show, as thrilled and bursting with the excitement over my work as I was, I was equally without emotion at home," she wrote.

She then wed Grant Tinker, an ad agency executive who later produced her second hit. That relationship ended in an alcoholic blur. In her autobiography, Moore wrote that at the time she favored "fishbowl-sized glasses of vodka on the rocks." Her mother was an alcoholic, and she spent much of her childhood living with nearby relatives because her mother was so incapacitated. When she was six-years old, a trusted neighbor sexually molested her. When she told her mother, she replied, "It didn't happen."

Of her second marriage, she wrote, "We made these feeble attempts at self-counseling during the so-called happy hour, the only time we had courage enough to broach the subject....In case there's any doubt about the acute state of my alcoholism, and the insanity it produced, I can recall with sickening clarity that on more than one occasion I played Russian roulette with my car, and what's more, some unwary, innocent people played with me."

News of this would have been unbelievable at a time when Moore played America's sweetheart on Saturday night television. Finally, during her third marriage, she found the courage to enter the Betty Ford Center. Named after the former first lady, this Palm Springs, California, facility serves a wealthy clientele with substance abuse problems. Moore fled after only three weeks of the five-week program. After a conversation with Betty Ford, she returned to complete it. "That phone call saved my life," she said.

"The person I am"

She came to believe that she was glad she struggled

with—and conquered alcoholism. "Had I not been forced to confront myself," she wrote. "I might never have come to know and admire the person I am."

Moore, a lifelong dancer, also had a cigarette habit. She smoked two and even three packs a day. She had to find the courage to snuff out that addiction as well. It did not help that her third husband, a cardiologist, also smoked.

Diagnosed with diabetes while hospitalized following a miscarriage, she struggled to keep the disease under control most of her adult life, even though she knew her drinking could have caused "serious" health effects. "I was never scolded," she wrote. "I wouldn't have listened, anyway."

Her worst blow came in 1980 when her only child Richie, 24, died when a shotgun he was handling fired. The death was ruled an accident, and this firearm was later taken off the market because it had a "hair-trigger."

She felt she had failed as a mother. Several years earlier he had struggled with a cocaine addiction. At his funeral, she wept, telling God, " 'You take care of him,' I screamed at the sky."

She struggled with them all her life. "I've two very distinct inner spirits who live my life for me, playing hide-and-seek at times," she wrote. "There does seem to be one brooding, paranoid, and pessimistic Mary Tyler Moore....The other Mary is a supremely confident champion. They do battle with each other, one emerging to rule for a time depending on outside circumstance."

MORAL: Have spunk.

Chapter 38

John Brown

Two Ends of a Chain?

Was he a terrorist or freedom fighter?

"My sympathy with the oppressed and the wronged...."

God told him to kill his enemies. Nothing could be clearer than that. He and his sons and their followers dragged evildoers from their beds in the middle of the night and hacked them to death with swords. That was only the beginning. He then schemed for years, developing a mad plan designed to throw his country into utter turmoil, causing bloody upheavals across the map.

Towards that end, a shadowy cabal of wealthy supporters came to his aid. They all lived far from where the mayhem would occur, and they secretly provided him with weapons and huge sums of money. When this evil genius finally carried out his bloody plot, it failed miserably, and he was hanged. Most of his money men fled the country, denying any knowledge of his plot.

Yet he lit a fuse that months later would explode into a savage war that ripped the country in two. Even the nation's future leader, who some thought was an ally of the madman, called him "insane." Even the man who would later gun down that leader called this religious fanatic a "terrorizer."

What's more, the wife of one the money men wrote a blood-curdling anthem praising the fiend. Its lyrics were blasphemous, comparing him to God. The regime's soldiers marched into battle singing her crazed song with lust.

This radical religious terrorist was John Brown, the most controversial figure in American history, a man who committed acts of terrible violence and martyred himself for the cause he believed in—the end of slavery.

The future leader was Abraham Lincoln. In December 1860, Lincoln denounced Brown—and any effort to free slaves—saying, "Emancipation would be the equivalent to a John Brown raid, on a gigantic scale." And he said all the charges against him and his party were "inexcusable" and "malicious slander."

Piercing Eyes

Brown was a compelling figure. He was well spoken and lean with piercing eyes. He had a hawk-like nose, a massive white beard, and a great shock of hair. A radical Abolitionist, he had pursued the goal of ending slavery for years with the white-hot religious passion that Americans would today associate with a radical Islamic terrorist like Osama bin-Laden. In a letter Brown wrote from prison shortly before his execution, he told a Quaker woman who expressed disapproval of his violent tactics, "You know that Christ once armed Peter. So also in my case I think he put a sword in my hand, there continued it so long as he saw best, and kindly too it from me. I mean when I first went to Kansas."

In the 1850s pro-slavery and anti-slavery settlers flooded into the new territory of Kansas. It would soon seek statehood. Whether it would be a free or slave state was unclear. Around the nation, people called it "Bloody Kansas" or "Bleeding Kansas" because of the violence there.

The most notorious event occurred in May 1856 when Brown and his raiders killed five pro-slavery settlers in the middle of the night. They slashed and stabbed their defenseless victims. Brown himself performed the coup de grace on one victim, shooting the wounded man in the head at close range. This lurid event shocked the nation and became known as the Pottawatomie Massacre.

For the next few years he traveled extensively in New England, secretly meeting with supporters. His most prominent backers became known as the "Secret Six." They gave him thousands of dollars, weapons, and ammunition. One of its members was the Boston physician Samuel Gridley Howe. His wife Julia Ward, a banker's daughter, would write "The Battle Hymn of the Republic" in 1862.

It took three years for Brown to develop his plan for his raid on Harpers Ferry. (Although it is now in present day West Virginia, at the time it was in the slave state of Virginia.) The town was strategically located where the Potomac and Shenandoah rivers combined, and it served as a railroad hub where trains going north and south and east and west met.

This bold raid, said Smith, "would strike terror into the heart of the slave States." He focused on the federal armory there, planning to seize thousands of muskets and huge quantities of ammunition.

Years later his daughter Anna detailed the plan and its goals. Her father would "secure firearms to arm the slaves, and to strike terror into the hearts of the slaveholders; then to immediately start for the plantations, gather up the negroes, and retreat to the mountains, send out armed squads from there to gather more, and eventually to spread out his forces until the slaves would come to them, or the slaveholders would surrender to them to gain peace."

On October 16, 1859, Brown and 18 other men botched the plan. They took at least 30 hostages in the armory, killing four and wounding nine in the process. They got bogged down. Instead of becoming a guerilla warrior, he and his compatriots became trapped inside the armory.

Upon seizing the building, Brown told its watchman, "I came here from Kansas, and this is a slave Sate; I want to free all the Negroes in this State; I have possession of the United States armory, and if the citizens interfere with me I must only burn the town and have blood."

Soon 90 Marines arrived. In one of American history's great ironies, the troops were led by Brevet Colonel Robert E. Lee, then an officer in the Union Army. He, in turn, sent his aide J.E.B Stuart, a future Confederate general, to order Brown to surrender. (Thomas "Stonewall" Jackson, a student at the Virginia Military Institute, would later witness Brown's execution.)

The Marines attacked. Brown was stabbed by a sword in the abdomen, injuring a kidney. After his capture, he was interrogated by military leaders and Henry Wise, the governor of Virginia. Although all those who were present were pro-slavery and loathed Brown for his beliefs and what he had done, all came away impressed by his steely demeanor, calmness, and mastery of theological issues.

His questioning had the flavor of a religious inquisition. Some of the dialogue recalls what Jesus experienced in his last hours. "Upon what principle do you justify yourself?" Brown was asked.

"It is my sympathy with the oppressed and the wronged, that are as good as you and as precious in the sight of God," Brown replied.

Governor Wise reviled Brown, calling him and his band "murderers, traitors, robbers, insurrectionists." But he also said Brown was "a man of clear head, of courage, fortitude and simple ingenuousness. He is cool, collected, and indomitable."

News of the raid and Brown's capture hit the nation like lightning, capturing in one blinding, brutal instant the divide the separated Americans. Southerners already lived in fear of slave revolts, but they were appalled when they heard the reaction of prominent Northerners.

"That new saint..."

Essayist Henry Thoreau gave a lecture in Massachusetts two weeks later during Brown's trial, saying "Some eighteen hundred years ago Christ was crucified; this morning perchance John Brown was hung. These are two ends of a chain to which I rejoice to know is not without its links."

Ralph Waldo Emerson, widely regarded by many as the nation's most prominent intellectual, was even more blunt, calling Brown "that new saint, than whom none purer or more brave was ever led by love of men into conflict and death, —the new saint awaiting his martyrdom, and who, if he shall suffer, will make the gallows glorious like the cross."

Meanwhile, a Virginia reporter spoke for many Southerners when he wrote that "Abolitionism...must be strangled and crushed if we are to live together in peace and harmony as members of the same political brotherhood."

To Northerners, Brown was a selfless martyr akin to Christ. To Southerners, he was a villain, no better than vermin.

Brown was charged with treason against Virginia, murder, and leading a conspiracy with slaves to overthrow their masters. When Brown testified, he said that he regretted the loss of life but said that the killings were unforeseeable.

"I did no wrong, but right," Brown told the court. "Now, if it is deemed necessary that I should forfeit my life for the furtherance of the ends of justice, and mingle my blood further with the blood of millions in this slave country whose rights are disregarded by wicked, cruel and unjust enactments, I say, let it be done."

Many Americans were even more unsettled when on November 15 a rare daytime fireball blazed across the sky in the eastern United States and then exploded making the sound of rapid cannon fire.

Brown was hanged on December 2, 1859, and among those in the crowd witnessing the event was John Wilkes Booth.

As Brown walked to the gallows, he handed his guard a note which read: "I John Brown am now quite certain that the crimes of this guilty, land: will never be purged away; but with Blood. I had as I now think: vainly flattered myself that without verry much."

In 1860, a "procession of meteors" (actually one object breaking up in the atmosphere) streamed across the evening sky looking like a comet. Walt Whitman and Herman Melville both wrote poems about the event, and both men connected this bizarre celestial happening to Brown. "Year of comets and meteors transient and strange," Whitman wrote in "Year of Meteors."

During that year's election campaign, Democrats did their best to convince voters that Republicans had something to do with Brown and his raid. No connection has ever been shown. At the time candidate Lincoln's proposed policy was to pay slave owners to give up their property. "Even though [Brown] agreed with us in thinking slavery wrong," he said, "that cannot excuse violence, bloodshed, and treason."

Nonetheless, Southerners viewed Lincoln as a radical Abolitionist of the same vein as Brown. They felt they would receive little, if any, sympathy from his administration. South Carolina seceded on December 26, 1860, and on January 9, 1861, its forces fired on the strategically located Ft. Sumter, which guarded the entrance to Charleston harbor. Lincoln was inaugurated on March 4, and he ordered the Navy to defend the fort. Following the first battle of the civil war on April 12, Confederates seized control of the strategic fort.

After Brown's execution, people in the North and South spontaneously began to sing songs about him. Some were sarcastic, others humorous. All followed the tune of an existing popular song. The lyrics to "The Battle Hymn of the Republic" came to Julia Ward Howe in her sleep in 1862. Unlike other similar songs, her words integrated Brown and his mission with the Union cause and the will of God.

In her mighty hymn, John Brown becomes the personification of God who "hath loosed the fateful lightnings of His terrible swift sword." He angrily "trampl[es] out the vintage where the grapes of wrath are stored." He delivers "his righteous sentence" and preaches "a fiery gospel." He is a threatening God—"With you my grace shall deal" the song proclaims. It concludes with the chilling words "As he died to make men holy, let us die to make men free."

In Lincoln's Second Inaugural Address in March 1865, he viewed the Civil War in a religious context: "Neither party expected for the war the magnitude or the duration which it has already attained....Both read the same Bible and pray to the same God, and each invokes His aid against the other....The prayers of both could not be answered....The Almighty has His own purposes."

Unlike Brown, Lincoln spoke of a forgiving God and not of a nation of Northerners and Southerners but of one people, united in their suffering, frailties, and capacity for greatness.

"With malice toward none, with charity for all, with firmness in the right as God gives us to see the right, let us strive on to finish the work we are in, to bind up the nation's wounds, to care for him who shall have borne the battle and for his widow and his orphan, to do all which may achieve and cherish a just and lasting peace among ourselves and with all nations."

MORAL: Vow to resolve disputes peacefully.

Chapter 39

Ulysses Grant

Taken for Granted

This general was so sensitive he never hunted.
He personally arrested soldiers for abusing horses.

*"Labor disgraces no man; unfortunately,
you occasionally find men who disgrace labor."*

"He habitually wears an expression as if he had determined to drive his head through a brick wall," said a friend.

In 1854, a failure, Ulysses Hiram Grant returned from two years out west, having resigned his commission as an Army officer. Had he not done so, he might otherwise have been court-martialed.

He then failed as a farmer, while his father-in-law, a neighbor, watched. Times were worse than hard. To feed his family he was reduced to selling firewood in the muddy streets of St. Louis. He pawned his gold watch. His father could not take him on at the family store. He failed as a rent collector because he was too soft hearted.

When he finally got work, the store owner died a month later, leaving him again jobless. Ultimately, he sold saddles in his brothers' store.

The Master Horseman

Though he had grown up on the frontier, he hated hunting. His sensitive soul, patience, and insight made him a master horseman. He could train the wildest colt, a skill that won him much respect.

His family had a vast frontier library—35 books. As a child, he loved to read. His father won him an appointment to West Point—without telling him. When told he was going, the young man dutifully did so.

Upon picking up his steamer trunk, to his dismay he found that the shopkeeper had embossed his initials incorrectly. The brass tacks read "H U G" for Hiram Ulysses Grant. Afraid of being mocked at school, he had the peaceful combination of letters rearranged to read "U H G." But when he got to the military academy, he found that its paperwork had gotten his name wrong. Uncle Sam said his initials were "U S G." This inadvertent symbol of patriotism won his classmates' admiration and gave him a new appellation—U.S. Grant—that would forever associate him with patriotism and the union.

"Ministering Angel"

As a lieutenant, Grant went to war in Mexico. He saw little glory, serving as a quartermaster, procuring mules and wagons, duties that kept him from the battlefield. Later, as a leader of thousands of men, his organizational skills would prove immensely valuable.

His career stalled. The Army stationed him far from his family in remote Oregon and northern California. Journeying west via the Isthmus of Panama with 750 other travelers, cholera hit, killing a third of them. Grant was a "ministering angel" caring for the afflicted, said one who was there. Ultimately, however, it's believed that boredom, isolation, and depression on the distant frontier led to dissolute living, namely heavy drinking, and his resignation.

Nonetheless, when the Civil War started in 1861, townspeople back home in Ohio nominated the disgraced officer, the man they knew as a saddle salesman and firewood dealer to serve as a colonel and raise a company of men. A slight man, only five-foot seven, Grant at first went unnoticed among other officers. Soon victories in small skirmishes made his superiors see his true stature. Battle revealed his taste for swift action, cunning feints, and his cool head.

Major victories followed as did rumors, perhaps spread by jealous officers that he was a drunk. Wrote one of his staff officers: "If Grant ever tasted liquor of any kind during the war, it was not in my presence, and I had the best position possible for observing his habits."

Grant never cursed. His strongest oaths were "By lightning!" and "Confound it!" Twice when he saw soldiers abusing mules, he personally arrested them. When he saw a straggler assaulting a woman, he leapt off his horse and rescued her.

President Lincoln promoted him to Lieutenant General, commander of all Union armies, and his leadership proved decisive to the war's outcome. Most of all, over and again, it was his humility and quiet demeanor as much as his military prowess that impressed others. Wrote one biographer: "He would never dwell on past mistakes, never wallow in its wounds."

MOTTO: When life has you selling firewood
in the muddy streets of life,
make matches and start the fire
that will change the world.

Chapter 40

Virginia Apgar

New Breath of Life

All newborns breathe easier thanks to this physician.

"Women are liberated from the time they leave the womb."

Dr. Virginia Apgar never held her breath when it came time to start something new. She began taking flying lessons when she was in her 50s. She often joked that her goal was to one day fly under the George Washington Bridge that spanned the Hudson River in New York City. She was no *under* achiever. During her long career, she flew higher than most physicians.

Her interest in medicine began because, as a child, her brother was chronically ill, and she took a loving interest in his condition. She could have done most anything in life. In school she was irrepressible, playing seven sports, acting in stage plays, working on the school newspaper, and playing violin in the orchestra. She did do poorly in one subject—home economics. Friends said she never learned how to cook.

There were few female doctors when she started medical school in 1929 at New York's Columbia College of Physicians. By the time she graduated (fourth in her class), she had amassed debts totaling nearly $4,000 (or $60,000 in 2018 dollars), an astounding amount at the time. She wanted to become a surgeon. Opportunities were few in that specialty, and with pressing economic needs, she turned to anesthesia, a field more open to women.

"Stag Dinner—MAD!"

But that was a struggle, too. At the time, nurses often performed anesthesia, and surgeons looked down on doctors who were anesthesiologists. Professional dinners were held at men's clubs which forbid entry to women. In her diary, Dr. Apgar once wrote, "Good meeting. Stag dinner—MAD!"

Anesthesiology continued to be a neglected medical specialty, but Dr. Apgar worked tirelessly, becoming her alma mater's first female professor in 1949. Her research focused on anesthesia during childbirth. Though medical care had improved greatly since the early 1900s, infant mortality rates remained high—especially during the first 24 hours of life. In those days, many newborns were not routinely given immediate medical attention.

Apgar realized that a key to saving the lives of more babies was examining them closely and immediately after birth to see if they were breathing well and getting enough oxygen. At the time, various doctors used competing systems to determine whether or not a newborn was in distress.

"You'd Do It Like This."

Legend has it that one day in 1949 a medical student commented to her about the need to better evaluate newborns. Taking a piece of paper, Dr. Apgar said, "That's easy. You'd do it like this" and wrote down the vital signs that should be observed.

Word spread, but it wasn't until 1952 that her name actually became a word. That's when a Denver physician wrote her to let her know one of his residents had invented a clever way to remember her five scoring criteria: APGAR—Appearance (color); Pulse (heart rate); Grimace (reflex irritability); Activity (muscle tone); and Respiration.

She was most amused to be honored by this eponym. (That's the technical term for an acronym named after a person.) In short order, doctors around the nation adopted the APGAR Score. Today all newborns are evaluated and rated using these criteria one minute and five minutes after birth. "Every baby born in a modern hospital anywhere in the world is looked at through the eyes of Dr. Virginia Apgar," says the National Library of Medicine's website.

Dr. Apgar lived to bring the breath of life to millions. She made a point of this in her work as a clinical instructor. Because resuscitation is an essential aspect of anesthesiology, she demanded that her students be ready to resuscitate anyone at any time anywhere. That's why she always carried with her a laryngoscope (for viewing the throat), an endotracheal tube, and a pocket knife for performing emergency tracheotomies (to open the windpipe). She told her students to be similarly prepared.

"Nobody, but nobody," she often said, "is going to stop breathing on me!"

MOTTO: Stay awake on the job.

Chapter 41

John Alcock & Arthur Brown

They Flew Upside Down

They were braver than Charles Lindbergh.
And luckier.

"Must see stars now!"

"Lone Eagle" Charles Lindbergh became the most famous man on Earth when he landed in Paris after his 33-hour solo non-stop trans-Atlantic flight. Met by an uproarious mob, the first thing he said was, "My name is Lindbergh. I have come from America. Alcock and Brown showed me the way."

Who in the world are Alcock and Brown? Eight years earlier in June 1919, Captain John Alcock and his navigator Lt. Arthur Brown showed Lucky Lindy the way to Europe. They made the first non-stop flight across the ocean, flying from Newfoundland to Ireland in sixteen-and-a-half hours.

A British newspaper had offered a hefty prize to the first aviators to make the trip. Some didn't take the offer seriously. After all, the challenge had appeared in the paper's April 1, 1913, edition.

They had only flown together three times. Their craft, a Vickers Vimy WWI bomber, was little more than a kite with engines. This two-engine biplane was only 43 feet long, the length of two cars. Canvas covered its hollow wood-and-steel frame wings, and the pilots had to squeeze onto a bench in an open cockpit between its two roaring Rolls-Royce motors. Top speed? About 100 miles an hour.

"Piece of Cake"

The night before they departed the duo dined at the home of Brown's fiancée Kathleen. When her father asked Brown if he was worried, he replied, "Piece of cake." Shortly before they took off, Kathleen gave Alcock a good luck gift—a stuffed cat named Twinkletoes.

Alcock and Brown would need all of its nine lives.

"We have had a terrible journey," Alcock told the press upon arriving. "The wonder is that we are here at all. We scarcely saw the sun or the moon or the stars. For hours we saw none of them.

We looped the loop, I do believe, and did a very steep spiral. We did some very comic "stunts," for I have had no sense of horizon."

Their first terror happened when an engine's exhaust pipe blew up, shooting out flames that threatening to set the wing on fire. Later, hail, rain, and lightning whirled the fragile craft into a dizzying spiral. It cascaded down thousands of feet in seconds. Before Brown could regain control, the Vimy came within 60 feet of the waves while flying on its side nearly perpendicular to the ocean

"The salty taste we noted later on our tongues was foam," said Alcock. Once the calamity had ended, they discovered that they had gotten turned around and were heading back to Newfoundland!

More Trials Lay Ahead

After again heading east, they had no idea if they were on course. Only briefly did the clouds part so Brown could navigate. "Must see stars *now*!" he scribbled on a note to Alcock. Finally, the Moon beamed down on them, and Brown, finding the North Star on his sextant, determined they had flown 850 miles— halfway to their goal with only another 1,000 miles to go.

Unbelievably, more trials lay ahead. Heavy snow and sleet drenched the Vimy. "We froze like young puppies....For four hours the machine was covered in a sheet of ice caused by frozen sleet," said Alcock. "The sleet was so dense that my speed indicator did not work." Weighted down, they plummeted. The freezing snow began clogging the engines' air intakes, threatening to choke the motors.

Desperate, Brown crawled onto the top of nose of the aircraft and then down onto the right wing. Fighting blinding waves of snow, he clambered from strut-to-strut. Clinging for his life with one hand on a cable, he opened his penknife with his teeth and chipped furiously at the ice in the intakes. Having cleared them, he then went to the left wing and did the same. But he wasn't done. Later he repeated the entire perilous process on both wings a second time.

The trip was not entirely without its pleasures. Brown and Alcock dined on sandwiches. The stoic Twinkletoes proved to be an amiable and fearless companion. Alcock enjoyed a beer, and Brown spiked his coffee with whisky. He even felt high-spirited enough to serenade the irritated Alcock with a folk song whose lyrics went "She's like the swallow that flies so high. She's like the river that never runs dry."

In the 1950s, London's airport accepted public donations to build a monument to honor Brown and Alcock. Who sent in the first check? Charles Lindbergh.

MOTTO: Sometimes you have to go out on a limb. Or a wing.

Chapter 42

A. Philip Randolph

Carrying the Load

His father was a pistol-totin' minister.
He grew up to organize a great civil rights rally.

"No earthly price can stop us."

His father was a minister with a shotgun. One evening Asa Philip Randolph watched as his father handed the loaded weapon to his mother. She sat with it across her lap on the porch. Then he watched as his father tucked a pistol under his coat and headed into the night.

His destination? The local jail near Crescent City, Florida, where a black man was held accused of rape. His father and his friends kept a vigil until dawn. They did so to deter any lynch mob, if it gathered, from dragging the man out to his doom.

When Randolph saw his father walking home the next morning, he was overjoyed. His father had helped saved a man's life. Randolph would go on to save and uplift the lives of many more men.

He was a bright little boy. But he couldn't go through the doors of the public library much less borrow its books. His parents were poor. They couldn't buy Randolph good clothes, but they could give him excellent moral instruction.

"You Are as Able..."

"We never felt we were inferior to any white boy," he remembered. "We were told constantly and continuously that "You are as able, you are as competent, you have as much intellectuality as any individual, and you are not supposed to bow and take a back seat for anybody."

He got the benefit of a sterling education. His parents introduced him to Shakespeare and Dickens, and he attended a high school run by the American Missionary Association. It had a white faculty from New England. Randolph was the class valedictorian in 1907.

That didn't mean he got to go to college or even get decent work. He did odd jobs. He stacked logs at a lumberyard. He pushed a wheelbarrow at a factory. He a water boy for a company laying railroad tracks.

After making his way north, he found work as an elevator operator in Harlem. The pay? Four dollars a month. His ambition was higher than the top floor. He wanted to make his mark in the world. In jest he wrote on a wall of the apartment building: "Philip Randolph swept here."

Mocked as 'String Bean'

Soon he was publishing a gazette called the *Hotel Messenger* to try to improve the lives of 'Negro' hotel workers. His tall willowy build led some to mock him as "String Bean" Randolph. Gradually he began to meet porters who worked the swank whites-only Pullman sleeper cars on long-distance trains. They worked 70 hours a week for low wages, and they lived in fear of hunger, never knowing when they might get a new assignment.

Randolph began visiting the porters secretly. After three years, he had organized 5,000 men. It took 12 years, but in 1937 he won legal recognition for the Brotherhood of Sleeping Car Porters, guaranteeing its members a 40-hour work week and decent pay.

"Freedom is never granted; it is won," Randolph said. "Justice is never given; it is exacted. Party has no weight with us; principle has."

Dignified, even serene, his friends marveled at his self-control. Said another labor leader: "Randolph learned to sit erect and walk erect. You almost never saw him leaning back, reclining. No matter how enjoyable the occasion, you look around, and there's Randolph just as straight as if there was a board in his back. He can't relax the way you and I do when we're sitting around talking. The man had so much dignity."

That Barrier Fell, Too

In June 1941, he worked to force Uncle Sam to allow blacks to find employment in defense factories. He threatened to lead a march of 100,000 men on Washington. Fearing violence, Eleanor Roosevelt pleaded with him not to do so. "No earthly price can stop us," he said, and soon FDR issued an order requiring factories to drop their color barriers. After the war, he urged Truman to integrate the armed forces, and that barrier fell, too.

Randolph was a gifted orator. He once spoke to an audience of 250,000 people. After all, he was the co-organizer of the 1963 March on Washington where Martin Luther King gave his famous "I have a dream" oration. It took 22 years, but Randolph's personal dream of a civil rights march in the nation's capital had finally taken place.

"We are the advance guard of a massive moral revolution for jobs and freedom," Randolph told listeners gathered around the Lincoln Memorial's Reflecting Pool. "This revolution reverberates throughout the land, touching every village where black men are segregated, oppressed and exploited."

MOTTO: Have a dream. But be patient.
It might take 22 years to come true.
Possibly longer.

Chapter 43

Robert Soto

Free as a Bird

The undercover federal agent halted the church
service to seize the minister's clothes.

"I wanted a ruling that was going to help all of Native America."

"Operation Powwow" sounds like a joke. But it was
nothing to laugh about when a federal undercover agent raided
Pastor Robert Soto's church service in 2006. His Grace Brethren
Church in McAllen, Texas, is a syncretic denomination. That
means its members are Christian, while their rituals incorporate
traditions of the Lipan Apache Tribe of Texas.

The agent saw Soto wearing a headdress that displayed
two feathers from a gold eagle. Soto's brother-in-law was also
wearing eagle feathers. Like many American Indian tribes, the
Lipan Apache hold eagles sacred and use eagle feathers in their
religious rituals because they believe this majestic bird's high-
flying ways put it close to God.

"The agent threatened to arrest me if I didn't allow him to
go into [our worship] circle," Soto recalled. "That's when I found
out that I was facing up to 15 years in federal penitentiary and
up to a $250,000 fine for having those feathers."

Severe Penalties

Federal law forbids the possession of eagle feathers
unless one has a permit, and these are typically only issued to
tribes for religious purposes. At the time, however, only the state
of Texas recognized the Lipan Apache as a tribe. Because the
tribe was not recognized by Uncle Sam, it held no permit,
because it could not apply for one.

(The law calls for severe penalties because when it was enacted, eagles were near extinction. Today, however, eagles are no longer on the federal government's list of threatened or endangered species. In fact, federal law allows eagles to be legally killed or injured by high-speed energy-producing wind turbines. The precise number killed this way each year is unknown. Some speculate the number may be as high as 4,200.)

Soto felt as though his spirituality had been stolen from him. "If I remember anything of that day, it was the children running around. Some were crying, and some were trying to hide," he said. As a result of the raid, his congregation shrank. Plans to pay him a salary were abandoned, and he developed heart trouble which he says was caused by the stress of his legal woes.

"The Way He Created Us"

Soto and other plaintiffs filed a suit in federal court alleging that the seizure of 42 eagle feathers violated their right to the Free Exercise of their religious beliefs guaranteed by the Constitution.

"If I got caught speeding, I deserve a speeding ticket, but if I get caught worshipping God the way He created us as native people, that's not violating the law," Soto said. "If anything, the government is violating my rights because [it's] interfering with my rights to worship God the way He created us."

Soto's case wound its way through the federal court system. After nine years, the Supreme Court ruled that because the federal government allowed other tribes to possess eagle feathers it had failed to show that it had a "compelling interest" in denying the Lipan Apaches the same treatment.

"We are free to dance, to worship, and to honor our God as native people," said Soto. "The fight wasn't for the feathers. It was for the religious rights for native peoples."

**MOTTO: Bring eagle feathers into your life,
not bull feathers.**

Chapter 44

Franklin Roosevelt

Standing Up to Fear

When shame befell this prominent New York
politician, his handlers lied to the press.

"When you reach the end of your rope, tie a knot in it."

Franklin Roosevelt was a man's man, but you wouldn't
have known it the way some people talked about him. When he
was a young man, an acid-tongued cousin called him "Miss
Nancy," implying that he was gay. When he was at Harvard, the
F.D. in F.D.R. stood for "Feather Duster." Other students thought
he was a glad-hander and a lightweight—a phony who cared
more about looks than anything else.

No question about it, he was one handsome guy. All his
life, he had a great head of hair, a brilliant smile, and that famous
jaunty jutting chin. But try and tell President Wilson that FDR
was just another pretty face. He invited Roosevelt to serve as
Assistant Secretary of the Navy for eight years—and that
included during World War I.

In the summer of 1921 with the Republican Harding in
the White House, Roosevelt was 39 and in peak condition. When
he wasn't thinking about running for governor of New York, this
a strapping six-foot one-inch tall man led an incredibly athletic
life. Golf, tennis, field hockey, baseball, chopping wood, sledding,
sailing—you name the activity, and FDR loved it.

The Worst Heat-Craze

And he loved the Boy Scouts, so much so that he chaired a
local Scout council. In the midst of the worst "heat-craze" in
years, he sailed his yacht up the Hudson River to Bear Mountain
State Park where 2,100 scouts had convened.

FDR and Scouts weren't the only thing on the move. So was the polio virus. It loves hot weather and unsanitary conditions. The disease is contracted when the virus enters a person's mouth. No one knows how he became infected, but while at the camp perhaps FDR shared a cup with an infected Scout or touched a dirty faucet.

After leaving the jamboree, he took his yacht to his family's estate on Campobello Island off the Maine coast in New Brunswick, Canada. Upon arriving, he took a dip in the frigid ocean. He said he didn't feel "the glow" he'd expected from that brisk swim. He was too tired to dress himself. He skipped dinner.

The next morning, he awoke to "stabbing pains" in his legs. The day after that he could barely stand. He could not hold a pencil. At bedtime, he could not stand.

The Terrible Diagnosis

Roosevelt was no stranger to illness. He had weathered typhoid fever, scarlet fever, the deadly Spanish flu, tonsillitis, mumps, and the measles. Because of his remote location, it took more than 10 days for the terrible diagnosis to be made. By that time, he had to be spoon fed. He could not sit up. Doctors ordered him to lie in bed for 23 hours a day. For weeks on end.

The press was told his malady was a "slight" case of infantile paralysis and that he was making a "very rapid and very complete recovery" and would soon be walking. It was unthinkable to tell the public the truth. People associated polio with the 'dirty' children of immigrants living in squalid, unsanitary slums. Few employers—much less voters—would trust a hopeless "cripple" with any job, much less that of governor.

Yet over the months to come, FDR's indomitable will and good cheer convinced family, friends, and voters that he was up to any task. When things looked the worst, he told a golfing buddy, he'd soon be teeing up. "I appear to have inspired the doctors," he told a banker.

But it took FDR five long years of physical rehabilitation and soul-searching to accept what had befallen him, according to one biographer. He learned to forget that he was a 'cripple.' His legs might have been useless, but he told himself that the essence of who he really was—his soul—was robust—and definitely most useful.

Once he stilled his own fears, he realized he could be as active and successful as the next man. In 1928 he charmed the voters of New York into electing him governor. He knew he had nothing to fear—just fear itself. He had learned that if you can conquer that, you can conquer any foe.

MOTTO: Face reality.
Find the good in it.

Chapter 45

Marty Mann

New Translation

Penniless in a sanitarium, she was given the manuscript
of a new book. It was her salvation.

"I wasn't alone anymore."

Bright and witty and beautiful, Marty Mann had
everything. And nothing.

Born to a wealthy family, she attended the best Chicago
schools. But just as she entered high school, she contracted
tuberculosis. Her parents sent her to recover in a California
sanitarium, although back then people euphemistically called
such a place a "Western ranch."

She married at 22. A year later, she divorced. Then her
father lost everything in the Crash of '29. The smart and stylish
Marty soon found work as an editor at a fancy magazine. She
lived the high life in Greenwich Village, and that involved lots of
bootleg gin. Soon she quit her job and moved to London. As did
her taste for liquor. She was drinking at noon, then secretly.
Then came terrifying alcohol-induced blackouts.

"Agony Past Bearing"

One summer afternoon in 1934 calamity struck. While at
a party at a country house, she staggered upstairs and fell off a
balcony. Whether she jumped or fell she never exactly knew. "At
times I feared life so much more than death that twice I sought
death," she recalled. "Suicide seemed a welcome release from a
terror and agony past bearing."

She awoke with a broken jaw and leg and spent six
months in traction.

Now penniless and unemployed, she spent her lonely, bleary days in Hyde Park sipping booze on the sly. Returning to America, she sought one psychiatrist after another, desperate to find out why she was drinking.

In those days the word 'alcoholism' was barely known. People thought alcoholism was caused a lack of morals and poor willpower. They called alcoholics bums, losers, and worse. And it was far more shameful for a woman to have drinking problem.

Then Marty met psychiatrist Harry Tiebout. He let her stay, free of charge, at his Connecticut sanitarium. He gave her the manuscript of an upcoming book from a new organization. Its name? "Alcoholics Anonymous." At first, its religious message urging alcoholics to seek the aid of a higher power upset her.

Then something happened: "You let God in," she said, "And He comes out of you." She almost seemed to faint. When she awakened, she was on her knees at her bedside, her pillow damp with tears. Wonderfully, she felt confidence and a sense of peace.

"I Wasn't Alone Anymore."

"I had come home at last, to my own kind," she said. "There is another meaning for the Hebrew word that in the King James Version of the Bible is translated 'salvation.' It is: To come home. I had found my salvation. I wasn't alone anymore.

"I wasn't the only person in the world who felt and behaved like this! I wasn't mad or vicious—I was a sick person. I was suffering from an actual disease that had a name and symptoms like diabetes or cancer or tuberculosis—and a disease was respectable, not a moral stigma."

She became one of the first women to join AA. She dedicated her life to helping other alcoholics. She founded the National Council on Alcoholism, becoming its long-time executive director, creating Alcoholism Information centers in cities across the U.S. For more than two decades she worked ceaselessly, traveling 50,000 miles a year, appearing on TV and radio, striving to convince Americans that alcohol abuse was a disease and one that was curable.

She gave many speeches. Whenever she addressed an audience, this elegant woman stood erect at the podium, and the first words she said—with pride—were, "My name is Marty Mann, and I'm an alcoholic."

MOTTO: Coincidence is when God winks at you. Wink back.

Chapter 46

Pablo Picasso

View Askew

His world fell around him. Did it fracture his mind or give him courage to see as no one had ever seen before?

"Others have seen what is and asked why.
I have seen what could be and asked why not."

He was born dead. Then he breathed life—and revolution—into art.

His story begins at 11:15 p.m. on October 25, 1881, in Malaga, Spain. The delivery had been difficult. Now the baby boy lay motionless, stillborn. The midwife gave up all hope on him and ministered to his mother.

As fate would have it, though, the boy's uncle was a doctor, and he had attended the birth.

But how to get the lifeless infant to breathe?

"Doctors at that time used to smoke big cigars, and my uncle was no exception. When he saw me lying there, he blew smoke into my face. To this, I immediately reacted with a grimace and a bellow of fury."

Later the world would react with astonishment, amazement, and even outrage at the limitless hurricanes of art produced by this feisty painter. His greatness is as overwhelming as his baptismal name—Pablo Diego José Francisco de Paula Juan Nepomuceno Maria de los Remedios Cipriano de la Santísima Trinidad Martyr Patricio Clito Ruíz y Picasso.

Aficionados of the occult believe some eerie conjunction of planets and stars swirled as he was born, and that the midnight moonlight bathed the city's white houses with supernatural force.

Could that explain why so many of Picasso's paintings depict people with fractured, shattered faces—eyes lopsided, noses jagged, teeth jittery—their features frantic and flattened?

There's more to the story. On the night of Christmas 1884 when Picasso was three, a savage earthquake rocked his town, killing more than 800 people across Spain. "My mother wore a handkerchief on her head, I had never seen her like that before," he recalled a half century later. "My father seized his cape from the coat-stand, threw it round his shoulders, took me in his arms and rolled me in its folds, leaving my head exposed."

Once safely at the rock-solid home of a friend, his very pregnant mother experienced her own tremors, giving birth to her second child three days later—on a basement floor.

Psychoanalysts of the professional (and amateur variety) have speculated that the traumatic birth, the calamitous quake, and witnessing of the bloody throes of delivery birthed in Picasso some psychic dislocation, giving him an inspired and distorted vision of reality.

True or not, Picasso gave the art world jolts throughout his long life. His styles were indeed born and reborn every few years.

Even as a child Picasso was the essence of art itself. Young Pablo was drawing before he could speak. (His first word was *lapiz*—pencil.) He delighted his family with paper cut-outs of animals and flowers. He signed and dated one of his earliest drawings when he was six. Fittingly, the fairly well drawn "Hercules with his Club" depicted the muscular and bearded divine hero (nude except for a fig leaf) wielding his weapon as confidently as Picasso would use a paint brush.

"I never did children's drawings," said Picasso. "Not even when I was very small—never." No wonder that this great master also said, "All children are artists. The problem is how to remain an artist once we grow up."

**MOTTO: When someone blows smoke in your face
or the world is falling down around you,
see the beauty of your situation.**

Chapter 47

Charlie Chaplin

The Silent Star

His stepmother made him sleep in the gutter.
He grew up to become a 'bum.'

"Nothing is permanent in this wicked world—
not even our troubles."

He made millions laugh, but Charlie Chaplin's London childhood was nothing to laugh at. "To gauge the morals of our family by commonplace standards would be as erroneous as putting a thermometer in boiling water," he recalled. Born to music hall performers, Chaplin rarely saw his father, an alcoholic who was estranged from his family.

Though he had lovely memories of riding with his mother Hannah "on top of a horse-bus trying to touch passing lilac trees," she had little ability to provide for her children. Her voice failed her. She could no longer perform.

Unable to care for Charlie and his brother, she took them to a workhouse when he was six. He stayed there for 18 long and miserable months. Then he was sent to another home for destitute children. At bedtime he and 20 other little boys knelt in the center of their ward in their nightshirts and sang hymns.

"Help of the Helpless"

"Abide with me. Fast falls the eventide. The darkness deepens. Lord, with me abide. When other helpers fail and comforts flee, Help of the Helpless, O, abide with me," he remembered singing.

"I felt utterly rejected. I did not understand the hymn," Chaplin remembered. "The tune and the twilight increased my sadness."

Worse was to come. Hannah was committed to an asylum, her madness possibly brought on by syphilis. Not yet eight years old, he was sent to live with his father. And he was rarely in the hovel he shared with his new wife. She was also a drunk. She hated the boys. After forcing them to sleep in the street, the police visited the squalid home.

Luckily, as if in a movie, Hannah regained her sanity and was able to care for the boys for a few more years, until finally succumbing to insanity and spending the last 23 years of her life confined in an asylum.

The Clog-Dancer

She encouraged her nine-year-old Charlie to try the stage. Soon he joined a traveling clog-dancing troupe. This led to bit roles in plays and then to comedic roles in vaudeville. Tours to America followed as did a meeting with famed silent film director Mack Sennett.

"Put on a comedy make-up," Sennett barked at the newcomer. "Anything will do."

Thus, on the spur of the moment, Chaplin threw on baggy pants, floppy shoes, a too tight coat, and a derby hat a size too small. He pasted on a brushy moustache and twirled a cane, and the look was complete. He had become...the Tramp, one of the first world-famous movie characters.

"This fellow is many sided," said Chaplin. "A gentleman, a poet, a dreamer, a lonely fellow, always hopeful of romance and adventure."

Transcending his terrible childhood trials, Chaplin knew how to bring joy to millions. "Laughter," he said, "is the tonic, the relief, the surcease for pain."

MOTTO: When darkness deepens, laugh at your misfortunes. If that doesn't work, try clogging.

Chapter 48

Juliane Koepcke

When Lightning Struck

On Christmas Eve, she fell 21,000 feet without a parachute
and landed safely in the Amazon jungle.
No food. No glasses. One shoe.

"I don't give up."

Juliane Koepcke's white high heels matched the white fabric of her thin sleeveless summer mini-dress. It was her high school graduation dress. She had just graduated, and she and her mother were flying on Christmas Eve 1971 to meet her father for the holidays.

They were on Flight 508 from Peru's capital Lima to remote Pucallpa on the Amazon. Juliane sat next to her mother in the window seat of a four-engine Lockheed Electra turboprop passenger plane. At 21,000-feet over the mountainous rainforest 36 minutes after the stroke of noon in the midst of a furious storm, Juliane saw lightning—"a glistening light"—hit one of the engines on the plane's right wing.

Metal Confetti

"This is the end of everything," she thought. The wing snapped off. The plane nosedived. A huge roar filled the cabin as the fuselage shredded, bursting into metal confetti.

Still strapped to her seat, her mother no longer by her side, Juliane remembers falling, falling, falling, the sky quiet around her. Then she looked down and saw the rainforest canopy—its trees as thickly packed "like green cauliflower, like broccoli"—rushing to meet her.

When she woke up, she was upside down and still buckled in. Other than some gashes, a broken collarbone, and an eye swollen shut, she was unharmed. She cried out for her mother. No answer. She searched for her for a day. She saw no survivors or wreckage. She did find a bag of candy. She ate a piece and only one piece, saving the rest.

As horrific as Juliane's situation was, she had one big advantage. She had grown up in the jungle with her biologist father, and her mother, an ornithologist. She knew what *not* to be afraid of. Animal sounds that might have terrified another teenager did not scare her. She knew how predators behaved and which insects and plants were the most dangerous.

She heard planes overhead, but she knew they would never see her through the 'broccoli' overhead. She understood she would have to do something to survive.

She Knelt and Drank

Famished, she licked drops of water off leaves. Then she saw a trickle of water. She knelt and drank. Her father had told her that if she were ever lost in the jungle to head downhill and follow water. It might grow into a stream, and the stream might grow into a river, and if she kept to the river, she might find a settlement or someone who would rescue her.

Though her injuries were minor, she had lost her glasses and a sandal. For the next 11 days, she felt the blurry way ahead. The trickle did turn into a stream. The stream became a river, and she started swimming, knowing piranhas congregate only in still water. She had no worries about caiman alligators. Experience had taught her they leave people alone.

The worst of her ordeal was the hunger (the bag of candy did not last long), the ceaseless rain, the cold chill of night, the millions of mosquitoes torturing her, and never knowing whether her odyssey would end in lonely death or rescue. "I don't give up," she told herself again and again.

A Bizarre Insect

Wriggling leeches fixed themselves to her. A bizarre insect laid eggs in her skin. Days later its maggots were born and writhed in her flesh as they ate their way out. No matter how hard she tried with a stick, she could not force out the maddening worms.

At last, she saw a primitive shelter on the riverbank. A motorboat was moored there. Crawling ashore, she found a can of diesel fuel. She remembered her father had once smeared gasoline on a dog's hair to rid it of skin parasites. She dashed the vile liquid on her body. She counted 35 worms emerge from one arm alone.

Of the 92 passengers and crew on the plane, only Juliane left the jungle alive. A few others, including her mother, had survived. None had been as bold as Juliane. (Her mother had been too injured too move.) Juliane took decisive action. Her courage saved her life.

MOTTO: Fortune favors the prepared mind. Stay calm and look for a motorboat.

Chapter 49

John Wayne

Real True Grit

He made 53 movies—all stinkers— before he had a hit.

"Courage is being scared to death but saddling up anyway."

"Nobody's coming around with plums on a silver platter," Marion Morrison often heard his father Clyde say. In their Winterset, Iowa, home, the family got more than its share of raisins, not plums.

Easygoing Clyde failed as a druggist. He had to declare bankruptcy. A friend recalled: "If he only had four bits in his pocket, he'd give a quarter to a friend, buy a beer for himself, and sit down and talk."

The family had to move in with his wife's relatives. Clyde's father bought 80 acres of land near the Mohave Desert and set up his son as a homesteader. Their new house was a "glorified shack." It had no running water, no electricity, no gas.

After two years, Clyde failed at farming, possibly because he had tuberculosis or because the land was poor. He was put in a veteran's hospital, and the family moved near Los Angeles.

His Feminine Name

Farm life did one thing for young Marion—It taught him to be a good shot with a rifle. Always hunting plums, in his new hometown, he got up every day at four to deliver newspapers. After school ended, he made deliveries for a druggist on his bicycle. He was, of course, a Boy Scout. And, of course, his feminine name caused the usual playground miseries.

In high school, he was a natural for the football team. "He could have been a great football player," recalled a teammate. "But he never wanted to hurt anybody. He must have knocked a few heads on the field because he won a football scholarship to the nearby University of Southern California.

He was six-foot three-and-three-and-a-quarters-of-an-inch tall with massive shoulders, giant hands, a barrel chest, and a slender waist. His character was gracious and gentle. he had a kind look in his eyes and an easy grin. Girls on campus swooned.

He Lost His Plums

Even with the scholarship, money was a problem. He worked as a bus boy for free meals. It embarrassed him that he had to stuff cardboard in his shoes to cover holes in their soles. One day he went to the nearby Fox studio where silent films were made. They got jobs moving props, sets, and equipment.

But during his junior year what plums he had fell from his grasp. He broke his collarbone bodysurfing, and he lost his scholarship. Forced to drop out, he hoped to earn enough money hauling movie gear full-time to finish school.

Soon directors like the young John Ford started noticing the good-looking young man with the big yet graceful way about him. "The son of a bitch looked like a man," said director Raoul Walsh. The studio arranged a screen test. He passed, and he got a new name, one a bit more masculine—John Wayne.

By 1931, he had made 20 films, forgotten flicks like *Cheer Up and Smile*, *The Drop Kick*, and *Hangman's House*. His growing 'star' appeal won him the top role in an epic western *The Big Trail*, one of the first movies shot on location. Filmed in a new widescreen 70mm process, it was going to be shown onto panoramic screens.

Hopes were high. Wayne knew he was on the brink of being a major star. The problem was few theatres had wide-screens. The movie bombed. It didn't look right on the small screens of the day. Wayne was unfairly blamed for the disaster.

"Girls Demand Excitement"

For the next eight years, plums turned not to raisins but to ashes. During the 1930s he appeared in 61 shoddy films like

Girls Demand Excitement, Two-Fisted Law, The Sweetheart of Sigma Chi, and *Pals of the Saddle*. It was the only work he could get, and what work it was. One day a director shot 114 scenes.

Wayne earned little in the way of money, but what he earned in experience was priceless. "Doing those B Westerns, he learned how to be resilient," a co-star said. "Doing those quickie Westerns, he learned how to be *John Wayne*."

In 1938, John Ford took a chance and offered him the role of the Ringo Kid, an outlaw in his new western *Stagecoach*. The industry thought the genre was kaput. Ford had a hard time getting funding, especially since he wanted to shoot at extra cost on location in the now mythic Monument Valley. Plus, he was taking a risk casting Wayne who, of course, was washed up.

The movie only did modestly at the box office, but it gave Wayne a new start. "John Wayne is so good in the role of the outlaw that one wonders why he has had to wait all this time since *The Big Trail* for another such opportunity," raved *The New York Daily News*.

This time Wayne was ready. "Tomorrow is the most important thing in life," he told an interviewer in 1972. "Comes into us at midnight very clean. It's perfect when it arrives, and it puts itself in our hands. It hopes we've learned something from yesterday."

MOTTO: Act naturally.

Chapter 50

Ron McNair

Booking It

When he went to check out books,
the librarian called the police.

*"Before you can make your dream come true,
you must first have one."*

When Ronald McNair was nine-years-old, he almost got arrested for trying to check out books from the library. He had walked a mile to get there, and there was no stopping him.

Except for the two policemen. This was 1959 in rural Lake City, South Carolina.

The Rev. Jesse Jackson said Lake City was so remote, it was "several miles deeper than the country." The library was segregated, and when young Ron innocently walked in, white people actually chuckled.

An elderly librarian told him, "This library is not for coloreds." She warned him that if he didn't leave right away, she would call the police.

"Lordy, Jesus"

"I'll wait," McNair replied, and he proceeded to sit on the librarian's check-out counter.

A second phone call was made—to Ron's mother. "Lordy, Jesus," she thought. "Please don't let them put my child in jail."

When she and two huge white officers arrived, the policemen quickly appraised the severity of this law-breaking attempt. One of them said to the librarian, "Why don't you just give the kid the books?"

After all, McNair could read when he was three. In second grade, he carried a slide rule, the device mathematicians used to make calculations before calculators were invented. In short, he was a nerd. Friends called him "Gismo."

He wasn't a total bookworm. His father Carl Sr. taught him the meaning of hard, hard work. "During the summer my sons worked sunup to sundown picking cotton and beans—all for just $4 a day." Meanwhile, he learned the value of education from his mother. Getting ahead was so vital to her that when her children were in grade school she commuted 600 miles every week to earn her master's degree in education.

Mother Toughened Him Up

His goal topped his mother's. He wanted to major in physics or engineering in college. When predominately white universities in South Carolina wouldn't admit him, he went on a full-scholarship to the mostly black North Carolina AT&T. Then came a PhD in Physics from MIT.

If his mother toughened him up for school, his father's lessons paid off, too. McNair also had the intense self-discipline to study karate through college, becoming a fifth-degree black belt.

One day a letter came from NASA inviting him to apply to be an astronaut. Out of 8,000 candidates, he was one of 35 selected. After training for six years, he first flew into space in 1984 aboard the Space Shuttle *Challenger* becoming the second African-American to go into orbit.

"He was absolutely phenomenal," said fellow astronaut Charles Bolden. "I know he slept, but I'm not sure when."

Saxophone Serenade

During his 191 hours in space on that mission, McNair played the lead role in acoustic levitation and chemical separation experiments. And he conducted "experiments" of a musical nature. (McNair loved music so much he had considered making that his major in college). He serenaded his fellow space travelers with his saxophone, making that a first in space.

"God chose a laser physicist to defy the odds of oppression," said Rev. Jackson, preaching a memorial service to McNair. His second flight into space was aboard STS-51, the 1986 *Challenger* mission that ended in a massive explosion 73 seconds after lift-off, destroying the Shuttle and killing all seven of its astronauts.

"The true courage of space flight is not strapping into one's seat prior to liftoff. It is not sitting aboard six million pounds of fire and thunder as one rockets away from the planet," said McNair. "The true courage comes in enduring and persevering, the preparation, and believing in oneself."

MOTTO: Dare great things.

Chapter 51

Cole Porter

Just One of Those Things

His songs were bliss. His legs crushed,
he wrote in pain for 20 years.

*"I can't stand hobbles. I can't stand
fences. Don't fence me in."*

It's not every boy who goes off to boarding school with an upright piano. But that's what Cole Porter of Peru, Indiana, did. Born into a family that had made its fortune in timber, oil, coal, and gold mining, Porter's early life was, as he wrote in one of his songs, "a trip to the Moon on gossamer wings."

"I inherited two million dollars," he said. "People always say that so much money spoils one's life. But it didn't spoil mine. It simply made it wonderful."

One of America's premier composers and songwriters, his songs effervesced like bubbles in champagne. Their elegance graced more than 30 Broadway shows and musicals. At Yale, he wrote 300 songs, including two fight songs whose wacky lyrics include "Bingo, Bingo, Eli Yale!" and "Bull dog! Bull dog! Bow wow wow!"

"Life's Great, Life's Grand..."

With maturity came standards like *Begin the Beguine, It's De-Lovely, Night and Day, You're the Top*, and *Just One of Those Things*. Without them, the world would be far less merry. Or gay, to be precise, for Porter was about as out of the closet as one could be in his day.

"I never sat down just to write a hit," he once said. Porter's sublime early days could have been summed up by lines from his song *Don't Fence Me In*: "Life's great, life's grand,

Future's all planned, No more clouds in the sky. How'm I ridin'? I'm ridin' high."

Unlike many Broadway composers, he wrote both the lyrics and the music for his songs, sometimes crafting a gem in less than a half hour. No one but no one else could so effortlessly spin off lines like "Do do that voodoo that you do so well"…."You're the top. You're the Tower of Pisa. You're the smile on the Mona Lisa"…"Birds do it. Bees do it. Even educated fleas do it. Let's fall in love."…"They say that bears have love affairs and even camels; we're merely mammals. Let's misbehave!"

"The instant happiness that Porter gave his audience is the kind that becomes history," said literary critic Alfred Kazin.

He didn't just write about high society. He *was* high society. (In fact, who else but Porter could have written the music for the Frank Sinatra musical *High Society*?)

He lived at the pinnacle. In 1931 *Vanity Fair* wrote, "He has often played for the King and Queen of Spain and the Prince of Wales….His Paris house in the *rue Monsieur* has a room done entirely in platinum…He averages at least two baths a day and owns 16 dressing gowns and nine cigarette cases."

While in Manhattan, he ensconced himself in the Waldorf Towers. He had fresh orchids, gardenias, and roses brought in daily, and they were always white orchids, white gardenias, and white roses. A typical evening might find him dining with Diaghilev, Lady Cunard, William Randolph Hearst, the Gershwins, or the Vanderbilts.

Life Was a Song

Porter and his songs were erudite, erotic, exotic, and, above all else, as elegant as "the nimble tread of the feet of Fred Astaire" as he wrote in a song.

You might say his life was a song. Until the summer of 1937.

While visiting a Long Island riding club, he was warned not mount a horse known to be skittish. Being impetuous, he did so. Something spooked his steed. It threw him, fell on top of him, and then rolled over him, causing compound fractures in both his legs.

Over the next three decades, Porter suffered through more than 30 operations, chronic bone disease, constant pain, depression, and ultimately the amputation of his right leg in 1958.

He Loved the "Bitch"

To help take away the misery, he used humor. He gave each leg a name. The left was adorable Josephine, the right Geraldine, a monster. Nonetheless, he assured friends that he loved the "bitch" and was very *attached* to her.

He managed to be as stoic as he could about his medical woes. When he was a boy, his mother had told him that a gentleman keeps his personal problems to himself, otherwise he only distresses his friends.

He told everyone that while waiting for the ambulance to arrive—while under a horse—he slipped out his notebook and wrote lyrics for "At Long Last Love." His biggest Broadway hit was 1948's *Kiss Me, Kate*. He told a correspondent he wrote it carefree songs in "terrific hell" from pain.

"Why do you start me on stories about these legs?" he asked a friend. "They don't depress me in the least, luckily."

MOTTO: "Be a clown. Be a clown. All the world loves a clown. Be the poor silly ass, and you'll always travel first class."

Chapter 52

Jane Addams

Clean Up Artist

She collected garbage, and she collected
the Nobel Peace Prize.

*"Nothing can be worse than the fear
that one had given up too soon and left one
unexpended effort which might have saved the world."*

She was the first woman to serve as the Nineteenth Ward
Garbage Collector, and it was one of her proudest achievements.

In 1895 in Chicago, half of all children died before their
fifth birthdays. That meant 10,000 to 12,000 deaths a year, half
of all deaths in the city. A major cause was disease due to
horrible sanitation. The Chicago River was a "cesspool, seething,
boiling and reeking with filth, which fills the north wards of the
city with [noxious] gases," a contemporary account said. What's
more, corruption and incompetence plagued the city's sanitation
department.

Jane Addams wouldn't stand for it. She filed 700
complaints with the city, and the mayor, weary of fielding her
grievances, gave in, and put her in charge of garbage collection in
her neighborhood.

The Garbage Buggy

Every day thereafter she and her colleagues rose at dawn
to pile into their official garbage collection buggy to follow the
ward's garbage collectors. She handed out 300 official junior
garbage collector badges to children, so they could collect tin

cans for recycling. She hauled landlords into court and nearly doubled the number of collection wagons in her area.

Indefatigable. Relentless. Unstoppable. That was Jane Addams. "If she began doing it," said a childhood friend, "You couldn't make her quit."

A tireless advocate for the poor, she won the Nobel Peace Prize in 1931. She is regarded as the mother of social work in America.

She was born to it. She adored her father—a staunch abolitionist. When she was two years old, she witnessed her mother's death in the throes in premature labor. An obituary noted her mother's "constant willingness" to aid "the suffering."

Her Deformities

From her earliest days, she felt sympathy for the weak. At the age of four, she contracted tuberculosis of the spine, which left her with deformities. She often called herself an 'ugly duckling.' She knew what it was like to be 'different,' to feel shame through no fault of one's own.

"I prayed with all my heart," she wrote, "that the ugly, pigeon-toed little girl, whose crooked back obliged her to walk with her head held very much upon one side, would never be pointed out to visitors as the daughter of [my father]"

When she was six and her father took her on a buggy ride to the poor part of town, she felt wounded. "I remember launching at my father the pertinent inquiry why people lived in such horrid little houses so close together," she wrote in her autobiography. She told him that when she grew up her home "would not be built among the other large houses but [would be] right in the midst of horrid little houses like these."

"Dangerous" Ideas

True to her prediction, in September 1889 she founded Hull House in a "congested quarter" of Chicago. She called it a settlement, and she likened herself and her co-workers to "pioneers in the midst of difficult surroundings." Why this neighborhood? The poorest immigrants lived there. Mud was thick in the streets. Few homes had tap water. The stench from garbage and human sewage was sickening. She had found her home.

Over the next 40 years she fought against dishonesty in government and for sanitary codes. She helped win the vote for women and build playgrounds. She demanded factory safety laws and urged an end to child labor. Her enemies said she had "dangerous" ideas. She co-founded the ACLU. She advocated world peace and pacifism and was called unpatriotic. In a word, she was fearless, the embodiment of courage.

Perhaps a phrenologist knew her best. When she was 16, he read the bumps on her head to estimate her character. (This quack practice was taken seriously back then.) His conclusion: "If she builds castles in the air, she always has some good foundation for them."

MOTTO: Someone else's garbage can be your gold.

Chapter 53

Ida B. Wells

A Sit-Down Stand

She fought for civil rights tooth-and-nail,
and the railroad conductor had the marks to prove it.

"The way to right wrongs is to turn the light of truth upon them."

Rosa Parks wasn't the first African-American to make a stand by sitting down. Eight decades before Parks' famous bus ride, newspaper writer and teacher Ida B. Wells fought tooth and nail for equality.

Born a slave in Mississippi in 1862, both of her parents died of yellow fever when she was a teenager. Her five siblings stayed with her grandparents, while Wells worked as a teacher to support her brothers and sisters.

"I came home every Friday afternoon, riding the six miles on the back of a big mule," she recalled. "I spent Saturday and Sunday washing and ironing and cooking for the children and went back to my country school on Sunday afternoon."

Dressed Like a Lady

Separate-but-equal railway accommodations angered her, as did the oppression blacks faced in all aspects of their lives. Now living in Memphis, the 21-year-old Wells went to the train station carrying a parasol and dressed like a lady, wearing a hat, gloves, and a corseted dress. She wanted there to be no question that she deserved to be treated with dignity.

She deliberately sat in the whites-only car with the first-class ticket she had bought. The conductor told her he wanted to treat her like a lady but to do so she would have to go to the 'colored' car.

"I replied that if he wished to treat me like a lady, he would leave me alone," Wells recalled.

He asked again. When she would not budge, he tried to yank her out of her seat. But he succeeded only in ripping off the sleeve of her dress. Then things got serious. She bit his hand.

She Drew Blood

"The moment he caught hold of my arm, I fastened my teeth in the back of his hand," Wells wrote. "I had braced my feet against the seat in front and was holding to the back, and as he had already been badly bitten, he didn't try it again by himself."

In fact, she bit him so hard she drew blood. Finally, the conductor and several passengers dragged her out. Incensed at the thought of sitting in the colored car, she left the train.

Later, Wells filed suit against the railroad and won $500 in compensation. "DARKY DAMSEL GETS DAMAGES" declared a local paper. Three years later, however, a higher court ruled against her, and she had to pay $200 in court costs.

Fearing reprisals, local blacks did not rally behind her. "So, I trod the winepress alone," she wrote.

By the time she was 25, she had become editor and co-owner of a local newspaper. She won the nickname "Princess of the Press," thanks to her hard-hitting reporting and editorial appeals for justice. Her bravery, however, would eventually force her exile from Memphis.

"Die Fighting"

In 1892, a white mob dragged three black men from jail and lynched them, gouging out one victim's eyes. A furious Wells wrote that lynchings were an abomination whose one and only purpose was to make it easier to subjugate blacks.

"Lynchings," she said, are "an excuse to get rid of Negroes who were acquiring wealth and property and thus keep the race terrorized." She led a black boycott of the city's trolley cars that crippled downtown businesses, infuriating white merchants.

Then in 1895 while out of town, her newspaper offices were looted. She was warned that if she returned, she would be lynched. Her response? She bought a pistol and vowed to "die fighting against injustice [rather] than die like a dog or a rat in a trap."

Reluctantly, she then took up her fight in Chicago, becoming editor of that city's first African-American newspaper. She crusaded against voting discrimination, fought for women's rights, and wrote scathing diatribes against lynching.

Someone "must show that the Afro-American race is more sinned against than sinning," she wrote. "And it seems to have fallen to me to do so."

**MOTTO: Dress like a lady,
but be prepared to use your teeth.**

Chapter 54

Al Haynes

Crack of Doom

An explosion rocked a DC-10 at 37,000 feet,
leaving the aircraft uncontrollable.

*"It's about luck, communications, preparation,
execution, and cooperation."*

A billion to one. According to aviation experts, those are
odds against what happened to Flight 232 on July 19, 1989. On
that lovely, sunny day, this United Airlines McDonnell Douglas
DC-10 was bound from Denver to Chicago with 296 passengers
and crew on board. At 37,000 feet flying at a groundspeed of 560
miles per hour, passengers felt and heard what seemed like an
explosion in the tail. Then they felt a sinking feeling as the DC-10
lost altitude.

Soon the confident voice of Flight Engineer Dudley
Dvorak told passengers the aircraft had "lost" its number two
engine. They would continue to on to Chicago, he said, at a lower
altitude and a slower speed.

A DC-10 has three seven-foot diameter General Electric
turbofan engines; one is mounted under each wing, and the third
(the number two engine) is in the tail. A fan blade in the tail
engine had shattered, hurling shrapnel that severed all of the DC-
10's stainless-steel hydraulic control lines.

Fall Out of the Sky

To their horror, Captain Al Haynes and First Officer
William Reynolds watched the hydraulic fluid gauges show
lower and lower levels before falling to zero. Just as cars use
pressurized hydraulic fluid to ease braking and steering, aircraft
use hydraulic systems as well. Elevators move a plane's nose up

or down and ailerons and rudders enable it to turn. Without such aids, the aircraft was crippled and should have been un-flyable.

"Al, I can't control the airplane," said Reynolds. The DC-10 started to fall out of the sky. It wanted to roll to the right even though Reynolds was trying to get it to do the opposite—climb and turn left.

Within minutes, Dennis Fitch, a United DC-10 flight instructor who had been sitting as a passenger, entered the flight deck, joining Haynes, Reynolds, Dvorak, and Jerry Lee Kennedy, a new pilot who was aboard to observe the flight.

Fitch said what he saw on the flight deck was "unbelievable. Both the pilots were in short-sleeved shirts, the tendons being raised in their forearms, their knuckles were white."

"We have almost no controllability," Haynes told air traffic control. "Very little elevator, and almost no ailerons. We're controlling the turns by power…We can only turn right. We can't turn left." A moment later, he added, "I have serious doubts about making the airport."

"An Extension of Me"

Having lost normal control of the aircraft, they kept it aloft by applying asymmetric thrust, increasing the thrust of one engine while lowering the other's thrust and alternating the process to keep the DC-10 from rolling over.

"It just became like the airplane was an extension of me," Haynes said. "I could feel these stimuli coming at me before I actually felt them or saw them. It struck me like a thunderclap—Dear God, I have 296 lives literally in my two hands."

The pilots communicated with United's Systems Aircraft Maintenance office, home to its best engineers. Its experts could not believe what the pilots were telling them. Over and over they asked Haynes to confirm what had happened because it was impossible for all hydraulic systems to fail, and even if that had happened, it would be impossible to fly the DC-10 without them.

The engineers had no advice. What was happening could not be happening.

Ground controllers diverted the flight to Sioux City, Iowa. Amazingly, 285 members of the Iowa Air National Guard and rescue personnel had gathered there that day for a training exercise.

Breaking the Tension

For 45 minutes, the white-knuckle struggle to keep the jet flying continued. As it entered its final approach, the air traffic controller said, "United Two Thirty-Two Heavy, the wind's currently three-six-zero at one-one. Three-sixty at 11. You're cleared to land on any runway."

Breaking the tension, Haynes joked, "You want to be particular and make it a runway, huh?"

As the DC-10 neared the airport, it looked as though it would make a normal landing but at a high speed—250 miles per hour—and that alone was dangerous. The pilots no longer had the use of the plane's hydraulically-powered brakes.

A few seconds before landing 100 feet above the ground, with the runway dead ahead, Fitch and Haynes, struggling with the controls, applied more thrust. The DC-10's right wing dipped 20 degrees (either due to the added thrust, the plane's instability, or both), and the wingtip caught the runway. The DC-10 then cartwheeled, pirouetted onto its nose, toppled over, exploded into a fireball and ripped apart.

Of the 296 passengers and crew onboard, 185 survived, including all of the flight crew. Haynes suffered a concussion and required 92 stitches in his scalp and surgery to have his left ear, which had been 90 percent torn off, reattached. He resumed flying three months later.

Under Terrific Pressure

Investigators later found that the titanium alloy fan blade shattered because it had been made of contaminated metal which, nonetheless, had passed multiple factory inspections. The impurities had caused a pit to form on the surface of the 10-pound, 28-inch-long blade. Every time the engine ran during its 18-year history, the defect grew larger and larger. No one ever noticed it during regular inspections.

At the time of the accident, the tiny cavity measured only three-hundredths of an inch in circumference (0.030) and fifteen hundredths of an inch deep (0.015). Fatigue cracks had begun to radiate from around it, and they caused the blade to shatter while rotating under terrific pressure—3,500 times a minute.

To recover from the trauma of the experience, Haynes gave more than 1,500 speeches, recounting what had happened. "I tell people it's about luck, communications, preparation, execution, and cooperation. You can apply that to any business and your life....

"I feel guilty about 232. [I] didn't do the job the company paid [me] to do—to get from Point A to Point B...The captain gets all the credit, like a quarterback on a football team who won the big game. But it's a team effort—that's what I stress."

MOTTO: Steer any way you can.

Chapter 55

Ida Rosenthal

Uplifting Responsibility

"Down with the czar!" yelled the Russian girl.
But she found her calling supporting American women.

"I wasn't meant for snow shoveling."

Ida Rosenthal wanted to foment a revolution against Russia's czar. Instead she sewed a revolution in fashion. Born 1886 in a small town near Minsk, she went to high school and worked as a seamstress in Poland. While there, the Jewish teenager became exposed to radical notions such as women's rights. Upon returning home, she dared make fiery public speeches urging the tsar's ouster.

She towered four-foot 10-inches tall and had a full, rounded figure—*zaftig* as one might say in Yiddish. Her feminine feistiness and form appealed to a young listener named William Rosenthal. He, too, had a radical bent. Fearing the tsar's wrath, they emigrated to Hoboken, New Jersey, and were soon wed.

Ferocious for her independence, Ida refused to slave in a sweatshop for 12 hours a day. "I don't want to work for anyone else," she vowed. She couldn't read or speak English, but she did have the moxie to gamble on her business prowess—She bought a sewing machine on an installment plan. Thus, she began making inexpensive knock-offs of stylish frocks she saw in magazines. Fast forward a few years, and she had 15 employees.

This Wise Decision

Fate in the form of a heavy snowfall intervened. A cop on the beat told her to shovel the snow in front of her business. The drifts were half as tall as she was, and the job was an ordeal, even for someone as tough as her.

"I wasn't meant for snow shoveling," she decided and soon moved to Manhattan. This wise decision led her to more affluent customers, and now she turned out more fashionable clothes at higher prices.

Around this time, Uncle Sam decided to muscle in on the fashion business. World War I meant America needed more steel for more battleships. In those days, all women wore corsets, and most had steel boning. When women did as Uncle Sam commanded, that freed up 28,000 pounds of steel for cannons and tanks and turrets.

In the process, women were freed, too, literally. The loose-fitting flapper look became the thing. Women flattened their breasts with bandage-style bandeaux to get that "boyish" look.

Women, Not Boys

That didn't work so well for *zaftig* ladies like Ida, and lots of women wanted to look like...women, not boys. Her business partner started sewing the bandeaux into dresses. William hobby was sculpting, and he fashioned a make-shift brassiere with soft-knitted pockets.

At first, her company sewed bras into dresses with no thought of selling them separately. Then they gave them away. Sensing that demand might bust out, they started selling them for a dollar a piece. In 1922, Ida launched a new company—Maidenform.

That's when the worries really began. The company was tiny, and if the whims of fashion shifted, Ida would be broke. Luckily, being based in Manhattan meant being near the theatre district and its open-minded vaudevillians. Once women on Broadway wore bras, Hollywood took notice, and once movie stars became customers, the rest is fashion history.

Ida gradually got out of the dress business. When the Crash of 1929 hit, most dressmakers went belly up, while Maidenform found itself well-supported financially. During the Depression, it made a half million or more bras a year. (The company did make one misstep during WWII. After winning a contract to make underwear for GIs, it learned that soldiers didn't particularly care to have the words MAIDENFORM BRA COMPANY stamped in their boxers.)

While Ida did not invent the brassiere, her chutzpah made it a must item in every woman's wardrobe. Her Russian spirit of revolution and her American zeal for innovation made her a melting pot success story, or as *Fortune* magazine put it, she's "as bright as a Christmas sparkler and as nicely rounded as a bagel."

MOTTO: Do what the policeman says.

Chapter 56

Babe Ruth

Slugger's Battle

He was one of the first patients to receive
experimental chemotherapy.

*"You just can't beat the person
who never gives up."*

Everything about him was big. His whole life was big, and
in September 1946 the pain in his head was big. The agony
behind his left eye wouldn't go away. The whole left side of his
face was swollen. His left eye had clamped shut. His whole head
ached, and he was hoarse and couldn't swallow.

At first, the doctors thought it was merely a sinus
infection. Then they guessed some of his teeth had gone bad, so
they pulled three. Then came the diagnosis—a rare cancer in the
back of his nose and throat—nasopharyngeal carcinoma. Only
about 1,000 Americans are diagnosed with it every year.

Babe Ruth would be dead 21 months later at the age of
53.

He fought hard, just the way he'd battled to win all
through his life. He was one of the first patients in the world to
receive experimental chemotherapy. Some researchers think he
was the first patient with his type of cancer to be given both
chemotherapy and radiation.

A Tough Old Ox

Maybe he was in the right place at the right time. Maybe
the doctors thought he was such a tough old ox that he would
thrive in the face of unknown treatments.

He asked no questions about what his doctors were
doing. He knew that the daily injections of teropterin might help

him or that they might make his condition much worse. He had been told the drug had rarely been given to humans before. (It is related to methotrexate which today is used to treat cancer.)

"I realized that if anything was learned about that type of treatment, whether good or bad, it would be of use in the future to the medical profession and maybe to a lot of people with my same trouble," Ruth wrote in his autobiography.

To say that Ruth was tough would be the understatement to end all understatements. Casual baseball fans and experts agree he was the best who's ever played the game, and you don't win that sort of universal acclaim unless your hard-won achievements prove it ten times over.

An Olympian Record

When he started in the major leagues in 1914, the record for home runs hit in a year was 27. He hit 27 in 1919. The next year he slammed an amazing 54. His all-time high of 60 came in 1927, and he closed his career with 714 dingers, an Olympian record that stood for 47 years.

Want more? He led the league in homers 12 times. He played on seven world championship teams.

What's more, before he was the king of sluggers, he was one of the best pitchers ever. His lifetime ERA (Earned Run Average) of 2.28 over 1,221 innings ranks him as the third best pitcher ever in major league baseball.

He loved everything about life from hot dogs and women to fast cars and fancy clothes. Most of all, he loved kids. In the 1926 World Series, he even performed something close to a miracle for a seriously ill boy named Johnny Sylvester. On his death bed (or what the press said were his final hours), Johnny asked his father if he could have a ball autographed by Babe Ruth. The press got the story, and the Babe said he could do better than that—he would hit a home run for Johnny. And Babe Ruth being Babe Ruth, he hit three home runs in that game. Johnny Sylvester lived until 1990.

What explains the Babe's affection for children? When he was seven, his father took him by the hand to St. Mary's

Industrial School for Boys in Baltimore. It was an orphanage. Ruth would spend the next 12 years there. He was on its books as "incorrigible."

No one knows why he was sent there. His father was a saloon keeper. Maybe the police told his father his joint was just too rough to have a child around. On the other hand, Ruth told reporters no one could make him go to school and that he had learned how to hold a beer mug before most kids could hold pencils.

"I hardly knew my parents," he wrote in his autobiography. "I had a rotten start, and it took me a long time to get my bearings." Rarely did his parents visit him. "I guess I am too big and ugly for anyone to come to see me. Maybe next time," one of the other boys remembered him saying.

Ruth may have started out rotten, but he ripened into one of the world's greatest athletes and most beloved celebrities. His appetite for life was insatiable. "I swing big with everything I've got," he said. "I hit big, or I miss big. I like to live as big as I can."

MORAL: If you play for one run, that's all you get.

Chapter 57

Mark Rothko

Intergalactic Explorer

Haunted by childhood horrors, he fought back,
creating works of haunting spirituality.

"Unknown adventures in an unknown space"

Artist Mark Rothko would sometimes show people the scar on the tip of his nose. One of his earliest childhood memories was being carried in his mother's arms. Suddenly, a Cossack thundered past on his horse. He slashed wildly at them, the tip of his whip just catching the toddler's face.

"Kill the Jews to Save Russia" read signs in Dvinsk, the town where his family lived. Most Jews there lived in poverty working 14-hours a day in factories. Rothko was born in 1903, and two years later, pogroms in nearby towns killed thousands. Though no Jews in Dvinsk died, Jews lived under martial law.

Rothko's father was politically active and an Orthodox Jew. When his son was five, he enrolled him in a religious school, so he could memorize the Talmud. A deep spirituality would stay with him all his days. Two years later, his family emigrated to America. His father died six months later.

Rothko spent the rest of his life reliving those fearful times through his art, almost as though he were trying—but never succeeding—to exorcise them. He said he saw pits dug in the forests where Cossacks buried Jews they had kidnapped and murdered. Historians agree he would have been much too young to have seen such things but instead must have heard stories about such grim events.

Whatever the truth, critics think Rothko was haunted by these rectangular maws—dark open wounds in the earth, explaining why his best-known works are rectangular and large enough to fall into. By repeating the format over and over, it was as if he were saying again and again to viewers, "See! Look at what I suffered! Feel! Experience what I experienced!"

His 45-year career saw him first paint as Realist and Surrealist. In the 1930s and 1940s his work was a riot of archetypal images conveying pain, passion, and violence—a reflection of the times. Starting in 1948, he ascended to his mature period with his 'color field' paintings. These massive unframed works are shimmering windows to the infinite. They have deceptively banal titles like 'Black in Deep Red,' 'Untitled (Black and Orange on Red),' 'Untitled (Violet, Black, Orange, Yellow on White and Red),' and 'No. 6 (Yellow, White, Blue over Yellow on Gray).'

Lozenges of fog, sometimes divided by bright bands that crackle with energy, they contain no images, no symbols, only colors. They radiate. They blush. They burn. Some of these paintings evoke joy. Some feel sad. They almost feel alive. All overwhelm.

How did he do it? He worked on specially prepared canvases and applied many layers of paint applied so the finished works feel both deep and transparent. That Rothko had been a set designer accustomed to working on a large scale helped, too, as did secret ingredients in the paint such as tomato soup and beet juice.

"Tragedy, Ecstasy, Doom"

"Euphoric veils of diaphanous color" is how the Guggenheim describes his work. "You can *fly* through" a Rothko, wrote Tom Wolfe. "Look at that 'airy' quality, those 'areas floating in space,' those cloud formations, all that 'illusionistic space' with its evocations of intergalactic travel."

"Unknown adventures in an unknown space" is how Rothko described his art. Indeed, he hurled himself into orbit and beyond before any astronaut got there.

He denied he was an Abstract Expressionist. "My work is not abstract," he said. "It lives and breathes." And he added: "I'm interested only in expressing basic human emotions—tragedy, ecstasy, doom, and so on."

Rothko believed that viewing his work should be a spiritual experience. Deeply concerned with how his work was exhibited, he insisted that the lighting and other conditions help viewers feel joy, awe, mystery, and dread.

His paintings have been known to make people cry. It was as though they caused some viewers to be engulfed, overwhelmed, and gripped in their deepest, most profound emotions. "The people who weep before my pictures," said Rothko, "are having the same religious experience I had when I painted them."

**MOTTO: You don't need a priest for
an exorcism to be performed.**

Chapter 58

Zachary Hood

First-Grade Legal Case

Zachary's first-grade teacher wouldn't let him
show his art. So his mother went to court.

"Students may express their beliefs..."

When first-grader Zachary Hood of Medford, New Jersey, got in trouble in 1996, he didn't go to the principal's office. He went to a federal court of appeals.

It may be incorrect to say that his teacher punished him, but Zachary felt that way. He went home crying and feeling humiliated. His mother Carol was furious.

Here's what happened—Zachary's teacher wanted to reward her students for learning to read. She told them to each bring in a story from home, so they could read it aloud to the class. There were only two rules, she said: The story had to short, and it had to be on a first-grade reading level.

"Don't Be Angry Anymore"

Zachary chose a story from *The Beginner's Bible*. It recounted the rivalry of the brothers Jacob and Esau in the Book of Genesis and their reconciliation. Here is what Zachary wanted to read to his classmates:

"Jacob traveled far away to his uncle's house. He worked for his uncle, taking care of sheep. While he was there, Jacob got married. He had twelve sons. Jacob's big family lived on his uncle's land for many years.

"But Jacob wanted to go back home. One day, Jacob packed up all his animals and his family and everything he had. They traveled all the way back to where Esau lived.

"Now Jacob was afraid that Esau might still be angry at him. So, he sent presents to Esau. He sent servants who said, 'Please don't be angry anymore.'

"But Esau wasn't angry. He ran to Jacob. He hugged and kissed him. He was happy to see his brother again."

To Zachary's dismay, the teacher told him he couldn't read the story because of its "religious content." The principal agreed, telling Zachary's mother passage was "the equivalent of praying."

She filed suit in federal court alleging that her son had been denied his First Amendment rights. She was doubtless doubly upset. According to her, the principal told her that she and her son didn't "appear to be public-school material." To make matters worse, Zachary's mother also said the principal told her, "I have enough trouble with Jews," a statement the principal denied making.

A Less Conspicuous Place

This wasn't exactly poor Zachary's first offence. He got in trouble the first time the year before at Thanksgiving. He and his fellow kindergarteners had to draw a picture of something they were each "thankful for." Zachary drew a picture of Jesus. At first, his teacher displayed it with the other children's posters outside the classroom. Then the school took it down. That upset Zachary, and the teacher hung it again but in a less conspicuous place.

A federal court ruled against Zachary. It held that although nothing in the story was overtly about religion (it made no mention of God, Christianity, or Judaism), his classmates might have concluded that if their teacher had allowed him to read it, they might have thought the school was endorsing his religious beliefs.

A federal court of appeals affirmed the decision without hearing any oral arguments. Then, after a rehearing was requested, the appeals court heard oral arguments from both sides. It again ruled in favor of the school, voting 6-6, thus upholding the lower court's decision.

In its ruling, the court stated that students possess only limited free speech rights in school and that the school and its teacher had properly exercised their legitimate discretion in forbidding Zachary to read the story. In a dissent, Justice Samuel Alito (who was later elevated to the Supreme Court) contended that "public school authorities may not discriminate against student speech based on its religious content." Ultimately, the Supreme Court declined to hear the case.

In a way, however, Zachary actually won. In response to this case, the Department of Education issued guidelines saying public schools should permit students to express their religious beliefs. Its "guidance" to schools says, "Students may express their beliefs about religion in the form of homework, artwork, and other written and oral assignments—free of discrimination based on the religious contents of their submissions."

Zachary Hood's parents later enrolled him in a local private school.

MORAL: Sometimes you can win by losing.

Chapter 59

Zabadiel Boylston

"Just and True"

City leaders called the doctor's therapy "malignant filth."
His ally? A fanatic who led a witch hunt.

"But see, think, judge; do as the Lord our healer Shall direct you."

Bright red flags went up over more and more front doors of Boston homes in 1721. Some had the words "God have mercy on this house" emblazoned on them. Smallpox had returned. The flags meant: "Quarantine. Do Not Enter."

The plague had struck this thriving city of more than 10,000 colonists years earlier. Remembering its horrors, more than 1,000 people fled to the countryside. "This grievous Calamity of the Small-Pox has now entered the Town," wrote the prominent minister Cotton Mather. He called the disease "the destroying Angel." Smallpox typically killed half of all the children and old people who contracted it and about 15 percent of all other sufferers.

Mather had a rare knowledge of smallpox. Five years earlier when a journal published one of his essays, he chanced up an article in the same issue describing the strange Turkish practice of "Inoculation" against the disease. The report said that when liquid from the pox (or material from their resulting scabs) was placed under the skin of those who had not had the disease, a great number of the resulting cases were less severe than if the disease had been contracted naturally.

"be WARILY proceeded in"

Mather had evidence of this in his own home. Years before he had bought a slave and named him Onesimus which means "Beneficial." How fitting it was, for Onesimus told Mather that he had been inoculated and showed him the procedure's scar.

He did further research and learned that this strange ritual was performed among the "heathens" and "'primitives" not only in Africa but also in Asia and Russia. Mather then wrote a leading Boston physician. "How many Lives might be saved by it, if it were practiced?" he asked and recommended that it "be WARILY proceeded in."

When the letter was forwarded to other doctors, none showed an interest—except the surgeon Zabadiel Boylston. Perhaps the others were wary of being associated with Mather. He had been a leading figure in the Salem Witch Trials, and his efforts had led to 20 executions.

Boylston was controversial, too. He had recently performed the first mastectomy in America, removing a woman's cancerous breast. Other doctors were appalled, saying that it was impossible to cure the disease that way. He had also removed bladder stones from children, a practice associated with quacks.

He clearly didn't care what others thought. He charged more than other physicians and had no qualms about suing patients who failed to pay. He also had the weird habit of changing his clothes and bathing after visiting patients. Perhaps worse, he had not studied at Harvard.

"Ravings and Deliriums"

Boylston knew first-hand what smallpox could do. He was a smallpox survivor. His case had been horrendous and had left him with a ravaged pockmarked face.

Here is how he described the symptoms of smallpox in the worst cases: "Purple spots, the bloody and parchment Pox, Hemorahages of Blood at the Mouth, Nose, Fundament, and Privities; Ravings and Deliriums; Convulsions, and other Fits; violent inflammations and Swellings in the Eyes and Throat; so that they cannot see, or scarcely breathe, or swallow anything, to keep them from starving. Some looking as black as the Stock, others as white as a Sheet; in some, the Pock runs into Blisters, and the Skin stripping off, leaves the Flesh raw....Some have been fill'd with loathsome Ulcers; others have had deep, and fistulous Ulcers in their Bodies, or in their Limbs or Joints, with Rottenness of the Ligaments and Bones: Some who live are Cripples, others Idiots, and many blind all their Days."

He had another reason for wanting to pursue inoculation. None of his six children had had the disease. He decided to perform the procedure on his adult slave Jack, the slave's son, and Thomas, his six-year-old son. He could not expect Bostonians to submit to the procedure unless at least one of his family members had undergone it, a sign of his own faith in the procedure. As for his slaves—they were, in the thinking of the day, his valuable property, and he did not want to lose them.

Mather implored Boylston to proceed, writing him, "See, think, judge; do as the Lord our healer Shall direct you."

Thomas and the other child developed fevers and twitchings lasting more than a week before the children regained full health, while Jack barely became ill.

When Bostonians learned what Boylston had done, "the immediate reaction was shock," one historian wrote. He published a statement saying he was on solid medical ground because the accounts from far-away lands were "just and true" and his three patients had survived without lasting ill effects.

"Infusing...Malignant Filth"

Boston's leading citizens convened a hearing. Boylston suffered through its verbal abuse. Its report declared that he was "infusing...malignant Filth" in patients and that what he was doing was well known to have "prov'd the Death of many Persons." Two days later Boylston was inoculating others.

Someone hurled a firebomb into his home, according to one account. It failed to explode. Another person wanted to embarrass Boylston by secretly spreading tar on his saddle. The dirty deed failed when the vandal accidentally put the tar on another man's saddle and "spoil'd his Breeches."

Over time, Boylston inoculated 280 people. Only six died or 2.4 percent, far lower than the usual fatality rate. Acclaim followed. Boylston wrote the book *An Historical Account of the Small-Pox Inoculated in New England*. In it, he offered a 15-step guide to performing inoculations. He described each of his cases and made conclusions based on a statistical analysis (at a time when the word 'statistics' did not exist). He even proposed that tiny, unseen creatures caused the disease by entering its victims via skin contact, respiration, or through contaminated food or water.

Sometimes it's courageous to get under people's skin, but it helps if you are a medical professional.

MORAL: Your mother was right—
Wash your hands.

Chapter 60

Alex Haley

Haley's Comet

He was going to jump overboard into the Atlantic.
Then voices spoke to him.

"Find the good and praise it."

No matter where he lived, Alex Haley hung a strange framed collage in his home. It consisted of two unopened sardine cans, three pennies, a dime, and a nickel. Before he won fame and fortune as the author of the best-selling book *Roots*, that's all the food and money he had at one point while trying to eke out a living as a writer. He only made enough from freelance writing "to hang on by [his] fingernails."

Growing up in the tiny west Tennessee hamlet of Henning, Haley didn't know what to do with his life. He entered college at 15 and remembers being "easily the most undistinguished freshman" there. When he was 17 in 1939, he dropped out to join the Coast Guard and served as a cook. During World War II, the Navy took command of the Coast Guard's ships, and Haley did fairly hazardous duty on an ammunition ship in the south Pacific.

On a lark, before shipping out, he bought a portable typewriter. To while away the lonely hours, he obsessively wrote 30 to 40 letters a week to friends and relatives. The resulting deluge of replies did not go unnoticed by shipmates starved for letters from loved ones. Soon they asked him to write love letters for them.

"A Wall of Rejection"

When Haley wasn't peeling potatoes, he was the chief cook and bottle-washer for the ship's newsletter which contained news, personal profiles, and humor. After the war ended, Haley worked in the Coast Guard's Manhattan public relations office and became its Chief Journalist.

Year after year, he dashed off submissions to all manner of magazines, even the lowliest celebrity and romance publications. The result? "A wall of rejection notices," a friend recalled.

He never gave up and continued trying to break into big magazines after retiring from the Coast Guard in 1959. "When I first got bold enough to try [to sell a story to] *Reader's Digest*, I received a rejection slip with a very different, rather august approach," Haley recalled. It read—'Dear Mr. Haley: We're sorry, but this does not quite jell for us.' That would just frustrate the hell out of me, because I had been a cook, and I would get an image of too much water in the Jello."

Slowly, his persistence paid off, and he placed stories in *The Christian Science Monitor*, *The Atlantic*, *The Saturday Evening Post*, *Cosmopolitan* (which was then a general-interest magazine), and, indeed, *Reader's Digest*.

Finally, Haley rose to prominence by conducting Playboy Interviews, the most notable of which were with Martin Luther King (the longest interview he ever gave) and Malcolm X. He then wrote *The Autobiography of Malcolm X* which became a best-seller.

As a child, Haley spent hours listening to his relatives tell tales of family history, and he had long wanted to write a book that explored his family's history. On the strength of his success with his Malcolm X book, Doubleday gave him an advance of $5,000 ($40,000 in 2018 dollars) to write a book titled "Before This Anger."

It took 11 difficult years for Haley to complete what would become *Roots*. He had severe writer's block and was swamped by the research he felt he had to do to ground the book in reality. (He slept in the un-airconditioned hold of a freighter, so he could get a sense of what it might have been like to have been a captive African making the Middle Passage.)

He insisted that his book be marketed as non-fiction, even though scenes and dialogue set in the distant past were clearly fictional. This decision would later bring Haley much grief when he faced two lawsuits alleging plagiarism. (One was dismissed, and Haley settled the other.)

The Lord's Design

On at least one occasion, his writer's block was so horrendous, he contemplated suicide. He was returning to the U.S. via freighter after spending time in Liberia traveling and talking with oral historians. Frustrated by his inability to put pen to paper and mounting personal debts, he found himself standing by the ship's rail.

"The Lord's design...put me to a severe test," Haley remembered. He felt he was "just a millimeter from dropping into that sea." Then he says the voices of his characters spoke to him, and that gave him the confidence to proceed.

When *Roots* was published in 1976, the book was a sensation—like a comet crossing the American consciousness. His motto had always been "Find the good and praise it." Now he had done more to improve race relations than almost anyone else in American history.

Haley won a Pulitzer and the National Book Award. *Ebony* magazine said it was the nation's number-one topic of discussion. The resulting TV miniseries spanned eight evenings—and the history of Haley's family from Africa to his birth—and was watched by 50 million people. Overnight, Haley became not just a celebrity (and wealthy) but also the nation's most prominent African-American.

"All that money has almost no meaning to me," he said at the time. "I was broke for so long that I got used to being without money."

He lived lavishly and flew on *Reader's Digest's* corporate jet. "I walked up the runway into the plane, and I looked around at seats for about 14 people, but there was nobody but me.... There was a silver tray with all kinds of little sandwiches cut in circles, diamonds, and everything.

"You can't comprehend what's happening to you. All your life you've been wishing to God somebody'd read something you wrote, and then all of a sudden this is happening." Then Haley remember his first letter from a *Reader's Digest* editor. "And the thought just came to me: 'Well, I guess it finally jelled.' "

**MORAL: Better to try and be rejected than never
to have tried at all.**

Chapter 61

James Bond Stockdale

Strength in Unity

This fighter pilot mastered a stern philosophy.
As a POW, no torture could break him.

*"Do the right thing, even if it means dying like a dog
when there's no one there to see it."*

"I was just a blind, crippled animal, shitting on the floor....I had crotch rot from continuous filth. My pajamas were caked with pus."

That's what happens when you are tortured and then held in leg irons for days on end while chained to the cold, filthy concrete floor of a windowless cell measuring three feet by nine feet.

That was the plight of James Bond Stockdale, winner of two Purple Hearts and the Medal of Honor, America's most prestigious military decoration. He was the highest-ranking U.S. Navy officer held prisoner during the Vietnam War. A carrier-based fighter pilot, Stockdale had flown nearly 200 combat missions before being shot down in 1965.

Stockdale even took part in the infamous Gulf of Tonkin incident. A U.S. destroyer in a thunderstorm mistakenly reported that North Vietnamese ships were attacking it. As part of an urgent nighttime 'rescue' mission, Stockdale and other fliers shot at what their radar told them was firing at the ship. They later realized that their gear—and the ship's sonar— had created imaginary targets. No enemy ships. No attack.

But the Johnson Administration used the event as a pretext for massively escalating the war. Stockdale was furious, writing in his memoirs that "it was a bad portent that we seemed to be under the control of a mindless Washington bureaucracy, vain enough to pick their own legitimacies regardless of evidence."

"Punched Out"

A bad portent indeed. Soon thereafter while on a mission over North Vietnam, anti-aircraft fire peppered his fighter, and Stockdale "punched out," ejecting himself and parachuting into a small village. His parachute still billowing, a dozen men fell on him—"the quarterback sack of the century" Stockdale called it. They beat him senseless, shattering his leg, injuring his knee (which never healed), dislocating his shoulders, and breaking a bone in his neck.

Much worse came, following his arrival at the Hoa Lo Prison, what POWs dubbed the "Hanoi Hilton." He spent seven-and-a-half years there in captivity, four of those years in solitary confinement.

"I was tortured 15 times," Stockdale recalled. "That's total submission. They did that with shutting off your blood circulation with ropes, giving you claustrophobia and pain at the same time and bending you double."

Stockdale knew he held priceless secret information. If torture broke him and the world learned that no North Vietnamese attack had taken place in the Gulf of Tonkin, it would be "the biggest Communist propaganda scoop of the decade," he wrote. "In this war, it was already becoming clear that it was the propaganda bombs, not the TNT bombs, that were going to make the difference."

"A Reverse Cherokee"

He kept his mouth shut. To keep from being used as a propaganda pawn, he nearly mortally injured himself. He slashed his filthy scalp from front to back with a razor, creating what he called "a reverse Cherokee" haircut, making a bloody mess of himself. Then he disfigured himself by punching himself in the face again and again until his hands and face were sore.

Why? To prevent the North Vietnamese from putting him on international TV.

Stockdale's will to resist gave other prisoners hope. They saw his resolve. And Stockdale was wise enough to use his authority to relax the military's code of prisoner behavior, giving his fellow POWs permission to reveal information, so long as what they 'confessed' to was harmless.

"Unity was our best hope," Stockdale said. "A life of perfection was out of the question, but [the POWs] elected to take pain in a unified resistance program....Their self-esteem could be maintained, and they could sleep with a clean conscience at night."

A student of the Greek Stoic philosopher Epictetus, Stockdale held fast to this belief—"Look not for any greater harm than this: Destroying the trustworthy, self-respecting, well-behaved man within you."

**MORAL: In a crisis, people look for leadership.
Be that leader.**

Chapter 62

Charles Schulz

The Nobody Who Became a Somebody

For this artist, grief was good. No one would
buy his work. Until he got his big break.

*"Life is like a ten-speed bicycle. Most of us have gears we never
use."*

He thought of himself as "a nothing young man" or just "a nothing" or "a nobody." In seventh-grade, he was too puny to get the honored post of crossing guard. A friend said he "was a genius at becoming invisible." Of his high school years, he recalled "I wasn't actually hated. Nobody cared that much." His high school yearbook rejected his drawings. When asked in school if he wanted to be an artist when he grew up, he replied, "No." Later, he recalled, "I didn't want to be accused of thinking I was better than I was."

What accounts for *this* outlook? Many things, undoubtedly. His Norwegian grandmother told him cheerful things like "If you're too happy today, something bad will happen to you tomorrow" and "If you laugh at the dinner table, you'll cry before bed."

This shy and timid loser was a real Charlie Brown. He was the real Charles Schulz who created Peanuts. He once told an interviewer: "I suppose there's a melancholy feeling in a lot of cartoonists, because cartooning, like all other humor, comes from bad things happening."

"They Were What Sold"

When it was at its peak, this comic strip whose main character always fails at almost everything ran every day in 2,600 papers in 75 nations in 21 languages. It is estimated that the strip along with licensed product and endorsements generated revenues of more than $1 billion a year, with Schulz taking home as much as $40 million annually.

Why was Peanuts such as massive hit? "If you're going to create cartoon characters, you can create them only from your own personality." That is what Schulz did. Lucy, Linus, and the gang weren't really children—they were adults who looked like children. He had no particularly affinity for children, saying "I drew them because they were what sold."

Schulz said he succeeded because his strip relied on the "real minimum gag…. No one had ever done this type of humor before." In what other comic strip would characters say existential things like "What's the matter with me? Where's my sense of responsibility? …. Is it really my fault when I do something wrong? Must I answer for my mistakes…. Who is responsible? Who is accountable?"

Schulz and only Schulz would have written such dialogue.

He was his father's son. Schulz revered his father, a barber who never graduated from high school. His father never took a vacation in 45 years. Similarly, Schulz wrote, penciled, inked, and lettered Peanuts without an assistant for nearly 50 years, taking only one vacation. The last of his 17,897 strips appeared the day he died.

"I Became a Man"

He knew from his earliest memories that his destiny was to be a comic strip artist. After all, his kindergarten teacher had told him, "Someday, Charles, you're going to be an artist." After high school, his father enrolled him in the home-study Federal School of Illustrating and Cartooning, and he had a tough time making the monthly $10 payments.

The rejection was ceaseless, but he had toughened up since his school days. He had been drafted into the Army in 1942. Being in the service changed him. He put on 25 pounds—all muscle, and he rose to the rank of sergeant. He went in "a young guy who nobody ever thought would amount to much," and it gave him the opportunity to spend time "with a bunch of men." The result? "I became a man."

But Disney didn't want him. Neither did Classics Illustrated comics. After being hired as "junior artist," he learned the only implement he would be wielding was a broom so he could sweep the offices. At his next job, he addressed labels.

He took twice-a-week evening classes at the Minneapolis School of Art. The woman who kept attendance remembered thinking, "He'll never amount to anything."

He submitted ideas for strips to the Chicago Tribune-New York News Syndicate. "Not professional enough," it said. *The Chicago Sun-Times* syndicate agreed.

Every week from 1947 into 1950 he sent submissions to magazines. "This way you are never without hope," he said.

His Big Break—Broken

Finally, in 1948, he got his big break—the E.W. Scripps syndicate in Cleveland offered him a one-year contract for a comic strip and flew him to its offices. It was Schultz's first trip on an airplane. Once back home, he got the contract in the mail, signed it, and sent it off. The syndicate took Schulz's photo for a sales brochure. Then just like Lucy yanking away the football, it cancelled the deal. Its salesforce didn't think it could get enough newspapers to sign on.

"I was never discouraged," Schulz recalled. "I always knew that I was getting closer and closer." He had so much confidence that when Disney asked him to move to Los Angeles to work as entry-level artist, he declined, preferring to stay with in Minneapolis where he had made a circle of friends.

Slowly, a trickle of success came. The local newspaper ran his cartoons. Finally, in 1950, United Features saw what a gem he was. There was one condition: He had to change the name of his strip from "Li'l Folk" to "Peanuts." He loathed the title and resented it to his dying day. But he was smart enough to take the deal.

First only seven papers took the strip, then 35, and soon enough, the strip was a sensation. Charlie Brown even went to the Moon. The astronauts of Apollo 10 named their command module after him, and they named their lunar module Snoopy.

Happiness, as Schulz was famous for saying, is a warm puppy, and happiness is also having the courage to stick with your dream until it comes true.

MORAL: If life pulls away the football before you can kick it, listen to Beethoven.

Chapter 63

Stanislav Petrov

Haste Makes Waste

His patience prevented global thermonuclear war.

"I didn't want to make a mistake."

The button in front of him pulsed, glowing red as if it had a wicked life of its own. On it one word was written: "Start."

As in start World War III.

A klaxon blared the alarm to Stanislav Petrov, a 44-year-old lieutenant colonel in the Soviet Air Defence command. He was the duty officer in charge sitting in a now less-than-easy chair in Serpukhov-15, a secret underground bunker located 100 miles south of Moscow. From this command center, the U.S.S.R. monitored satellites positioned over the U.S. which would give it early-warning of American missile launches. It was 15 minutes after midnight on September 26, 1983.

The Cold War that year was colder than ever. Soviet leaders feared that President Reagan wanted war. In March, he denounced the U.S.S.R as the "focus of evil in the modern world...an evil empire." The U.S. had begun placing Pershing II nuclear missiles in Germany in response to the Soviet redeployment of its nuclear missiles in Europe. The U.S. Air Force was routinely testing Soviet air defenses with bomber missions that diverted away from the Russian border at the last moment. Worse, on September 1, the Russian air force shot down a Korean Airlines 747 that had strayed over Russian territory, killing all 269 aboard.

"Every second counted," Petrov recalled. "My cozy armchair became a hot frying pan."

Two massive green electronic maps of the Soviet Union and the U.S. spanned the wall in front of him. On it, Petrov could see nine American military bases. "When the "Start" button in front of me began blinking, I immediately looked at the map. I could see on it that a military base on the east coast was also blinking—a signal that a missile had been fired, aimed at us."

Now—again and again and again and again and again—five more warning lights flashed red. The sirens continued to blast. The screen showed that the United States had launched five more Minuteman intercontinental ballistic missiles (ICBMs), each tipped with three to five independently targetable nuclear warheads in the 300 kiloton to 500 kiloton range. (The A-Bomb that destroyed Hiroshima had a yield of only 15 kilotons.)

The screen flashed the words "Missile Attack." Because multiple launches were now seen, the computer automatically notified the general staff of the Russian military. Petrov knew it would need his confirmation before contacting Yuri Andropov, the General Secretary of the Central Committee the Communist Party.

Petrov called a superior officer to ask his opinion. The officer was drunk and asked Petrov: "Can it wait until tomorrow?"

Petrov spent five agonizing minutes trying to figure out what was going on. "I had a funny feeling in my gut," he recalled. "I didn't want to make a mistake. I made a decision, and that was it."

No Funnel-Shaped Tail

His decision was to tell his superiors the warnings were a false alarm. They were. There had been no U.S. missile launches. Petrov was experienced—and cool-headed—enough to know that the U.S. would be unlikely to launch an attack with so few missiles.

He was also suspicious of what the computer was telling him. On the monitors in front of him, he saw no visual confirmation of missile launches—the funnel-shaped tail of fire that would trail behind the ascending ICBMs. Plus, the early warning system had just been installed. Petrov didn't trust it. As it turned out, atmospheric and orbital conditions caused its sensors to interpret high altitude clouds as missiles.

Had Petrov authenticated the launches to his superiors, he said, "All our forces would have been brought into combat readiness, with more than 11,000 missiles... complete overkill."

Afterwards, his colleagues embraced him and justly called him a hero. Petrov swigged a pint of vodka "as if it were a glass," he says, and then slept for 28 straight hours. As a reward, his comrades chipped in and got him a Russian-made portable TV.

Petrov went on to live as a pensioner in Russia. Danish movie director Peter Anthony interviewed him at length for a documentary about the incident. "I felt like I was meeting Jesus when he answered the door, yet he was living like a street person," the director said. "He would make soup by boiling a leather belt in water to give it flavor."

MORAL: Think before you press the panic button.

Chapter 64

Clarence Birdseye

No Chicken

He really liked cold food.
The problem was no one else did.

*"Anyone who attempts anything original in
this world must expect a bit of ridicule."*

Clarence Birdseye was obsessed with food. He would eat anything. "Scrumptious" was how he described lynx marinated in sherry. He sampled seal meat, owl, polar bear, filleted rattlesnake sizzled in pork fat, hawk, porcupine (de-quilled, presumably) and skunk (but mercifully only its front half).

He even made a string-powered gizmo to catch starlings in the yard of his Massachusetts home. Whether the device's purpose was to rid him of pests, provide dinner, or both is lost to history.

The editor of his college yearbook teased him by putting this phony quote by his photo: "I ain't afeer'd o'bugs, or toads, or worms, or snakes, or mice, or *anything.*" Indeed, when he was 10, he wondered if there might be a market for muskrat. It turned out there was, and with the proceeds from the beasts he trapped and sold, he bought a shotgun.

4,495 Ticks

His college nickname was "Bugs." This turned out to be prescient. His family's financial woes forced him to drop out. Soon he found work as a naturalist out west. He helped researchers study Rocky Mountain Spotted Fever and was at liberty to kill any animal that might be carrying the creepy creatures. He shot more than 1,000 deer, elks, mules, and mountain sheep, as a result, collected precisely 4,495 ticks. To his credit, his report did much to advance medical and scientific knowledge about the disease.

Later he bred foxes for their fur. This led him to Labrador where he saw something that would change his life. He watched the Inuit ice fishing. When they yanked fish from the ocean, the 30-degree-below zero air made the fish freeze rock solid almost before they hit the ground. Then, wonder of wonders, when the fish thawed, they tasted fresh.

Frozen food already existed, but no one had mastered the process. It was so appallingly bad not even prison inmates would eat it. Wanting to ward off riots, New York state banned it in its penitentiaries. Stores selling frozen food had to display signs in their windows that resembled warning labels.

Starting around 1915 Birdseye started to experiment, first with cabbage and then with caribou in sea water and ice. In 1922 an ice cream company gave him permission to run experiments in its plant. The next year Birdseye started his own company.

To simplify production, he decided to sell his frozen foods in uniformly-sized small rectangular boxes. Then he had to master multiple challenges. He perfected waterproof inks. He devised glues that would withstand freezing. He conjured up filleting machines, and he designed wrappers. (His persistence led DuPont to invent cellophane for that purpose.)

Frozen into Tidy Blocks

The key to his manufacturing process lay in his invention of the "multi-plate freezing machine." It compressed whatever was being frozen into tidy blocks, thus preventing germs from entering and making the shipping easier.

As clever as Birdseye was, no one wanted to buy his food. Railroads shunned his wares fearing they'd make a mess. Sanitation officials, wary of disease-carrying food, didn't like the idea. Stores had no freezers, and shoppers were no different from prison convicts. They also loathed all things frozen whether they were haddock or green peas.

Enter Marjorie Merriweather Post, the grand dame of The Post Company, famed for its many breakfast cereals. Legend has it that when her yacht sailed into Gloucester, Massachusetts, where Birdseye had his factory, her cook served her goose for dinner. It wasn't just any goose. He had bought one of Birdseye's frozen birds at the market.

She loved it, and after nagging her father for three years, she got him to buy Birdseye's company for the then fantastic sum of $22 million. The truth is that she was smart as a whip and, goose or no goose, saw a smart business move and made the deal happen all by her self.

"A Scientific Miracle"

Birdseye went to work for Post and lived happily and wealthily ever after. Its financial wherewithal created the infrastructure that allowed the industry to grow. Post gave grocery stores display freezers. It taught clerks how to use them and sell the chilly food. It sold grocers frozen food on consignment to minimize their risk. Lavish advertising promised housewives the best of summer's luscious fruits in winter. Stamping its good journalism seal of approval, *The New York Times* raved in 1932 that frozen food was "a scientific miracle in home management."

"Change," said Birdseye, "is the very essence of American life." What he neglected to add was that to make that change happen it takes someone with the courage to defrost old-fashioned thinking.

MORAL: In a crisis, be cool, but don't freeze.

Chapter 65

Jimmy Stewart

The Liberator

He wanted to fight. His boss said that would ruin his career.
His career was ruined, but he had a wonderful life.

"I prayed that I wouldn't make a mistake."

"Airplanes were the first thing I thought of every
evening and the first thing I thought of every morning," said
movie star Jimmy Stewart, recalling his childhood. When
Lindbergh conquered the Atlantic in 1927, nine-year-old Jimmy
eagerly listened to every radio news flash. In the 1930s while
making pictures for MGM, the young star found the time to earn
his commercial pilot's license, sometimes flying cross-country to
visit his parents.

"You're like a bird up there," he said. "It's almost as if
you're not part of society anymore. All you can think about is
what you're doing, and you have a complete escape from your
worldly problems."

But when FDR instituted the draft in 1940, Stewart
wanted to fight, not escape. Military service was a tradition in his
family. His great-great-great grandfather fought in the
Revolution. Both of his grandfathers served in the Union Army in
the Civil War. (One was at Appomattox Courthouse when
Confederate general Robert E. Lee surrendered.) He watched his
father go off to fight in Europe in the Great War.

Stewart, however, had to fight Uncle Sam before he could
fight Nazis. At 32, he was far older than most enlistees who
wanted to fly (and beyond the regulation age limit for pilots).
Worse, he flunked his physical. He was six-foot three-inches tall
and weighed 138 pounds. The Army said he was a "health risk."
Using a Hollywood diet coach and lots of milkshakes, he packed
on the pounds, and after pulling a few strings, he was reclassified
as 1-A.

He certainly wasn't in it for the money. His salary fell from $12,000 a week to $21 a month. MGM threw him a going-away party. Stars Rosalind Russell, Judy Garland, Lana Turner, and Ann Rutherford all kissed him, and Russell used her handkerchief to wipe off their lipstick from his cheeks. After writing each woman's name by her lipstick smear, Russell gave the handkerchief to Stewart. He kept it as a lucky charm, and it flew with him on all his combat missions.

Even though he was now in the Army, he still had to fight to get to Europe. Uncle Sam assigned him to a Motion Picture Unit in Dayton, Ohio, to make morale films. Angry, he met with the commanding officer. Convinced that Stewart wanted to see action, he urged his superiors to transfer Stewart, writing, "He wants to be treated exactly as any other American boy drafted into the service of his country."

In the fall of 1943 at the advanced age of 35, Stewart became the commanding officer of the 703rd Squadron of the 445th Bomb Group of the Second Combat Wing of the Second Bomb Division of the Eighth Air Force, rising from private to captain in two-and-a-half years.

He led a squadron of 15 B-24 Liberator bombers and became known for his crisp flying skills and quick-thinking. His men liked him. "I always got the feeling that he would never ask you to do something he wouldn't do himself," a flier recalled.

During his 15 months in action over Europe, he flew more than 20 combat missions. They included strategic strikes in Germany, Holland, and France against a U-Boat base; naval shipyards; a V-1 missile launch site on Christmas Eve; a chemical factory belonging to I.G. Farben, the maker of cyanide gas used in death camps; a Nazi air base; bomber and fighter plane factories; and an incendiary raid on Berlin. As D-Day approached, his group went after tactical targets in France, including another V-1 launch site. Promoted to colonel 12 days before D-Day, he flew on the day of the invasion itself on a bombing mission just north of Omaha Beach.

On each flight, Stewart took with him a copy of the 91st Psalm which his father had sent him. Its verses read: "Surely, he will save you from the fowler's snare and from the deadly pestilence. He will cover you with his feathers, and under his wings you will find refuge; his faithfulness will be your shield and rampart. You will not fear the terror of night, nor the arrow that flies by day."

"Just remember you can't handle fear all by yourself. Give it to God. He'll carry it for you," said Stewart. "Fear is an insidious thing. It can warp judgment, freeze reflexes, breed mistakes. Worse, it's contagious. I felt my own fear and knew that if it wasn't checked, it could infect my crew members."

The trauma of combat was severe. Stewart couldn't eat. A friend said he survived the war on ice cream and peanut butter. B-24s had no heat. Temperatures in the bombers at 20,000 feet fell to 40 below zero, and Stewart wore an oxygen mask and an electrically-heated flying suit.

That wasn't nearly the worst of it. The terrors of air combat were constant. A Nazi fighter tore past his plane so close to the cockpit that Stewart could count the rivets on its underbelly. After missions, he regularly found gashes in his plane so big he could put his hand through them.

On one occasion, flak tore a hole in his cockpit floor two feet across only a few inches from his feet. After one flight, his B-24's flak-riddled fuselage split open on the runway. "Somebody sure could get hurt in one of those damned things," Stewart said to a sergeant standing nearby. On one flight, he barely limped back to base when one engine iced up and flak took out another.

"All I wanted to do was keep [the men in my squadron] alive and do our job," said Stewart. "I didn't pray for my own life. I prayed that I wouldn't make a mistake."

When bombers in his squadron were shot down—a regular occurrence, Stewart's responsibility as squadron leader included the grim task of writing hand-written letters to the parents of each airman. It was lonely being a leader. "You can't make the men you command into your friends," he said.

Loneliest Man

The press was always after him. He subscribed to his home town paper, *The Indiana Evening Gazette*, and in one issue, the headline of a story read: STEWART SAID LONELIEST MAN—INDIANA CAPTAIN TOO BUSY TO TALK TO NEWS WRITERS. Throughout his four-and-a-half years in the service, Stewart avoided all contact with reporters, unless he was ordered to do so.

After flying 20 combat missions (as well as others that went uncredited), his commanding officer saw the terrible effects of combat in Stewart's face. "I just told him I didn't want him to fly any more combat," he recalled. "He didn't argue about it."

When his parents first saw him when he came back to the States, they noticed that his hair was graying, and he was thinner. They thought he looked as though he had aged two decades.

He refused to capitalize on his combat heroism. When he learned that MGM wanted to make *The Jimmy Stewart Story*, a movie celebrating his exploits, he nixed the idea. A clause in all of his movie contracts said that his war record could not be used in publicizing his films.

He rarely spoke of his wartime experiences. "I saw too much suffering," he said. "It's certainly not something to talk about." Psychologically, his experiences haunted him, and he became deaf from his long hours near the roar of airplane engines.

After the war, he couldn't get work. Neither could director Frank Capra. He talked Stewart into starring in his new film *The Greatest Gift*. After Capra told Stewart its plot, he asked him what he thought. "How do I know?" Stewart replied. "I can't make head nor tail of the damn thing!"

Retitled, the film was released as *It's a Wonderful Life*, the story of a man haunted by failure who realizes that anyone who has friends is a success.

MORAL: Trust the Director.
He knows the role you should play.

Chapter 66

Cabeza deVaca

He Found the Real Treasure

The explorer's mission to Florida failed. Nine years later,
he emerged in California a changed man.

"I preferred risking my life to placing my honor in jeopardy."

The Spanish slave raiders were speechless. It was April
1536 on the Pacific coast of present day Mexico. Skilled in the
dark art of burning Indian villages to kidnap men, women, and
children into slavery, the cavalrymen were out seeking new
captives.

Now they saw a group of Indians walking towards
them—unafraid. But one of them was black. Another was white.
Both were barefoot and wore only animal pelts. The white man's
hair had grown to his waist, and his beard hung down to his
chest.

"They remained looking at me for a long time, so
astonished that they neither talked to me nor managed to ask me
anything," wrote Cabeza de Vaca. He and 300 other men had left
Spain in 1527 on a mission to colonize Florida. Now nine years
later, only de Vaca, the expedition's Royal Treasurer, and three
other men had survived.

Hammered by a Hurricane

After being hammered by a hurricane in Cuba, the
explorers landed on Florida's west coast near present day St.
Petersburg. The expedition's leader Narvaez decided to send half
his party by ship to Panuco, a distant Spanish outpost on the far
side of the Gulf of Mexico.

He, de Vaca, and others would head inland in search of
gold. With misgivings, de Vaca followed orders. "I preferred

risking my life to placing my honor in jeopardy," he would write in his account of his odyssey.

For months, the party fought Indians. "All the Indians we had seen from Florida to here are archers, and as they are of large build and go about naked, from a distance they appear to be giants," de Vaca wrote.

Finally, the exhausted explorers became lost in swamps, their numbers depleted from skirmishes with Indians. To survive, they had no choice but to eat their horses one by one. To reach Panuco more than 1,000 miles away, they decided to build five 33-foot-long rafts, each able to carry 50 men. They had no tools, so they melted their crossbows, spurs, horseshoes and all other metal and built a forge so they could fashion primitive axes and saws.

"It seemed impossible," he wrote, "as none of us know how to construct ships. We had no tools, no iron, no smithery, no oakum, no pitch, no tackling: finally, nothing of what was indispensable. Neither was there anybody to instruct us in shipbuilding, and, above all, there was nothing to eat, while the work was going on....

"Considering this, we agreed to think it over. Our parley ceased for that day, and everyone went off, leaving it to God, Our Lord, to put him on the right road according to His pleasure."

"The Isle of Doom"

Then they set to sea, hugging the coastline westward. "And so greatly can necessity prevail that it made us risk going in this manner and placing ourselves in a sea so treacherous," wrote de Vaca. "And without any one of us who went having any knowledge of the art of navigation."

Amazingly, they traveled 400 miles to the mouth of the Mississippi. There the strong current pulled the rafts in different directions, and Narvaez was carried out to sea and never seen again.

Now only 80 explorers were left alive near Galveston Island on an island they named Malhado, the Isle of Doom. Only 15 would survive the winter. Many died after resorting to cannibalism. "They were people beyond hope, and all died that winter of hunger and cold, eating one another," de Vaca wrote.

Indians captured and enslaved the survivors, putting them to work digging roots to eat and hauling timber. Killed for the slightest misstep or no reason at all, de Vaca and his weary group lived in terror.

For several years, the explorers lived as slaves, passed from one tribe to another. Finally, only four were left alive, and after escaping, they began a journey west that would take them through present day Texas, New Mexico, Arizona, and northern Mexico.

Then something miraculous happened. Indians observed the Spanish men performing Christian rituals and concluded that they were medicine men. At first, de Vaca would only make the sign of the cross over a sick Indian or blow on his body, fearing that if he did more he might be killed if his 'medicine' failed to work.

"The Children of the Sun"

Over time, he grew bolder. He used a knife to perform surgery on an Indian's chest, digging out a deeply embedded arrowhead and suturing the incision. When another Indian given up for dead had been prepared for burial, de Vaca made the sign of the cross over him. Hours later, he rose and went about as if he had never been ill.

"This caused great surprise and awe, and all over the land nothing else was spoken of," de Vaca wrote.

Now in awe of the men they called "the children of the sun" (because their appearance and ways were so alien), the Indians revered them. Instead of being sold to other tribes as slaves, the Spaniards led crowds of as many as 3,000 to 4,000 Indians from one tribe to the next, each tribe marveling at the strangers' mighty deeds.

"In this way Jesus Christ guided us, and his infinite mercy was with us, opening roads where there were none," wrote de Vaca. "And the hearts of men so savage and untamed, God moved to humility and obedience."

When the slave raiders rescued de Vaca, he had lived in the wilderness and among Indians for so long that he found Spanish ways strange. For days, he could not sleep in bed or wear clothes.

What's more, his long years with the Indians had given him great sympathy and respect for them. He was appalled by his countrymen's horrific treatment of Indians. He wanted Spain to peacefully partner with them.

Upon returning home, he made his case to the king and became governor of an area in South America which includes present day Argentina, Uruguay, and Paraguay. His hopes of working together with the natives proved naïve. The men under his command, eager for gold and power, took him prisoner and sent back to Spain where lived out his days in his ancestral village.

De Vaca was true to what his heart told him was right. He had found his treasure. "For myself I may say that I always had full faith in His mercy and in that He would liberate me from captivity, and always told my companions so."

MORAL: Walk it out.

Chapter 67

Barry Marshall

It Takes Guts

When no one would listen, this doctor
swigged a beaker of deadly bacteria.

"Now they might say, "It's so off-the-wall....Is it true?"

When Barry Marshall went to medical school, he
planned to become a general practitioner, not a Nobel Prize
winner. He got B's and C's in high school and felt lucky just to get
into med school. After growing up in remote Australian mining
boom towns with names like Kalgoorlie, Rum Jungle, and Kaniva,
he had set his sights no further than going into practice in Perth,
Australia's fourth biggest city.

Once there, he realized how hard it was to diagnose
patients. Not every patient fit the classic textbook models he
learned in school. This made him want to keep an open mind.

"As a trainee general physician with broader training, I
was comfortable with the notion of infectious disease and
antibiotic therapies," says Marshall. "I am told by others that I
have a lateral thinking broad approach to problems, sometimes
to my detriment. In school my grades always suffered because I
was continually mucking about with irrelevant side issues which
I often found to be more interesting."

He became troubled by the ulcer patients he saw. Some
were in excruciating pain, and many of those who underwent
surgery found no relief. In 1981, he partnered with his hospital's
pathologist Robin Warren who had discovered that such
patients' stomachs were awash with the bacteria *Helicobacter
pylori*. Marshall did his own research and found *pylori* in the
stomachs of patients with stomach cancer.

"We observed that everybody who got stomach cancer
developed it on a background of gastritis, an irritation or

inflammation of the stomach lining," Marshall said. "Whenever we found a person without *Helicobacter*, we couldn't find gastritis either."

Marshall became convinced that antibiotics represented a simple cure for ulcers and a potential way to wipe out stomach cancer.

"I had developed my hypothesis that these bacteria were the cause of peptic ulcers and a significant risk for stomach cancer," Marshall said. "If I was right, then treatment for ulcer disease would be revolutionized. It would be simple, cheap, and it would be a cure."

Up until this point, the medical community thought stress and other psychological maladies caused ulcers. After all, so many martini-swilling, two-pack-a-day big-city businessmen had ulcers. Then when researchers found antacids cured ulcers in rats, everyone thought they'd found the way to treat the problem

This became big business. Drug companies made millions from their antacid preparations. Other physicians routinely prescribed anti-depressants and tranquilizers for ulcers. The Mayo Clinic built its reputation on gastric surgery. In short, many of the biggest players in medicine had no incentive to look for another cure. No one believed that bacteria could thrive in the stomach's acid environment.

"[At the time], to gastroenterologists, the concept of a germ causing ulcers was like saying that the Earth is flat," Marshall recalls. "I had this discovery that could undermine a $3 billion industry, not just the drugs but the entire field of endoscopy. Every gastroenterologist was doing 20 or 30 patients a week who might have ulcers, and 25 percent of them would. Because it was a recurring disease that you could never cure, the patients kept coming back."

Marshall needed a guinea pig to test his theory. In 1984, he found one—himself. He first had an endoscopy to sample his stomach's contents. It found no *pylori*. He then took the *pylori* from a petri dish and mixed it with a cup of the standard beef extract solution his laboratory used to grow cultures of bacteria. He let the "cloudy broth" sit overnight and swigged it the next morning.

Three days later, his mother told him he had bad breath. "After five days, I started to have bloating and fullness after the evening meal, and my appetite decreased," he recalls. "I vomited clear watery liquid, without acid, each morning." Soon thereafter he had two more endoscopies. Both now revealed that *pylori* had invaded his stomach and were thriving there.

Recalled Marshall, "Rob blabbed the results of my still unreleased work, [saying I had found the cause of ulcers. He told reporters] "…. 'Barry Marshall has just infected himself and damn near died.' A slight exaggeration, but it made for good copy.

"What he didn't know was that the journalist he was speaking to was from the *Star* newspaper, a tabloid that often featured stories about alien babies being adopted by Nancy Reagan. This was right up their alley. The next day the story appeared, "GUINEA-PIG DOCTOR DISCOVERS NEW CURE FOR ULCERS … AND THE CAUSE."

"This became one of the serendipitous, life changing events in my life, and I have Rob's temper to thank for it…. I was contacted by a continuous line of patients in the USA who read the story and were desperate for treatment."

For the next 10 years, he and Warren worked to get physicians to accept their findings. During that time, he secretly treated patients with antibiotics because gastroenterologists would not prescribe them. Finally, in 1993 and 1996 the National Institutes of Health and the FDA announced they would investigate the Australian's findings, and in 2005, Marshall and Warren won the Nobel prize in Physiology for their pioneering work.

MORAL: You've got the stomach for it.

Chapter 68

Ringo Starr

One "Ring" to Rule Them All

He was so sickly other kids called him "Hospital Boy."
But love was all he needed.

"Remember—peace is how we make it."

"I wish I had brothers and sisters," little Richy complained. "There's nobody to talk to when it's raining." If that had been the worst problem this little boy had when he was growing up, his childhood would have been most uneventful.

Sadly, he was ill so much of his young life that other children called him "Hospital Boy" and "Lazarus." He had been healthy the first years of his life, but when he was six in 1947, he developed appendicitis. An ambulance raced him to the children's hospital, but it was too late—His appendix had burst, and he had developed peritonitis, a potentially fatal inflammation of the abdominal lining.

Three times that night the doctors told his mother Elsie he would not live until dawn. For the next few days he went in and out of a coma. In fact, for the next four months he continued to go in and out of consciousness.

To help the stitches heal, the doctors and nurses ordered him to lie still in bed. He hadn't yet learned to read or write. The boredom was excruciating. Then one day while trying to play with another child, he fell out of bed. His stitches ripped open, lengthening his hospital stay into 1948.

By summer Richy was home, but he had fallen far behind in school. His teachers ignored him. He would never catch up and, as a result, never learned to spell and wrote words phonetically. He rarely read anything besides comic books.

Then when he was 14 in 1954, ill health befell him again. He developed pleurisy, an inflammation of the lining of the chest around the lungs. After 10 weeks in the hospital, his doctors diagnosed tuberculosis. It was likely caused by the foul air pollution in his town and the close and damp living quarters in the Dingle, the slum where he lived. He would stay in a sanitarium through most of 1955.

From time to time, teachers came in. He learned crafts such as basket making and knitting. One day a music teacher came in with assorted percussion instruments. She quickly learned that Richy wouldn't take part unless she gave him a drum to play.

The sanitarium allowed the children to watch television for an hour a day. One evening Richy saw a drummer on a variety show twirl his drumsticks. "Wow! Look at this man," he said. "Twiddling the sticks!"

When he was released, he went back to school but only to pick up a document certifying his eligibility for the dole, unemployment money from the government. Getting the school to give him that piece of paper was problem, too. He'd been there so rarely, it had a hard time finding any record he'd ever attended.

He was homely looking and weak from his medical woes, which had left a grey streak in his hair above his left ear.

"I'm quite happy inside," he said. "It's just the face won't smile." The Dingle was rough. Most teens were in gangs. "You kept your head down, your eyes open, and you didn't get in anybody's way," he said.

Richy was good at running away, not fighting. "I got beaten up a few times," he recalled. "It's that terrible craziness, that gang situation, where, if you're not fighting an outsider, you get crazy and start fighting amongst yourselves, like mad dogs."

He spent his days idling about. He sang in a church choir. He wasn't strong enough to work at a job bundling newspapers. He couldn't pass the physical exam to become a railway worker and was laid off. He found work as a waiter on a ferry, but he quit, fearing that the Navy might draft him, thinking he was fit for sea duty. Finally, he got a job as an apprentice metalworker. He joined a union, and he learned how to use a lathe.

With what spare change Richy had, he bought a 50-inch diameter bass drum from a junk store, and he delighted in playing it on family occasions. "Used to drive 'em all mad," he recalled.

Perhaps because he lacked physical strength, he compensated by developing a flamboyant style. For his sixteenth birthday his mother gave him a signet ring. Then he got an engagement ring from a girlfriend. When his grandfather died, he started wearing his wedding ring, and, finally, for his twenty-first birthday his mother gave him another ring. People started calling him Ringo.

Tomorrow never knows, and soon thereafter and for eight days a week for most of the 1960s, with a little help from his friends, he became the most well-known drummer in the world in the most famous band in the world. He knew how to make the other guys in the group laugh. They became the brothers he never had.

"The feel I have...that just comes from God," Ringo once said. "I truly believe that my heartbeat keeps the tempo, because I naturally have great time....I just have great time, and that's the rhythm of my heart and my soul."

For Ringo Starr, nothing came easy. As he wrote in a song, "Got to pay your dues if you wanna sing the blues, and you know it don't come easy.... Remember—peace is how we make it. Here within your reach, if you're big enough to take it."

MORAL: Keep on smiling.

Chapter 69

Roberto Canessa & Steve Callahan

View of Heaven, Seat in Hell

When all is lost, sometimes you find
everything in nothing.

"Time will bring you answers."

People in the most extreme survival situations often find beauty, even joy, in their plight. Thus, courage arises from their contemplation of the majestic beauty of the world. They revel in the magnificence of creation and have near religious experiences. Having found manifestations of God in their midst, they go forward with renewed strength and hope.

The Miracle of the Andes occurred when a chartered plane carrying 45 people, mostly members of a Uruguayan rugby team, crashed high in the Andes in 1972. Of those aboard, only 16 lived long enough to be rescued more than two months after the disaster. Having quickly run out of food, they became cannibals, eating the flesh of the frozen corpses of their friends and relatives.

Realizing that all searches for them had long been abandoned and that they were all slowly dying, two of the passengers, Roberto Canessa and Nando Parrado, made a 10-day trek out of the high mountains, before finally encountering shepherds who took news of them to the outside world.

More than 30 years later, documentary filmmakers flew some of the survivors back to the crash site. In the resulting film *Stranded*, Canessa sits with his daughter, looks at a distant mountain, and says:

"Imagine the whole valley pure white everywhere. I felt privileged to be here. No one else but me was able to see this. I learned that when everything feels hopeless, if you wait a little, sometimes in the walls that seem to offer no way out, doors you never imagined may appear, if you know how to wait.

"When you're desperate and don't know what to do and think you're going to die, just wait a little, and time will bring you answers. That's what happened. The wind died. The moonlight was beautiful. It was horribly cold, and I felt close to God. I don't feel it now. Whoever made all of this, the Creator, was my friend."

Similarly, shipwrecked sailor Steve Callahan had a similar epiphany while floating in the Atlantic Ocean. He had sailed alone from Newport, Rhode Island, to England in a 21-foot sloop he built and designed himself. On his return in 1981, he sailed from Cornwall to the Canary Islands, heading for Antigua.

Seven days out, in a gale during the night, an unknown object (Callahan thought it was a whale) jabbed a hole in his boat. Watertight compartments kept it from sinking immediately. He scrambled into a six-person life raft that measured about six-feet across. Before his boat went down, he scavenged charts, a spear gun, and solar stills for generating fresh water. After 76 days, he had drifted across the ocean, and fisherman near the Caribbean island of Guadeloupe found him, thanks to the sea birds that hovered over his raft.

During the voyage he felt he had "a view of heaven from a seat in hell." In his book *Adrift*, he wrote: "In these moments of peace, deprivation seems a strange sort of gift. I find food in a couple hours of fishing each day, and I seek shelter in a rubber tent. How unnecessarily complicated my past life seemed.

"For the first time, I clearly see a vast difference between human needs and human wants. Before this voyage, I always had what I needed—food, shelter, clothing, and companionship—yet I was often dissatisfied when I didn't get everything I wanted when people didn't meet my expectations, when a goal was thwarted, or when I couldn't acquire some material good.

"My plight has given me a strange kind of wealth, the most important kind. I value each moment that is not spent in pain, desperation, hunger, third, or loneliness. Even here, there is richness all around me. As I look out of the raft, I see Gods face in the smooth waves, His grace in the dorado's swim, feel His breath against my cheek as it sweeps down from the sky. I see that all of creation is made in His image."

MORAL: Be grateful for the gift of life.

Chapter 70

Jack LaLanne

Pimples to Push Ups

When he opened the first 'fitness center,' people said he was crazy. After all, exercise causes heart attacks!

"Forget about what you used to do.
This is the moment you've been waiting for."

When he was 41, he swam from Alcatraz Prison to Fisherman's Wharf while handcuffed, and he wasn't an escaping convict. He was Jack LaLanne, the self-proclaimed Godfather of Exercise. In fact, he repeated the feat when he was 60 while handcuffed *and* shackled *and* towing a 1,000-pound boat. Known for his incredible feats of strength and endurance, when LaLanne was 70, while handcuffed and shackled he towed 70 rowboats, each carrying at least one person, for a mile.

A tireless evangelist for good health, LaLanne opened the nation's first health club in 1936. Back then, people thought he was nuts or a con artist. Most people thought lifting weights would cause heart attacks or impotence. LaLanne also had the crazy notion that women and the elderly should work out to stay strong, ideally through a combination of aerobic exercise and weight-lifting.

"Between your ears"

A national celebrity for decades, his TV exercise show ran for 34 years. It consisted of little more than the 5'6" LaLanne in a jumpsuit with a few props and boundless enthusiasm. In later years when he was introduced to younger people who didn't know who he was, LaLanne would joke "I spent a lot of time on the floor with your mother."

He was a founding member of the President's Council on Physical Fitness in 1963, and the American Medical Association, American Cancer Society, American Heart Association all honored him for his leadership of the modern fitness movement.

He rose every day at 4 or 5 a.m. to do a daily two-hour workout (an hour with weights and an hour swimming), and he did this every day for 73 years.

"Fitness starts between your ears," he said. "You have to figure out what you want and then go ahead and do it. Your body is your slave."

No kidding—LaLanne did 1,033 push-ups in 23 minutes on live TV in 1956. When he was 54, he beat Arnold Schwarzenegger, then 21, in a chin-up contest on Muscle Beach in Venice, California. Later when Schwarzenegger was the governor of that state, he called LaLanne "an apostle for fitness."

"I'm not afraid of anything," LaLanne said. "When you're in good shape, mentally and physically, you know you can cope with life's problems. You do your best with the equipment you have."

When he was in his early teens, he was bulimic and suicidal. "I was a miserable goddamn kid," he recalled. "I'd eat a quart of ice cream in one sitting, shove my finger down my throat, heave it up, and have another quart.

"There's nothing more addictive on this earth than sugar. Not heroin, booze, whatever. It's much worse than smoking. I had blinding headaches every day. I was mentally screwed up by sugar. I was psychotic. I was malnourished. I was always getting sick. I got kicked out of school. I wanted to die."

He was "a skinny kid with pimples and boils" when his mother took him to a lecture by famous nutritionist Paul Bragg, the first person to open a health-foods store. By the time they arrived, his speech had begun. No seats were left. The LaLannes were about to leave when Bragg invited them onstage.

"It was the most humiliating moment," LaLanne recalled. "I was so ashamed of the way I looked. I didn't want people to see me. Little did I know they had problems, too."

He heard Bragg say: "It doesn't matter what your age is, what your physical condition is. If you obey nature's laws, you can be born again."

LaLanne was reborn. He changed his diet and began to exercise. He became captain of his school's football team. "I had to take my lunch alone to the football field to eat, so no one would see me eat my raw veggies, whole bread, raisins and nuts. You don't know the crap I went through," he recalled. And when he was 19, he won the national World's Best Built Man contest.

He gleefully celebrated his 75th birthday saying, "No cake, no pie, no candy, no ice cream! It makes me feel great not eating birthday cake. That's the gift I give to myself." LaLanne never ate red meat, nor did he drink coffee. He ate two meals a day. They typically included fresh fruit and vegetables, fish, eggs, and a wine. "If man made it, don't eat it," LaLanne said.

He continued his two-hour daily exercise regimen until the day before he died at 96 from pneumonia. He had been sick for a week but had refused to see a doctor. "I can't afford to die," LaLanne often joked. "It'll wreck my image."

MORAL: Get off your butt.

Chapter 71

Squanto

Special Instrument

Kidnapped and taken across the ocean, when he returned, a plague had wiped out his civilization.

"He directed them how to set their corn…"

Imagine being kidnapped and taken in chains across the ocean. Six years later when you finally make your way back home, you find that in the interim your civilization has been annihilated, your villages littered with skeletons. This is what befell a Wampanoag Indian known as Squanto or Tisquantum. His name was spelled differently by different settlers, and it would seem unlikely that Tisquantum was the name he was given at birth. It means "the Wrath of God."

History records that without his aid, the Pilgrims might not have survived their first year in the New World. The Governor of the Plymouth Colony William Bradford said Squanto was "a special instrument sent of God for their good beyond their expectation."

He lavishly praised Squanto, writing that "He directed them how to set their corn, where to take fish, and to procure other commodities, and was also their pilot to bring them to unknown places for their profit.… Squanto stood them in great stead, showing them both the manner how to [plant corn], and after how to dress and tend it."

While Squanto did indeed do those things (and took part in the first Thanksgiving), history is complex, as were Squanto's motives. Consider the deprivations and horrors that he had endured up to that point—and the precarious position he found himself in. Both the Indians and the Europeans were suffering.

Consider the plight of the Pilgrims in early 1621. The facts of their 65-day storm-tossed voyage from Plymouth, England, are astounding. To begin with, their passage took twice the usual sailing time. The *Mayflower* was a cargo ship unsuited for the tempestuous north Atlantic.

Equally dreadful were the ship's crowded conditions. These families of religious separatists (and other settlers) had planned to travel in two ships, but when the *Mayflower's* leaky companion vessel the *Speedwell* had to return to port, so did the *Mayflower*, and all 102 travelers (none of whom were farmers), 30 crewmen, and livestock had to cram together below decks.

Besides its fitful voyage and delayed departure, to make matters worse, the Mayflower went off-course. Instead of landing at its planned destination—the warmer Virginia Colony, the Mayflower instead arrived at Cape Cod at the worst possible time—early November 1620, months later than they had planned.

Lack of provisions and the icy cold forced the settlers to winter aboard the ship. As spring approached, only about half the passengers and crew remained alive, and they were starving.

As bad off as the Pilgrims were, what had happened to the Indians was worse. In 1614, the year that he was kidnapped, more than 100,000 Indians lived in New England. The Wampanoag called the New England coast where they lived Dawnland, and they knew themselves as "The People of the First Light" because they lived where the sun rose.

Explorers such as Verrazano in the 1520s could smell their fires from hundreds of miles away at sea. During the early 1600s, literally hundreds of ships from Spain, Italy, Portugal, France, and England sailed to the New England area to fish and trade.

In 1614 Capt. John Smith landed in present day Massachusetts and was given a tour of an Indian community by Squanto. (This is the same John Smith who founded Jamestown in 1607, returned to England, and had now voyaged again to New England.)

After he sailed on, his lieutenant kidnapped Squanto and nearly two dozen other Indians to sell as slaves. This act so outraged the Indians that instead of welcoming future traders they killed them on sight.

Catholic priests from Spain bought him, took him to Spain, and converted him to Christianity, as the Pope had decreed that Indians were to be treated humanely.

Months later, Squanto convinced the priests to let him try to make his way back home. He traveled to London and worked there as a shipbuilder before finally sailing to Newfoundland and finding passage to Dawnland.

What he found upon his return was a land "utterly void" of human life, as another one of Smith's lieutenants put it. "Neere two hundred miles along the Sea coast, that in some places there scarce remained five of a hundred," wrote Capt. Smith.

An unknown disease—possibly smallpox, plague, or viral hepatitis—had burned through the villages, reducing the Wampanoag population from about 20,000 to about 1,000 between 1614 and 1620. (A smallpox epidemic in 1633 would further reduce their numbers to as low as 500.)

Skeletons lay in heaps in Indian villages. So rapidly had the holocaust done it work that "the living being (as it seemes) not able to bury the dead, they were left for the Crowes, Kites and vermin to prey upon," wrote one English settler. "And the bones and skulls upon the severall places of their habitations, made such a spectacle after my coming into those partes, that, as I travailed in the forest nere the Massachussets, it seemed to mee a new found Golgotha."

Now in March 1621, three Indians approached the Pilgrims' feeble settlement. They were Massasoit, the leader of the local Wampanoag coalition of tribes; Samoset, the leader of a tribes to the north; and Squanto, their prisoner, under suspicion because of his lengthy contact with Europeans.

Imagine the Pilgrims' astonishment when one of the Indians spoke English and could serve as an interpreter. The two groups had good reason to be wary of each other. The Europeans feared Indian attacks, and the Indians resented the Europeans' presence, but because Massasoit's tribes had been decimated by the plague, he feared that enemy tribes would finish off his people. He wanted to strike an alliance with the Europeans.

Gov. Bradford summed up the arrangement: "If any did unjustly war against him [Massosoit], they [the Pilgrims] would aid him; if any did war against them, he should aid them."

Thus, Squanto was the right man in the right place at the right time. Massasoit freed him, and Squanto became the Pilgrims' teacher, guide, and interpreter.

Massasoit and Squanto engaged in a power struggle, and two years later Squanto "sought his own ends and played his own game," Gov. Bradford wrote. Squanto told the colonists that Massasoit was conspiring with other tribes against them, while at the same time telling the Indians that the Pilgrims were plotting their demise.

Squanto and Bradford travelled together to Cape Cod to negotiate a new peace treaty with Massasoit. Despite the enmity he helped created, Squanto, now distrusted by both sides, was successful, and while returning to the Pilgrims settlement, he took a fever and died. His peace lasted 50 years.

MORAL: Give thanks.

Chapter 72

Patrick Henry

Price of Chains

He kept his wife locked in the cellar, and it
was for her own good.

"Is life so dear...?"

The great patriot and Founding Father Patrick Henry
kept his wife in the cellar. He and Sarah Shelton, "a woman of
some fortune," had been childhood friends. They married when
he was 18. She was only 16.

He wanted to be a plantation owner, but he failed at that.
His land, given to him by Sarah's parents, was poor, and his
manor burned to the ground. Then he tried his hand at being a
storekeeper. After two years, he failed at that, too. Some said he
was reduced to working as a barkeeper in his father-in-law's inn.

Patrick and Sarah had six children. The first two, Martha
and John, respectively, were born in 1755 and 1757.

He read for the law and passed his law exams—barely—
doing so "after much entreaty and many promises of future
study," said Thomas Jefferson.

In one of his first cases in 1763, known today as "the
Parson's Cause," he found his calling. He was a natural-born
rabble-rouser.

King George III had vetoed a popular law passed by
Virginia's House of Burgesses (legislature). It had capped how
much clergymen would be paid. When the King vetoed it, a
parson came forward suing for back wages. This would have cost
the colony's taxpayers more in taxes.

In court, Henry declared that the King had "degenerated
into a Tyrant" and thus had "foreit[ed] all right to his subjects'
obedience. People in the courtroom cried "Treason!" Henry lost

the case but won—The jury awarded the parson only a penny in damages.

And it was also in 1763 that Sarah and Patrick had their third child, William.

Two years later Parliament passed the despised Stamp Act. It taxed a variety of paper goods in the colonies to pay for the upkeep of British troops stationed in North America. Not only did the colonists see no need for such an army, they regarded this as taxation without representation because they had no representatives in Parliament in London.

Speaking again in the House of Burgesses, Henry warned King George that he risked being overthrown by heroes of the people. "Tarquin and Caesar had each his Brutus! Charles the first, his Cromwell," Henry cried. "And George the Third…

Before he could complete his sentence, delegates shouted "Treason!" When the uproar died, Henry finished his thought, calmly saying, "….and George the Third may profit by their example. If this be treason, make the most of it."

In Boston, when John Adams heard an account of Henry's speech, he said, "the eminent patriot Patrick Henry, Esq. who composed" those words revealed "the universal opinion of the continent." Founding Father George Mason said, "His eloquence is the smaller part of his merit. He is in my opinion the first man upon this continent, as well in abilities as public virtues."

The Henry family added two new members in the late 1760s—Annie in 1767 and Elizabeth in 1769, giving them five offspring.

A sixth child—Edward—arrived in 1771, and it was then that darkness fell in the Henry home. Sarah developed postpartum depression. She stopped speaking. She stopped feeding herself.

Worse, she believed she was being persecuted. She hallucinated and threatened suicide and even expressed a desire to kill her baby. Patrick Henry's "beloved companion had lost her reason" his doctor later told Henry's son. "[She] could only be restrained from self-destruction by a strait-dress" (an early type of straitjacket).

In 1773, the first hospital for "lunatics, idiots, and those of disordered minds" opened in Williamsburg. Henry toured it, but when he saw its barred windows and the iron rings where inmates would be chained in their cells, he realized he could never send his wife to such a place.

Upon returning to his estate, he converted part of its basement into an apartment for Sarah. It had a sunny view and a fireplace. A slave tended to her needs, and Henry visited her several times a day to be with her and help feed her.

In September 1774, he traveled to Philadelphia as a delegate to the First Continental Congress. British troops now occupied Boston in the aftermath of the Tea Party in 1773. The mood in the colonies had changed. More and more colonists now understood how right Henry had been when he said the King was a tyrant.

"We are in a State of Nature," Henry told the Congress. "Government is dissolved. The distinctions between Virginians, Pennsylvanians, New Yorkers and New Englanders, are no more. I am not a Virginian, but an American." At that time, this was a most radical thought—to be an American.

When he arrived home, he found that Sarah's condition had deteriorated. She died in early 1775. Some think she committed suicide. The location of her grave is unknown.

In those days to have a mentally ill relative cast shame on an entire family. By keeping her at home and caring for her as best he could, Henry showed extraordinary courage.

In March 1775, weeks after her death, he traveled to Richmond to take part at a convention of Virginia delegates at St. John's Church. While still grieving for Sarah, Patrick Henry told his fellow Virginians "Our chains are forged! Their clanking may be heard on the plains of Boston! The War is inevitable—and let it come!...Why stand we here idle!"

Then Henry slumped as though he were a slave weighed down by shackles or perhaps in part by the woes and miseries of his life.

He lifted his hands heavenward and raised his eyes and asked, "Is life so dear or peace so sweet as to be purchased at the price of chains and slavery? Forbid it, Almighty God! I know not what course others may take, but as for me—Give me liberty, or give me death!"

In a final touch, Henry thrust an imaginary dagger into his chest, just as the Roman patriot Cato had done by committing suicide rather than honor Caesar.

Instead of cries of "Treason!" now there was only silence. His listeners were awestruck. One delegate was so overwhelmed that then and there he declared, "Let me be buried at this spot!" Word of Henry's courage spread, heartening the colonists' resolve.

In later years, Washington asked him to serve on the Supreme Court. Henry, who once could barely pass his law exams, declined. And when he died, a local newspaper eulogized him, writing, "As long as our rivers flow, or mountains stand...Virginia...will say to rising generations, imitate your HENRY!"

**MORAL: Stand up for what you believe in.
Grief be damned.**

Chapter 73

Mike May

Willing to Fall

This blind spy held the world speed skiing record.
Then experimental surgery restored his sight.

"I was always happy I tried."

CIA analyst Mike May liked being a "human guided missile." That's why he won the world record for downhill speed skiing. As a boy, he climbed a 175-foot tall radio tower with no safety gear. Then his mother let him build an 80-foot antenna in the backyard.

After college, Hay lived in a remote village in Ghana for six months working as a laborer hauling buckets of dirt. He invented a portable GPS system when the technology was new, and he helped invent the world's first laser turntable. He also starred in a play for six weeks.

When he was in elementary school, he was a safety crossing guard. He rode a bicycle for three miles. He played baseball, tetherball, and kickball, and he rode a pogo-stick and had a skateboard.

Such things are not so unusual. May, however, had been blind since he was three. He had wanted to make mud pies in his family's garage. He needed a jar, and he found one filled with a hardened powder. It was calcium carbide. When he went to wash it out, the water and the powder combined, creating an explosive gas—acetylene. Chemical burns scarred his corneas, the transparent part of the eyes in front of the iris and pupils.

A Chance at Bat

Growing up, he let nothing stop him. When he played baseball, he might run into a tree instead of first base, but he didn't care. He wanted his chance at bat. The play he starred in was *Butterflies Are Free*, the story of a blind man trying to leave home. He commanded the stage with such abandon some in the audience feared he might topple into the orchestra pit.

"Sometimes I got bloody," May told Robert Kurson, the author of the book *Crashing Through* which tells his life story. "Sometimes I ended up on big adventures. But no matter what happened, I was always happy I tried...."

May didn't want to sit around his whole life wondering what might have happened if he tried something. He tried it. Even when he lost his left eye to infection as a young man, he kept going forward into the unknown and new adventures.

One day when he was 45, he began his greatest adventure. On a lark, he sat in an optometrist's chair. "I think you're going to find that I'm blind," May told the doctor.

The optometrist couldn't argue with that, and he asked May if he would like to see his partner, Dan Goodman, an ophthalmologist. After examining May's eye, Goodman said, "I think we can make you see."

And that is what Dr. Goodman did—he let May see again. He performed an experimental corneal epithelial stem cell transplant. The surgery grafted a ring of cells one-third of a millimeter thick around the perimeter of the cornea. After growing securely into place, they birthed new cells. A second operation then attached a transplanted cornea to the healthy outer ring.

May had many good reasons not to have the operations. The procedure had a 50 percent failure rate. His new vision, if any, might not last. Worse, he would be taking a dangerous anti-transplant rejection drug that could cause liver failure, kidney failure, and cancer.

May also wondered—did he really need vision to see? He knew he was married to a beautiful woman. He knew he had two beautiful sons. In his mind, he always "saw" them perfectly well. In the final analysis, however, in May's mind—as always—"Curiosity outweigh[ed] a mountain of reasons not to do it."

When the bandages came off, the first face he saw was that of his wife. He saw her blond hair, her blue sweater, her face, her lips, and later he saw all of her, and when they made love, he looked into her eyes.

He saw his 80-year-old mother for the first time in 42 years. When he noticed—for the first time—that one of his sons had freckles, his wife cried.

At first, he could only see things one at a time as though he were looking at photographs. His vision quickly improved, allowing him to play catch with his other son.

But as with other patients who have regained vision, he suffered from prosopagnosia, difficulty interpreting the world visually. He would never be able to drive or read. The portions of his brain that processed such visual activity never developed during his childhood.

When his body tried to reject the transplant, May endured a series of horrifically painful injections directly into the cornea. Putting medicine inside the eye was the only way to save it. Each time, he could see the gleaming needle coming at his eye, and each time the pain was shattering.

May's spirit wouldn't allow his body to give in to possibility of failure. The treatment worked, and his body's attempt to reject the transplant ended.

When he was a teenager, he worked as a camp counselor. Of course, the younger boys had asked him for life advice. Fittingly, he replied, "Have adventures. Speak to your curiosity. Be willing to fall down or to get lost. There's always a way."

MORAL: See what you can do.

Chapter 74

Andy Warhol

Soupy Sales

"Weak." "Banal" "Senseless."
That's what art critics called his work.

"I want to be plastic."

Clam Chowder. Chicken Noodle. Cream of Vegetable. Onion. Green Pea. Scotch Broth. Vegetable. Split Pea. Vegetable Beef. Bean. Cheddar Cheese. Tomato Rice. Beef. Cream of Asparagus. Cream of Celery. Black Bean. Turkey Noodle. Beef Broth. Chicken Gumbo. Turkey Vegetable. Chili Beef. Vegetable Bean. Cream of Chicken. Cream of Mushroom. Pepper Pot. Chicken. Consommé. Tomato. Minestrone. Chicken Vegetable. Beef Noodle. Vegetarian Vegetable.

Campbell's Soup Cans. All 32 varieties. 1962. Warhol.

These were the stars of his first solo show at a gallery in Los Angeles in July of that year. The purchase price for each 20 by 16 inch silkscreened-and-painted work: $100. An art gallery down the street mocked him. It offered for sale real soup cans—two for 33 cents.

Of the show, the art critic at *The Los Angeles Times* wrote "This young 'artist' is either a soft-headed fool or a hard-headed charlatan." *The New Yorker's* ruling? "Narcotic reiteration...a joke without humor."

Vogue Sniffed

"The air of banality is suffocating," said one critic. Another believed that the contemporary nature of Warhol's works "may render [him] unintelligible and thus obsolete in the future." *Vogue* sniffed "weak ways of seeing and feeling." *Time* magazine deemed his art "excruciatingly monotonous, [and] the apparently senseless repetition does have the jangling effect of the syllabic babbling of an infant."

Only six of the works sold. The gallery owner bought them back. Years later he sold the complete collection to the Museum of Modern Art for $15 million.

"I like boring things," Warhol once said.

It took guts to make and show art like "Campbell's Soup Cans."

A professionally trained commercial illustrator, Warhol was, during the 1950s, at the top of his game in Manhattan doing fashion and shoe illustrations for top department stores and fashion magazines. He wanted more. He wanted to make his mark on history.

Before his breakthrough in 1962, he tried three times to get a show at one New York City gallery. Each time the gallery rejected his delicate line drawings of young men French kissing. As one critic wrote, such art got him "precisely nowhere."

In the early 1960s he designed an issue of *C: The Journal of Poetry*. Its back cover depicted two men kissing. An early 1960s movie about sex never makes clear whether the those on screen are male or female.

Don't say Warhol didn't have guts.

He was inept at social relations. He was unable recognize friends. He became famous for his inarticulateness and monosyllabic attempts at conversation. He was obsessed with repetition and uniformity. He stared blankly into space at parties. He always bought the same brand of underwear, and they had to be green.

"It is fascinating how many of the things he did are typical of autism," said a British medical expert. "Warhol almost certainly had Asperger syndrome."

This progenitor of Pop was raised in a Pennsylvania mining town. His parents were struggling Czech immigrants. His father was a coal miner. He worked in West Virginia, and he died of drinking poisoned water when Warhol was 13. His mother, whose father beat her to get her to agree to marry, was then diagnosed with colon cancer, and soup may have been almost all he had to eat.

When young Andrew Warhola was in third grade he came down with Sydenham's chorea (St. Vitus Dance), a nerve disorder that causes involuntary movements in the legs and arms. Forced to stay in bed for at least a month, his mother Julia encouraged his interest in art, and he collected pictures of movie stars.

"A Good Supply"

One special thing his mother did to comfort him was to serve him soup in bed. To Warhol, soup became the quintessence of love. "Mother always served Campbell's soup," said Warhol's brother. "She always had a good supply."

Perhaps soup symbolized hard times to Warhol.

Perhaps there is another reason Warhol painted soup cans. Prior to those works, he had done a series of images inspired by comic book art, but fellow Manhattan Pop artist Roy Lichtenstein beat him to the punch, winning a show at a prominent gallery with similar images.

Struggling to think of what to create, Warhol asked a friend who was an interior decorator and gallery owner. She asked him what he loved the most. Warhol's reply? "Money."

She told him to think of something else, something simple that people see every day. *Voila*, soup cans. Said Warhol: "I used to drink it. I used to have the same lunch every day for 20 years."

Or maybe there were other reasons why Warhol did what he did. "I just do art because I'm ugly," he said, "And there's nothing else for me to do."

Then again, maybe it is as simple as this: "Art," said Warhol, "is what you can get away with."

MORAL: Soup's on.

Chapter 75

Calvin Coolidge

Greatest Grief

When his teenage son died suddenly, he found the strength to perform the duties of his most demanding job.

"Nothing in the world can take the place of persistence. Talent will not; nothing is more common than unsuccessful men with talent."

To most people, Calvin Coolidge is little more than a punch line. He may be best known for his supposed reply to a woman who is said to have approached him at a White House dinner saying, "My husband bet me I couldn't get you to say three words. "You lose," the taciturn president replied.

Though Coolidge was shy, in reality, he held press conferences twice a week. He let himself be photographed in a long Indian headdress and as a cowboy, and he often spoke on the radio. In fact, he's sometimes called "America's First Radio President."

Though Coolidge is little remembered, Ronald Reagan had good things to say about his fellow Republican. "I'd always thought of Coolidge as one of our most underrated presidents," Reagan said. "He came into office after World War I and faced a mountain of war debt but instead of raising taxes, he cut the tax rate and government revenues increased, permitting him to eliminate the wartime debt and proving that the principle ...about lower taxes meaning greater tax revenues still worked in the modern world."

Coolidge, who grew up on a Vermont farm, was a frugal Yankee, even in the days when government spent far less on fewer programs. He and his budget chief determined that federal workers would only be issued one pencil. Every employee was told to use his pencil down to its stub before asking for a new one. "Our item of expense for pencils is materially less," a federal report proudly stated.

Although the nation experienced boom times during Coolidge's presidency from 1923 to 1929, he had to contend with a mountainous problem far more intractable than debt.

His son Calvin Jr. died while he was in office.

Even his older brother John admitted that Calvin Jr. was his father's favorite. He had inherited his father's dry wit and stone-faced expression.

At age 16, he was a strong young man. The summer before, he had worked as a farm-hand on a Connecticut tobacco farm. He was "full of pranks" and lover of books.

On June 30, 1924, he and John, 17, played tennis on the White House lawn. A blood blister rose on the middle toe of his right foot. Calvin Jr. hadn't been wearing socks. At first, he didn't think much of it and told no one. Soon he was limping, and he developed a fever of 102. Red streaks went up his leg like crimson lightning.

He had sepsis (blood poisoning) caused by the bacteria *Staphylococcus aureus*. In those days, it caused many deaths. Penicillin or another antibiotic would have likely easily cured him, but such wonder drugs had yet to be discovered.

A few days later, doctors admitted him to the nearby Walter Reed Medical Center, home to some of the nation's best physicians. Calvin Jr. received blood transfusions and even had an operation.

The Fourth of July was the President's birthday. He used the occasion to write his father in Vermont, saying "Calvin is very sick, so this is not a happy day for me…. Of course, he has all that medical science can give, but he may have a long sickness with ulcers then again he may be better in a few days."

Calvin Jr. drifted in and out of consciousness, at one point blurting out on July 7 "Come on, help!" as if he were leading a cavalry charge. Then he relaxed and said, "We surrender!" His doctor said, "Don't surrender." But Calvin Jr. said "Yes" and died.

His doctor remembered, "It is commonly stated that President Coolidge is 'cold as ice,' but I had the opportunity of seeing him in his hour of grief and to know quite otherwise.

Indeed, it was the most touching and heart-rending experience of my whole professional career."

(Not since Lincoln's son William died of typhoid fever in 1862 had such a tragedy befallen a President. "He was too good for this earth," Lincoln wrote. "It is hard, hard to have him die.")

The Presidential election campaign was underway. When Calvin Jr. died, the Democrats convention was in its second sweltering week in Madison Square Garden. An announcement came over the loudspeakers. There was a "low, prolonged moan, almost a sob. Rancor ceased, and a wave of common sympathy swept over the vast audience."

Coolidge lost interest in campaigning. For weeks, he wore black armband for weeks. Many historians believe Coolidge fell into a depression which never lifted and may have even contributed to his death four years after leaving office.

In his autobiography, Coolidge acknowledged that a bright spark in his life had been extinguished. "The greatest grief that can come to a boy came to me," he wrote. "Life was never to seem the same again."

Most notably, he added "When [my son] went, the power and glory of the Presidency went with him." Perhaps Coolidge thought he was destined for ill fate. "I do not know why such a price was exacted for occupying the White House," he wrote.

Was Coolidge's presidency ruined by this tragedy? Biographer Amity Shlaes thinks not. "Like Lincoln, Coolidge lost a son while in office; like Lincoln, he pushed ahead and achieved much despite the loss, including fighting corruption and improving government services."

Whatever the truth, depression and grief were not as well understood—or treated—in the 1920s as they are today. Calvin Coolidge could have resigned the presidency. He did not. Coolidge, whatever one thinks of his political principles or accomplishments, upheld his duties as president to the best of his abilities.

MORAL: Fight the good fight.

Chapter 76

Brownie Wise

Sealing the Deal

"Now listen to me, woman!" her boss raged.
"I do the manufacturing, and you do the selling!"

"When you help someone up a hill,
you find yourself closer to the top."

Brownie Wise was going nowhere fast. In 1947, she was 34, divorced, working as a secretary, and had a son to feed. To make ends meet, she rented her attic to servicemen, and she made rhubarb wine which she traded for butter. (Her mother gave her the name Brownie because when she was born, she had big brown eyes.)

One evening a door-to-door salesman from the Stanley Home Products company came to her home, trying to sell her mops and brushes. When the luckless man left, Wise said to herself, "I could do better than that."

She got in touch with Stanley and started selling its wares. "I needed the money for me and my kid," she said. "I got out there and made it.

Soon she was promoted to branch manager, only to be told by the company's founder that "upper management is no place for a woman."

Before she left Stanley, a magic moment happened. During a sales meeting, she saw a curious plastic container on a snack table. In those days, plastics were rarely seen in home products. Another salesperson told her the containers were selling poorly at the local department store. She watched as it fell off of the table. It didn't shatter. Its lid stayed sealed.

It was Tupperware, the creation of taciturn New Hampshire entrepreneur Earl Tupper. (He had earlier invented—and struck out with—the fish-powered boat and the dripless ice cream cone.) In 1949, he patented Tupperware's unique lid. It sealed with a crisp snap and stayed sealed.

Tupperware held the promise of making leftovers last longer while also making heroes of thrifty housewives from coast-to-coast. Tupper had worked hard to create his seemingly indestructible air-tight brainchild. It was made of polyethylene, a waste product of World War II manufacturing. It was black. It was greasy. It smelled bad. No one wanted it. Tupper reformulated it. Now the problem was no one wanted to buy it.

Wise knew what to do. She combined her genius at home sales with Tupper's scientific wizardry. Within months, he noticed that her home sales had outstripped his department store numbers. He gave her the exclusive right to sell Tupperware in Florida.

She created a social marketing system—the 'party plan'—that gave housewives a rare outlet for business success in the 1950s. This Southern charmer from rural Georgia understood that housewives would have to see, touch, and feel the product to understand how marvelous it was.

She told her party givers that just touching Tupperware would bring them luck. Said Wise: "Get your fingers on it. Wish for what you want. Then work like everything, and your wish will come true."

"If you want to build a business, build the people," she said. Between 1951 and 1958, Tupperware became a social phenomenon. Wise had 10,000 home party saleswomen spreading her food storage gospel. Tupper smartly pulled his products from stores and only sold them through home-party sales.

Wise was a born preacher. Her mother was a union organizer, and young Wise spent hours watching her address crowds. Then she started giving them. "People were surprised someone so young could deliver a speech like a pastor," said Wise's biographer Bob Kealing.

"It is a proven fact that you will sell more to a group of 15 women than you will sell to them individually," Wise said. "The social spirit of a party tends to lower sales resistance of those present, as well as increase a competitive buying spirit."

Tupper hired her to be a vice president, and she ran her sales division, Tupperware Home Parties, from her Kissimmee, Florida, home. In fact, she did so well that the company built her a lakefront mansion. In 1954, she was the first woman to appear on the cover of *Business Week*.

She created an annual "Jubilee" national convention. Top sellers got lavish gifts such as motorboats, minks, and Cadillacs. They played games. One involved tossing around a Tupperware bowl filled with grape juice to prove it would stay sealed. To motivate saleswomen, she had them sing inspiring songs with lyrics like "I've got that Tupper feeling deep in my heart."

Tupper, though delighted with his company's incredible growth, was uneasy with the amount of publicity Wise received. The two fought. On one occasion, she protested his interest in a Tupperware dog food container. The stern northerner barked, "Now listen to me, woman! I do the manufacturing, and you do the selling!"

"Woman?" replied Wise. "Is that the way you address your wife?"

In 1958 Tupper fired her. She had held a Jubilee for 1,200 guests on Maui. A horrendous thunderstorm sent 21 guests to the hospital. Lawsuits ensued. Tupper and Wise had falling out. She owned no stock. As severance, she got only one year's salary—$30,000 ($270,000 in 2018 dollars). As a final blow, the company asked her to leave her mansion. (Though she lived in it, the company owned it.)

Later, Wise founded Cinderella, a company that sought to sell make-up on the party-plan system. It went nowhere. Though she never regained the heights she attained in the 1950s, she broke the mold (or perhaps snapped the lid) by having the courage and insight to create an entirely new way of selling products—home parties.

"Remember the steam kettle," Wise once said. "Though it's up to its neck in hot water, it continues to sing."

MORAL: Snap to it.

Chapter 77

Harold Russell

Hooked

His hands blown away,
he kept a steady grip on his new life.

*"It is not what you have lost
but what you have left that counts."*

Harold Russell had never acted before. He had never even been in a movie before, yet he took home not one but two Academy Awards—something that had not happened before and has not happened since—for his portrayal of sailor Homer Parrish in *The Best Years of Our Lives.*

This 1946 movie also won the Oscar for Best Picture, beating Jimmy Stewart's *It's a Wonderful Life.* It depicts the difficult transition of three soldiers returning to civilian life after World War II. Film critic Roger Ebert called *Best Years* "lean, direct, honest about issues that Hollywood then studiously avoided."

Russell won the Best Supporting Actor honor. Because the Academy thought he had no chance of winning that, it also gave him an honorary Oscar for "bringing hope and courage to his fellow veterans."

Like the character he portrayed, Russell lost both of his hands during the war. It wasn't a combat injury. Though he had wanted to be a paratrooper, Uncle Sam deemed he would better serve America as a demolition (and parachuting) instructor. On June 6, 1944—D-Day—he was stateside preparing to train soldiers. A fuse malfunctioned. It detonated the TNT he was holding.

Because of the day's events in Europe, an unusually long briefing kept Russell from his duties. "When [the meeting was] over, we've still got about a thousand troops to run through a live ammo, live explosives obstacle course," he said.

"I started helping the guys make up explosive charges...It's late in the day, and we have to hurry it up. What I didn't realize was those blasting caps had been sitting out in the sun on a blanket for two hours, and they were touchy. I put one in a quarter-pound of nitro-starch, and that was it."

Russell had signed up the day after Pearl Harbor. He'd been a meat cutter and manager in a grocery store. He didn't enlist for patriotic reasons. He did so because he thought he was a failure.

Recuperating in Walter Reed General Hospital, Russell sunk into depression. "I was one sorry sack [of shit]," he recalled. "If I'd had the guts, I would have killed myself."

Given a choice of steel hooks or plastic hands, he took the hooks. They were articulated; each tip had two gleaming prongs that allowed him to grasp objects. "I don't need to be beautiful," Russell said.

While in the hospital, he saw the morale boosting film *Meet McGonegal*. It was about a World War I vet who had lost his hands. "Turns out he's also a millionaire, made it all selling real estate in Southern California after the war," said Russell. "One day I hear McGonegal is coming to Walter Reed to talk to the vets, and I tell the doctor, 'I have to meet that man. This is like Santa Claus coming!'

"He was great. He told me the reason he was such a success as a salesman was that no one ever forgot him…. He taught me to put the hook out and shake hands, break the ice, get it over with. If people can't cope, you're better off finding out right away."

Russell learned how to use the hooks in six weeks. He became so deft with them the Army put him in the training film *Diary of a Sergeant*. It depicted how he went about life in an easy, graceful, even joyful way.

At the time, movie director William Wyler was casting *Best Years*. He happened upon the morale film, and Russell got an unexpected chance at stardom. Wyler said he "gave the finest performance I have ever seen on the screen" because of his "true depth of feeling." (Interestingly, the war also left Wyler handicapped. He lost all hearing in his right ear and lost some in his left due to exposure to roaring bomber engines.)

"Dependent as a baby"

In one of the film's many moving scenes, Russell's character invites his fiancée up to his bedroom. (She is literally the girl who lives next door.) He has no plan to seduce her. Instead he wants her to understand what living with him would be like.

He has her remove the harness that straps his hooks to his torso and arms. "This is when I know I'm helpless," his character says. "My hands are down there on the bed. I can't put them on again without calling to somebody for help. I can't smoke a cigarette or read a book. If that door should blow shut, I can't open it and get out of this room. I'm dependent as a baby that doesn't know how to get anything except to cry for it."

At a time when people with physical disabilities were never seen in movies, except as monsters or freaks, *Best Years* showed Russell going through life as normally. The movie shows him plucking a cigarette from a pack, dialing the telephone, and even slipping a wedding ring on his fiancée's finger.

Russell married his real-life sweetheart in 1947, and they remained together until her death in 1978. He became the national chairman of Amvets, a veterans' group, and founded the World Veterans Foundation. President Kennedy made him vice chair of the President's Committee on Employment of the Handicapped, and Johnson and Nixon reappointed him.

Russell took life in stride (except when he learned that his pay of $6,000 for his work in *Best Years* was far less than the $100,000 the film's other stars took home). He rose far above what others might think was a dis-abling event. He joked that he was so good at using his hooks he could pick up anything—except the dinner check.

MORAL: Be like Homer—run the bases.

Chapter 78

George Orwell

The Clocks Were Striking

Dying, he struggled to finish his novel. He thought
it was "a ghastly mess." Readers called it genius.

*"In a time of deceit telling
the truth is a revolutionary act."*

The manuscript of his novel was a disaster. Its tentative
title was *The Last Man in Europe*. He called it "that bloody book."
He had typed and re-typed it while lying in bed. Littered with
cross-outs and deletions, he said "It's a ghastly mess now."

"A good idea ruined" he called it. There was a part of him
that had always hated writing. In one of his essays he concluded
that, "Writing a book is a horrible, exhausting struggle, like a
long bout of some painful illness."

Now Eric Blair was indeed having a tortuous struggle
with a terrible malady—He was dying of tuberculosis. The first
sentence of his 'ghastly' book goes this way—"It was a bright
cold day in April, and the clocks were striking thirteen."

Eric, better known by his pen name George Orwell, had to
struggle to finish his novel *1984*. When he was writing it, he also
called this classic of world literature "unbelievably bad."

He started work on the book in 1947. It was a race to see
whether he would finish it or die trying.

Recent years had not treated him kindly. Only two years
had passed since the sudden death of his wife Eileen. She was
undergoing a routine hysterectomy. Immediately after being
given anesthesia and before the surgery began, she suffered
cardiac arrest. She was only 39. Orwell had had premonitions of
her death. He was devastated.

Now a single parent with a modest income he had to slam
out essays and reviews to pay the rent. He wrote 10 hours a day,

often suffering from bronchitis and confined to his bed for weeks.

He had been in poor health for years. He may have contracted tuberculosis when he was a child in India. During his life, he fought not only bronchitis but also dengue fever and bacterial pneumonia. He suffered constant coughing jags because his bronchial tubes were so scarred.

The Hot Smoke

Of course, he chain-smoked cigarettes. Even when he was diagnosed with tuberculosis, his doctors encouraged him continue. They thought the hot smoke was good for the lungs, believing that it helped TB patients cough up sputum.

And, of course, when he was in a sanitarium, the doctors took away his typewriter—so he could completely rest. When he continued to write using a pen, to put an end to that, they put his right arm in a plaster cast.

How did Orwell get to this point? He had atrocious eating habits. He worked all hours of the day and night, and he generally ignored his health. He wouldn't wear a coat in the winter.

Now he was feverish, losing weight, wheezing, gaunt, spitting blood, and struggling with night sweats. During his last months when he was in-and-out of sanitariums, a friend said he was "long-suffering, tired-looking, immensely thin, but gentle." He was almost six-foot three-inches, and he weighed less than 160 pounds.

Tuberculosis tortured him, and he felt tortured by his doctors. On at least one occasion they inserted a long scope into his esophagus to peer into his lungs. "It was a hideously painful thing, and very frightening," to Orwell, according to his publisher David Astor.

More than one literary critic has noted the physical resemblance between Orwell at the end of his life and Winston Smith, the hero of *1984*, after being tortured. Orwell described Smith this way:

"The truly frightening thing was the emaciation of his body. The barrel of the ribs was a narrow as that of a skeleton: the legs had shrunk so that the knees were thicker than the thighs...The curvature of the spine was astonishing. The thin shoulders were hunched forward so as to make a cavity of the chest, the scraggy neck seemed to be bending double under the weight of the skull.... He was aware of his ugliness, his gracelessness."

The diagnosis of tuberculosis came a few days before Christmas in 1947. Orwell had spent the bulk of the year in the worst possible place for a person with the disease. He had secluded himself on Jura, a remote windswept island off the Scottish coast. He lived there in a farmhouse owned by Astor at the end of a five-mile-long rutted dirt path.

To prepare for life on the island, he told a friend he amassed provisions as though he were going on an arctic expedition. The house had no electricity. Orwell used bottled gas to cook and peat and gas for heat.

The weather was "freezing cold," said a friend who visited. "It pelted with rain, slamming it into the side of the house which such force I thought it would blow the place down. He chose the place for its isolation and quietness, but for a TB patient, it couldn't have been worse. It was damp and cold most of the time."

The first winter there, Orwell said, was "quite unendurable." He was lucky just to survive the summer. In August, he nearly drowned when his rowboat (with an outboard motor) was swamped in a whirlpool at sea.

Unable to bear conditions there any longer, he entered the hospital for Christmas. The wonder drug streptomycin, a tuberculosis cure, had just been released. It was so hard to come by in England there was a black market for it. Orwell was treated with it only because of Astor's friendship with the Minister of Health.

The drug did no good. He may have received too strong a dose. He suffered agonizing side effects that included ulcers in his throat and blood blisters in his mouth and on his lips. "In the morning my lips were always stuck together with blood, and I had to bathe them before I could open my mouth," he wrote. "Meanwhile my nails had disintegrated at the roots & the disintegration grew, as it were, up the nail, new nails forming beneath meanwhile."

In July 1948, he was free again. Upon returning to Jura, he worked hours on end to re-type his 150,000-word manuscript. He finished it days before his December deadline.

"I began to relapse about the end of September," Orwell wrote. "I could have done something about it then, but I had to finish that wretched book, which, thanks to illness, I had been messing about with for 18 months and which the publishers were harrying me for."

Orwell's ordeal made him more empathetic to the suffering of his characters—and other human beings. The greatness of *1984* lies at least partly in the courage Orwell marshalled in the face of death.

In his last months, he knew he was a dead man. *1984* was published to immediate and great acclaim in the middle of 1949. Orwell died soon thereafter in January 1950. He was 46.

**MORAL: Write the book of your life
so it lasts for ages.**

Chapter 79

Dwight Eisenhower

The Hewer of Steel

He was "the conqueror of the conqueror of worlds."
His toughest battle? Controlling his temper.

*"He that conquereth his own soul is greater
than he who taketh a city."*

His name—Eisenhower—means "hewer of steel" in German. As a general in World War II, Dwight Eisenhower ultimately served as Supreme Allied Commander of the Allied Expeditionary Force in Europe, overseeing the destruction of Nazi Germany. Shortly World War II ended, one of his military aides described him as "the conqueror of the conqueror of worlds."

Behind this future president's beaming smile lay the character of a supremely disciplined and brave leader. Yet here was a man who never showed courage in battle. In fact, he was never in a battle. No one ever took a shot at him, and he never fired a gun at anyone. Eisenhower's courage came in the form of the conquest of his own soul. He forged a will of steel.

He wasn't always that way. When he was nine and his parents wouldn't allow him to go trick-or-treating with his two older brothers, he flew into a rage. He stormed into the backyard and hammered his fists against a tree until his hands bled.

Later, his mother Ida, a pacifist, soothed him, saying "He that conquereth his own soul is greater than he who taketh a city." (She was paraphrasing Proverbs 16:32: "Better a patient person than a warrior, one with self-control than one who takes a city.")

Years later, Eisenhower would recall, "I have always looked back on that conversation as one of the most valuable moments of my life." He came to believe that "anger cannot win. It cannot even think clearly."

Eisenhower grew up with outdoor plumbing, one of five sons in a tiny house in Abilene, Kansas. His father was a mechanic in a creamery. "I have found out in later years we were very poor," Eisenhower recalled. "But the glory of America is that we didn't know it then. All that we knew was that our parents—of great courage—could say to us: 'Opportunity is all about you. Reach out and take it.'"

Sneak Out the Books

He wasn't above defying his mother—if slyly—to get that opportunity. As a child, he was a bookworm. Ida had to lock his books in the closet to get him to do his chores.

These were no picture books. They were about Roman and Greek history and contained detailed descriptions of great battles.

Eisenhower found the key his mother had tucked away and stole it. "Whenever Mother went to town to shop or was out working in her flower garden I would sneak out the books," he said.

As a politician, he enjoyed calling himself just "a simple country boy." One of his heroes—aside from Washington and Lincoln—was Themistocles, a general who used cunning and deceit to lure his enemies into thinking he was weak and unprepared.

When Eisenhower started high school, he had the opportunity to get bloodied. He took the challenge of becoming his school's designated warrior. The tradition in Abilene was that every year a freshman boy from the school on the south side of town would fight a boy from the school on the north side of town.

Their brawl lasted more than an hour. Witnesses said it was the "toughest kid fight" anyone had ever seen. Eisenhower's brother Arthur said he came home "beaten to a pulp. But never licked."

That same school year, Eisenhower had to show courage in another way—by standing up to two doctors. He scraped his knee, but his leg became infected. He went into coma, yet he heard the physicians telling his parents the leg would have to come off, if he were to live.

"You are never going to cut that leg off," he told them and his parents. He had a brother stand guard over his bed to ensure his vow was honored. After two weeks, the infection abated, and after two months of rest, he was back at school.

He became an outstanding football player in high school. When another team showed up with a black player, his teammates wanted to cancel the game. Eisenhower would have none of it. He shook the boy's hand before the game, and he switched positions from offensive end to center (the only time he ever did that), so that he could be opposite the black player, and when the game was over, he shook his hand.

Eisenhower faced great challenges to his self-control after graduating from West Point. After graduation, he wanted to fight in World War I. Instead, the Army gave him orders to report to Ft. Leavenworth where he oversaw the training of soldiers.

Finally, he became part of a tank battalion headed for Europe. At the last minute, however, his orders were changed, because of his "organizational abilities." Uncle Sam sent him to a ramshackle post at Gettysburg, Pennsylvania, to train tank crews.

Then, once again, he received orders to go to the front. The war, however, ended three days later.

Eisenhower's frustration was incredible. "I suppose we'll spend the rest of our lives explaining why we didn't get into this war," he said, and he vowed, "By God, from now on I am cutting myself such a swath and will make up for this."

Carving that path would prove horribly slow. Eisenhower stayed in the service, even though opportunities for advancement were greatly diminished after the war. Due to the demobilization, he was demoted from colonel to major, and he remained at that rank for 16 years.

He had to accept demeaning duty as a football coach at not one but two different posts.

The Army chastised him for writing a scholarly article on tank warfare. It predicted that in the future tanks must be "speedy, reliable, and efficient engine[s] of destruction." Instead of being praised for his foresight, his superiors told him his views were "incompatible with solid infantry doctrine." Worse, he learned that he would be court-martialed if he persisted in his "wrong" and "dangerous" ideas.

Slowly, senior officers saw what a gem he was. He was sent to Command & General Staff school—a plum assignment for future leaders. Out of 275 officers, he scored at the top of his class. He had duty in Europe under General Pershing, the leader of America's forces in World War I. While there, he wrote a guide to American battlefields in Europe, an experience which gave him first-hand knowledge of the continent's terrain and recent military strategy.

In 1929 just as the economy was collapsing, the Army put him in charge of a three-year study on how American industry might be mobilized in the event of war. He spent those years visiting factories and meeting with senior executives, experiences which prepared him for leadership.

"Magnificent Effort"

The Army chief of staff called his resulting report a "magnificent effort," and General MacArthur wrote that "this officer has no superior of his time in the army, distinguished by force, judgment, and willingness to accept responsibility."

Progress for Eisenhower remained slow, yet he showed courage by simply doing his duty and biding his time. He spent years in the Philippines working as MacArthur's aide. He loathed MacArthur's vainglorious, preening style, and he kept those views to himself.

When World War II started, instead of being given a field command, General Marshall, the Army's Chief of Staff, ordered him to Washington to serve as his right-hand man in the War Plans Division of the General Staff. Still Eisenhower chafed. "My God, how I hate this work by any method that forces me to depend on someone else," he said.

Patience paid off. By working for Marshall every day for six months, Marshall saw firsthand all of Eisenhower's talents—his aggressive combat instincts, his diplomatic finesse, his intelligence, his tolerance of stress, and his capacity for hard work.

In March 1942, he got his field command as Commanding General, European Theatre of Operations. The long years of staff duty proved he had the necessary character, demeanor, and experience for such responsibility.

He had a backbone of steel. When "pressure mounts and strain increases, everyone begins to show his weaknesses in his makeup," Eisenhower wrote. "It is up to the Commander to conceal his; above all to conceal doubt, fear, and distrust."

As president, he faced down the Soviet Union for eight long tense years during the Cold War. If that's not courage, consider how Eisenhower quit smoking. He was a four-pack-a-day man—smoking unfiltered cigarettes. He quit cold turkey in 1949, and he never picked up a cigarette again.

MORAL: Patience wins the game.

Chapter 80

Henry Moore

Holey Man

Gassed at the front, he dedicated
his art to peace.

"Everything I do is intended to be big."

The gas smells like garlic or horseradish. It might look yellowish. If you were exposed to it, you might not notice any effects for a few hours or even a day. Then loathsome red blisters would erupt all over your body and fill with yellow fluid. You might go blind temporarily or permanently. Blisters would form in your nose and throat, and your lungs might be so scalded, you would die.

This is what mustard gas does to people. It was the most widely used chemical weapon in World War I. The Germans used it on November 30, 1917, in the Battle of Cambrai against the British.

One of the soldiers in the front-line trenches that day was Henry Moore. The seventh of eight children of a coal miner from northern England, he was the youngest of all the men in his regiment, and he was one of only 52 out of 400 men who survived. Moore then spent two months in a hospital recovering.

But, truly, he never really recovered, physically or psychologically. His voice became permanently husky as a result of the gassing. When he was upset, sometimes he completely lost his ability to speak.

"A Disturbing Element"

He spent the rest of his life working through what he experienced that day. Today Moore is acclaimed as perhaps the greatest sculptor of the 20th century. He is known by most people as the creator of massive reclining figures, many of which have equally massive holes in them.

"When I carve into the chest," said Moore. "I feel as if I were carving into my own."

Over a career spanning 50 years, most of his works fall into three categories: mother and child, reclining figure, and heads. He worked in metals such as iron, lead, and bronze, stones such as alabaster and marble, and elm and cherry wood.

His life's course came to him one day in Sunday School when a teacher read an anecdote about Michelangelo describing him as "the greatest sculptor who ever lived." After that day, according to his biographer, whenever anyone asked him what he wanted to be in life, he would say "a sculptor."

Many of his works at first glance seem gentle and lovely in the smoothness of their simple swooping forms. Closer viewing, however, reveals in many of his sculptures faces that are emotionless or vacant and expressing shock or horror.

"I find in all the artists that I admire most a disturbing element, a distortion, giving evidence of a struggle," Moore said. "In great art, this conflict is hidden. It is unresolved. All that is bursting with energy is disturbing—not perfect."

Like many men of his generation, he rarely spoke of what he experienced during war. "But once he'd gone into his studio and shut the door, he found it very easy to get in touch with his subconscious, with his dreams and fears," said his daughter Mary. "He let these things flow through him, but he didn't talk about them. He was 50 when I was born. He and my mother behaved in a way that was typical of their generation. They never swore. They weren't touchy-feely. Things people would talk freely about today he channeled into his work."

In a letter he wrote in 1919, Moore told a friend, "The one great mistake in religion as I have known it is the belief it creates in one that God is Almighty. He is strong & powerful & good; but were he Almighty, the things I saw and experienced, the great bloodshed & the pain, the insufferable agony & depravity, the tears & the inhuman devilishness of the war, would, could never have been."

His near-death experience gave him a sense of urgency about his life. "I think, 'What has this day brought me, and what have I given it?' " he said.

There is no question that Moore understood that he was using his art to boldly confront and work through his traumatic experiences. In a notebook, he wrote "wounded man | reclining man | crawling man."

Many of his works are of deformed torsos, limbs without bodies, faces without features, and abdomens with holes blown through them. "There are universal shapes to which everyone is subconsciously conditioned and to which they can respond if their conscious control does not shut them off," said Moore.

"You can see echoes..."

Yet his work is about the power of life, not the negativity of death. Great sculpture, said Moore, has "a force, a strength, a life, a vitality from inside it, so that you have a sense that the form is pressing from inside trying to burst or trying to give off the strength from inside itself, rather than having something which is just shaped from outside and stopped."

During the 1940 German Blitz, he descended into London's Underground which thousands of people were using as air raid shelters. His resulting pencil sketches of indistinct cocoon-like figures huddling together proved popular in England.

"I think my father's shelter drawings of World War II – and actually, even when I look at family groups, plug into his seeing people dead and dying in the trenches, with their faces held in a rigor mortis, their mouths open," said daughter Mary. "He'd been gassed. [It] makes the limbs go rigid and the mouth hang open. You can see echoes of that in his sleeping figures."

Fears of war lingered in him for decades. After World War II, he made more than a dozen sculptures that mimicked the design of World War I German helmets. More ominously, some resemble mushroom clouds or skulls.

In the early 1950s, he created "Three Standing Figures," women who are all staring blankly at the sky, and Moore acknowledged that their anxious expressions were those of people expecting an air raid.

Moore was a fighter, and his fight, in his own way, was for peace. Said Moore: "If an artist tries consciously to do something to others, it is to stretch their eyes, their thoughts, to something they would not see or feel if the artist had not done it. To do this, he has to stretch his own first."

MORAL: Carve your place.

Chapter 81

Nelson Mandela

Jailed, Not Imprisoned

He took "a long holiday" in hell.

"I am the captain of my soul."

His birth name was Rolihlahla which means tugging on a tree branch or troublemaker. It was a fitting name for Nelson Mandela who devoted his life to ending South Africa's policy of apartheid and became his nation's first black president in 1994.

Prior to that triumph, Mandela sometimes joked that he "went on a long holiday for 27 years." He was sentenced to life in prison on May 1963 and remained confined until February 1990. He was a political prisoner, though the government never acknowledged that.

The first person in his family to go to school, Mandela would go on to found South Africa's first black-owned law firm. Political activity accompanied him all his adult life, and as a young man, he joined the African National Congress (ANC) whose goal was the abolition of apartheid.

He started out as a pacifist, believing in non-violent confrontation, in keeping with his views as a Christian. He also became a secret member of the Communist Party in South Africa. Though he was impressed by the ease with which its multi-racial members worked together, he opposed the Communists' goal of creating a class-free society

Mandela also stood against the use of violence against people. Instead, as a leader of the ANC in the 1950s, he advocated sabotage against property.

"It offered the best hope for future race relations," Mandela later said. He believed it was the smartest path to "scare away capital from the country" and that such a strategy would ultimately convince white "voters of the country to reconsider their position."

His objective? To create a "democratic and free society in which all persons live together in harmony and with equal opportunities."

Tantalized by the Sight

Understandably, the all-white South African government took a dim attitude towards anyone advocating sabotage. Mandela was tried on that that charge, and though he denied that he and the ANC planned guerilla warfare, he was sent to the prison on Robben Island. Like Alcatraz in San Francisco, it lies so close to Cape Town that its prisoners were tantalized by the sight of the city's high-rises in the distance.

"Going to Robben Island was like going to another country. Its isolation made it not simply another prison, but a world of its own," Mandela wrote in his autobiography.

Upon his arrival, guards taunted him saying, "This is the Island! Here you will die!" And he passed under a gate whose sign read "We Serve With Pride." He was now prisoner 46664, meaning that he was the 466th person to serve time there.

For the next 17 years, Mandela's home would be a seven-square foot cell. It had a one-square-foot window, and its walls were two-feet thick to prevent prisoners from communicating by tapping.

For many years, he slept on the floor on a bedroll. There were no beds. His cell's furnishings consisted of a stool and a "honey bucket" which he would empty every morning. (For the last 10 years of his sentence, Mandela was incarcerated at a prison on the mainland.)

His daily routine went this way. Prisoners were awakened at 5:30. They were expected to clean their cells between then and 6:45 when they were released from their cells for an unappetizing breakfast of corn porridge. Afterwards, Mandela typically took a half hour jog around the perimeter of the prison courtyard.

Guards then escorted prisoners to work. After lunch, they continued working until 4, at which time they had a half-hour to bathe before eating dinner alone in their cells. Meat was served only every other day.

"In those early years, isolation became a habit," said Mandela. "We were routinely charged for the smallest infractions and sentenced to isolation."

Work meant going to a lime quarry. Prisoners used pickaxes to pry the lime from the seams in the rock walls. Prisoners labored there for years without sunglasses, and the dazzling whiteness of the quarry permanently damaged Mandela's eyes.

Other tasks consisted of sitting silently and hammering rocks into gravel all day long.

Unlike some prisoners, Mandela enjoyed the daily 20-minute walk to the quarry, as it gave him an opportunity to spot deer, rabbits, and other wildlife running free.

"Wounds that can't be seen..."

"The months and years blend into each other" in prison, Mandela would later write.

He was not allowed to leave prison to attend his mother's funeral. He was diagnosed with tuberculosis (and cured), and he underwent surgery for an enlarged prostate gland. The psychological hardships of prison were worse than any physical pain. "Wounds that can't be seen are more painful that those that can be seen and cured by a doctor," Mandela said.

"To survive in prison, one must develop ways to take satisfaction is one's daily life. One can feel fulfilled by washing one's clothes so that they are particularly clean, by sweeping a corridor so that it is free of dust, by organizing one's cell to conserve as much as space as possible," he wrote. "The same pride one takes in more consequential tasks outside prison, one can find in doing small things inside prison."

The early years were the hardest. He was allowed only one visitor and one letter every six months. There was almost no reading material. Newspapers would arrive so scissored up (to remove political content), and they were nearly unreadable. In the late 1960s, prisoners were allowed more time to socialize and play cards and games, and Mandela became an avid gardener.

Prisoners were finally allowed newspapers and a small library. Mandela came across a poem by the Victorian-era British writer W.E. Manley. Its title was *Invictus* ("Unconquered"). Mandela was fond of reciting it to other prisoners. Its final stanza reads:

> It matters not how strait the gate,
> How charged with punishments the scroll,
> I am the master of my fate,
> I am the captain of my soul.

MORAL: Only you can imprison your soul.

Chapter 82

Julius Caesar

Greatest Unconcern

He laughed at thugs who kept him captive.
Then he killed them.

"I love the name of honor more than I fear death."

At the age of 25, Julius Caesar had won praise for his oratory. Many saw him as an up-and-coming politician in Rome. Life was good. His wife Cornelia had just given birth to their first child Julia.

Shortly after she was born, Caesar sailed to Rhodes, an island in the Aegean Sea, to learn more about the art of speechmaking under Apollonius, a rhetorician who had taught the great Roman senator Cicero.

It was the beginning of winter in 75 B.C., but Caesar did not make it to Rhodes. Cicilian pirates kidnapped him and held him on an island of the coast of southern Turkey north east of Cyprus in the Aegean Sea.

The pirates were not necessarily from Sicily. Bands of these sea-going thieves had roamed the waters of Aegean for decades. The Romans tolerated their presence partly because they were elusive and partly because they supplied Roman senators with slaves for their plantations.

"Burst out laughing"

The pirates gave the young nobleman a choice: Be sold as a slave or accept being held for ransom. When they told Caesar they would demand 20 talents of silver (roughly $600,000 in 2018 dollars), he "burst out laughing." So records the Greek author Plutarch in his *Life of Julius Caesar* (as translated by Robin Seager).

Caesar then told them that they had absolutely no idea who he was and how valuable a prize he was. He doubtless informed them that his family was of royal lineage and that he was a descendant of Iulus, the son of Aeneas, the legendary Trojan prince and warrior.

Incredibly, instead of begging for mercy as most captives would have done, Caesar told these "bloodthirsty" pirates that he was worth 50 talents and that he would have that sum delivered to them. They happily agreed, and Caesar sent most of his traveling companions back to sea, telling them to return with that amount. He kept with him only a friend and two slaves.

For the next 38 days, Caesar lived among the pirates as if he had not a care in the world—"with the greatest unconcern" as Plutarch says, for if his friends did not return, the pirates would surely kill him. He played games with the pirates and exercised with them.

He had the audacity to act as though he were their leader, not their prisoner. When he was tired and wanted to sleep, he would tell them to shut up. When he made speeches to them and recited poems that he had written for them, and they failed to be impressed, he mocked them, calling them "illiterate savages."

With much amusement, Caesar often told them that he would have them all put to death, if he had the chance. The pirates found all of his high-handed talk comical, attributing it to his youthful brashness.

When Caesar's friends returned with the ransom, the pirates did as they had promised and freed him. He immediately set sail for the nearby city of Miletus in present day Turkey. Once there, even though Caesar held no military rank and was not a Roman official, he immediately assembled several ships and manned with them sailors willing to confront the pirates.

True to his word

Returning to the place where he had been held captive, he found the pirate's ship anchored off-shore. He captured most of the barbarians. He also got back the 50 silver talents.

He took the pirates to Pergamon, another coastal city in modern Turkey, where he had them imprisoned. Before he could have them put to death, he needed the permission of Marcus Juncus, the Roman governor of Asia. Learning that he was not there but in nearby Bithynia, he sailed there.

Juncus refused Caesar's request. He told him that as governor he had the right to sell the prisoners as slaves, and after doing so, he would keep all of the proceeds himself.

This was not what Caesar wanted to hear. He rushed back to Pergamon before the governor's men could arrive to seize the prisoners. True to his word, Caesar removed the pirates from their cells and had them crucified, just as he had told them he would do. Because those being crucified typically spend several agonizing days suffering on their crosses, it is believed that Caesar may have shown them mercy and slit their throats instead.

Caesar bowed to no man. As Shakespeare would have him say, "I love the name of honor more than I fear death."

MORAL: Have a sense of humor. And beware of those who smile when they should not be smiling.

Chapter 83

August Landmesser

August Decision

He refused to salute a flag he hated.

"I have never done wrong."

The Nazis claimed that their infamous straight-arm salute had its origins in ancient Rome, but as with so much else about the Third Reich, that was a lie. Historians believe that Italian fascists first used it in the early 1920s to honor their dictator Benito Mussolini. German fascists admired the salute's militant posture and adopted it.

"It must be regarded as a survival of an ancient custom, which originally signified, " 'See, I have no weapon in my hand,' " said Hitler.

On June 13, 1936, Hitler visited the Blohm + Voss shipyard in Hamburg to witness the christening of the warship Horst Wessel. By a strange twist of history, a photograph taken on that day went relatively unnoticed until it appeared in a Japanese blog in 2011. (The blog's purpose was to boost recovery efforts from that country's recent earthquake and tsunami.

The black-and-white photo shows more than 100 men tightly packed together, their arms outstretched in the Nazi salute, undoubtedly chanting *Heil Hitler* (Hail, Hitler!) or *Sieg Heil* (Hail, victory!)

An Odd Expression

While there are a few men in the photo whose arms are not raised, one man stands out. His arms are crossed with seeming defiance. He has an odd expression, almost a grimace. None of the other men appear to want to stand next to him.

His name was August Landmesser, and he was a shipyard worker. He had joined the Nazi Party five years earlier hoping that doing so would help him find a good job.

In 1935, however, when he became engaged to Irma Eckler, the party expelled him. Why? She was Jewish. They were to be married in September of that year, but before they could exchange vows, the Nazis passed the infamous Nuremberg Laws which forbid Jews and non-Jews to marry and made legal other severe forms of discrimination against Jews Their first daughter Ingrid was born the next month.

In 1937 they lovers tried to flee to Denmark but were arrested at the border. When Eckler became pregnant again, the Nazi arrested Landmesser, accusing him of violating the Nuremberg Laws. He was tried and found guilty.

In a small gesture of leniency, the court accepted his assertion that he thought Irma was only part Jewish, and he was not jailed. She had been baptized as a Protestant when her mother remarried. As a parting gesture, the court warned him that if he continued on the same path, he would be imprisoned.

Racial Infamy

Two months later he was seized again. He begged the court for leniency, writing it, "My fiancée is expecting our second child any time now. Now I would like to marry her before this occurs and not leave her alone with the two children. I also ask that it be taken into consideration that I have never done wrong and that in this case the crime was committed thoughtlessly and, as it were, in a state of mental confusion, first due to the constant questions of acquaintances about how I'm going to manage and pay for everything once the second child arrives."

He was found guilty and sent to Borgermoor concentration camp where he served two-and-a-half years of a three-and-a-half-year sentence for dishonoring the Aryan race—racial infamy.

A newspaper account of the trial read: "In passing sentence, the Court maintained that if the purity of the German race is to be successfully maintained, then such violations of the Race Protection Law must be severely punished; that applies to Aryans as much as Jews. However, in this case the Court did not totally ignore the human aspect of the case. The Court was concerned not so much with the relationship of the accused with the woman involved, who is hardly a very worthy character, but rather his relationship with his children, for which the Court has every sympathy. However, the situation was aggravated by the defendant resuming the forbidden relationship and thus acknowledging neither restraint nor repentance. This was also the reason for the Court's decision to impose a sentence of penal servitude."

Landmesser never saw his wife again.

The Gestapo arrested Eckler and sent her to prison where she gave birth to her second daughter Irene. From there, she was sent to a series of concentration camps, finally ending up at Ravensbruck, a women's concentration camp, before being taken to the Bernburg Euthanasia Center where it is believed she was murdered in February 1942. (The Nazis used this facility primarily to kill mentally ill, sick, elderly, and disabled people as a part of its racial cleansing program. A total of 9,384 innocents were killed there in a gas chamber that used carbon monoxide.)

Freed from prison in early 1941, Landmesser worked as a laborer until being drafted in 1944 into a battalion composed only of former prisoners. Strapped for manpower and possessed with limitless cruelty, the Nazis used such battalions for dangerous missions, such as minefield clearing, where large numbers of casualties were expected. He survived until October of that year and died in combat in Croatia.

Ingrid and Irene had been sent to an orphanage prior to their parents' deaths. The Nazis allowed Ingrid to live with her Aryan grandmother, and she did so until her death in 1953.

A family friend took Irene to relative safety across the border into occupied Austria. When she returned to Germany during the war, she was put in a hospital which was told that her identity papers had been lost. Later both children were placed with foster parents. In 1958, Irene published her family's memoirs. They mostly consist of reprints of Nazi documents which starkly lay out the course of events that befell her family.

MORAL: Never forget.

Chapter 84

Alexander Selkirk

Not Such an Unsufferable State

A stranded hot-head learns that
courage lies in coolness.

"He is happiest who confines his Wants to natural Necessities."

He was a 28-year-old pirate and a hot head, and he was not the inspiration for Daniel Defoe's Robinson Crusoe.

Veteran navigator Alexander Selkirk left no written account of his solitary abandonment for nearly five years on Mas a Tierra, a volcanic island in the Pacific 400 miles west of Chile.

Thomas Stradling, the captain of his privateer, the *Cinque Ports,* left him on this forbidding 29-square-mile island on September 1704. More than five years would pass before he would be rescued on January 31, 1709, when Woodes Rogers, the captain of another privateer saw his signal fire. (Privateer is a genteel word for pirate ship, and in those days privately-owned British ships, with the government's approval, delighted in harassing Spanish merchants at sea.)

What we know of Selkirk comes from Rogers' book *A Cruising Voyage Around the World* and an interview he gave to essayist Richard Steele in 1711 for a magazine article.

Selkirk grew up in a Scottish fishing village and had a tempestuous relationship with his father and brothers before running away to sea at the age of 19. Eight years later he had earned the rank of sailing master (or navigator).

He sensed that his ship was in less than seaworthy condition. Its captain had died, and his successor Stradling had been the ship's 21-year-old lieutenant. The veteran Selkirk told the green captain that the mast and decks were so worm-eaten and in such a state of perilous decomposition that they demanded swift repair or else the ship would likely sink.

The argument grew to such a terrible pitch that Selkirk demanded to be put ashore on nearby Mas a Tierra (which Chile in the 1960s for touristic purposes renamed Robinson Crusoe Island).

Soon thereafter he thought the better of his ultimatum, but Stradling would have no more of him. He made an example of Selkirk, and if he thought some of his shipmates might accompany him ashore, he was most sadly mistaken. (The ship did indeed later founder. Most of its crew drowned, and those few who survived were imprisoned by the Spanish.)

The captain did kindly allow Selkirk to take with him the following items: Several books, including a Bible; a hatchet; a knife; bedding; clothes; several utensils; a musket along with bullets and a pound of gunpowder; mathematical instruments (presumably of a navigational nature); cheese; jam; some rum; and two pounds of tobacco.

His first months on the island were horrendous. Thousands of massive southern elephant seals, some nearly 20 feet long, had massed on the beaches to mate. Their bleating and honking drove him to distraction, forcing him to move inland.

Selkirk, wrote Rogers, "had to bear up against Melancholy, and the Terror of being alone in such a desolate place." It may be that he contemplated shooting himself to end his miseries.

For the next four years and five months, Selkirk saw not another soul, except on two occasions when Spanish ships anchored off shore. They sent parties ashore for fresh water and to hunt wild goats. He dared not surrender to them for fear that they would torture him to death or consign him as a slave to a Peruvian mine.

On one occasion, the Spaniards spotted him, and Rogers wrote that the sailors "not only shot at him but pursued him into the Woods, where he climb'd to the top of a Tree, at the foot of which they made water." Apparently, they did this not as an insult but because they were unaware he clung for dear life high above them.

Time passed, and he became accustomed to his solitary life. Rogers wrote, "We may perceive by this Story the Truth of the Maxim, That Necessity is the Mother of Invention."

From time to time, Selkirk made fires at high elevation to attract ships (and that is how Rogers ultimately spotted him). He built two huts, covered them with grasses and lined them with goat skins. He made fire by rubbing sticks together.

Food was plentiful. He shunned fish "because they occasion'd a Looseness, except Crawfish, which are there as large as our Lobsters." He feasted on turnips and cabbages. Most of all, he depended on wild goats for sustenance. They roamed the island in great numbers having been left there by ships' crews many years earlier. He kept track of how many he killed over the years—500.

When he ran out of bullets, he chased down the goats. On one occasion, his zestful hunt nearly killed him. He tackled a goat so close to the edge of a cliff that both he and his prey tumbled over the precipice. Rogers wrote that he was "so stun'd and bruis'd with the Fall, that he narrowly escap'd with his Life, and when he came to his Senses, found the Goat dead under him." Selkirk lay there for a full day before crawling to his hut where he convalesced for another 10 days.

He stayed in excellent physical condition. Walking and running "clear'd him of all gross Humours, so that he ran with wonderful Swiftness thro the Woods and up the Rocks and Hills." Rogers noted that "his Feet became so hard, that he ran every where without annoyance."

After his period of early "Melancholy" and "Terror," his mental condition became robust. To amuse himself, he sang Psalms and prayed. He told Rogers "he was a better Christian while in this Solitude than ever he was before, or then, he was afraid, he should ever be again."

"Cherish the Cats"

He was, however, plagued by rats. They "gnawed his Feet and Clothes while asleep." Mercifully, he had at hand an ancient solution for this woe. Countless cats also inhabited the island.

The midnight marauders "oblig'd him to cherish the Cats...[they] became so tame they would lie about him in hundreds, and soon deliver'd him from the Rats."

When his clothes fell to tatters, he remembered the skills his father, a tanner, had taught him. He painstakingly preserved goat hides and made for himself "a Coat and Cap of Goat-Skins" using a nail as a needle. When Rogers first spied the castaway draped in such garments, he said Selkirk "look'd wilder than the first Owners of them."

The experience made Selkirk a better man—physically and spiritually. He "bore up under such an Affliction, in which nothing but the Divine Providence could have supported any Man," Rogers wrote. "By this, one may see that Solitude and Retirement from the World is not such an unsufferable State of Life as most Men imagine."

The sea captain took pains to note that "It may likewise instruct us, how much a plain and temperate way of living conduces to the Health of the Body and the Vigour of the Mind, both of which we are apt to destroy by Excess and Plenty, especially of strong Liquor and the variety as well as the Nature of our Meat and Drink."

In his article, Steele concluded "he is happiest who confines his Wants to natural Necessities...or to use [the castaway's] own Expression, I am now worth 800 pounds, but shall never be so happy, as when I was not worth a farthing."

Selkirk swiftly returned to the pirate life. After sailing around the world, he briefly became a landlubber, enjoying the proceeds of the booty he had taken at sea. For reasons unknown, he decided to go straight and joined the Royal Navy. It was aboard one of its ships off the African coast that he died of yellow fever in 1721.

Scholars believe that Daniel Defoe would have surely known of Selkirk's experience, but his famed novel is more likely based on the experiences of many such castaways whose stories were well known in those days.

**MORAL: Don't let events get your goat.
Instead, get your own goat.**

Chapter 85

Edward Cave

Explosive Idea

He created something so dangerous,
it nearly got him beheaded.

"Must necessarily bear the stamp of the times"

The word *magazine* comes to English from Arabic via Italian and French words meaning warehouse or, more specifically, a place to store munitions.

In the hands of businessman Edward Cave a magazine was an explosive concept. He first published *Gentleman's Magazine* in January 1731, making it the world's first such publication.

He explained to readers that his invention was "a Monthly Collection, to treasure up, as in a Magazine, the most remarkable Pieces on the Subjects above-mentioned, or at least impartial Abridgements thereof."

Besides being its publisher, Cave was also its editor. He pushed his pen under the name Sylvanus Urban, reflecting his intention that the magazine appeal to both well-heeled city dwellers and rural lords and ladies.

"Our Magazine," he wrote, "must necessarily bear the stamp of the times, and the political, historical, and miscellaneous parts, dilate or contract in proportion to the reigning taste."

It covered all aspects of daily life—Parliamentary debates; reports on new inventions and medical treatments; natural history; archaeology; poetry; literary essays; news from the American colonies; agricultural prices; accounts of battles; sermons; lurid crime news; gossip; and listings of birth, deaths, ecclesiastical promotions, and obituaries. In short, it was an 18th century internet.

Here is a sampling of articles one might have found in the *Gentleman's Magazine*:

* An account of Edward Jenner's vaccinations against smallpox;

* An article about advancements in cataract surgery. (Doctors were now using knives to operate on eyes instead of scissors.);

* A discussion of where swallows went in the winter;

* A description of a balloon ride;

* Schematic drawings of a 30-hour sand chronometer and a "Centrifugal Engine for extracting water out of Ships";

* An exquisite illustration of an armadillo accompanied with an article about the characteristics of a specimen in Lord Southwell's possession: "This creature was brought hither from the Mosquito shore, upon the American continent...It is fed with raw beef and milk, and refuses our grain and fruits.";

* Tabloid tales such as this dreadful account: "A man at Farringdon Wash, near Fairford, having procured a ferret to hunt rats, the creature, while the family were busy, settled upon the cheek of an infant in the cradle, and could not be got of till it was choaked. The poor little infant died of the agony."

* An essay on "The capacity of Noah's Ark minutely considered." Its charts revealed where different beasts were housed;

* A design for a submarine. Yale University's library subscribed to the magazine. Yale student David Bushnell saw this 1747 story. He then wrote his master's thesis on a curious submersible contraption he called the *Turtle*. In September 1776, the Continental Army used it to attack a British warship.

* Missionary work among Georgia's Chickasaw Indians by John Wesley. (He would later found the Methodist Church.);

* A description of a cure for nervous spasms using "Russian Castor," a substance made from hairs plucked from the foreskins of Russian beavers. Presumably the beavers were dead when the plucking was done.

The magazine even published what might have been the world's first April Fool's story. It reported that a centaur had been born in England and would soon appear at Charing Cross in

London.

Cave's cornucopia of sublime insights and scandal made him wealthy. His magazine became the most influential publication in Georgian-era England. It had, for its time, a massive circulation—more than 10,000 copies. (Remarkably long lived, it ceased publication in 1922.)

Cave wasn't afraid of a fight. Before starting the *Gentleman's Magazine*, he published a newsletter while working as a postal clerk. Some accused him of opening people's mail to obtain news. Nothing could be proven.

His business plan beat *Reader's Digest* by more than a century. His magazine "contain[ed] the essays and intelligence which appeared in the two hundred half sheets which the London press then threw off monthly." In other words, some of its contents would be abridged. In many cases, he reprinted others' work with no alternations.

Other publishers were furious that this scoundrel would profit from their sweat. They filed lawsuits. Cave responded that it is "better that the proprietors should suffer some damage, than the acquisition of knowledge should be obstructed with unnecessary difficulties." In today's parlance, he would have said, "Information wants to be free."

A Nice Game of Shuttlecock

Cave was a big man, and not just because he was a media titan. He stood more than six-feet tall and was heavy set. He had his peculiarities—He only drank milk and water. For four years he was a vegetarian. He liked a nice game of shuttlecock. Like the fictional Perry White of Superman's *Daily Planet* newspaper, he was mean-spirited and pompous or so said his detractors.

He lived and breathed his magazine. His long-time reporter Samuel Johnson said Cave "never looked out of the window but with a view to the *Gentleman's Magazine*." Perhaps partly thanks to Cave's tutelage, Johnson become one England's renowned writers and the creator of the greatest dictionary the world had seen. Cave gave him his first job in publishing. One of Johnson's biographers said Cave gave his cub reporter Johnson assignments that were "almost unparalleled in range and variety."

One of Cave's great innovations involved reporting on Parliamentary debates. No one had ever done this before. Why? It was illegal. No matter—He sent friends and Johnson to sit in the galleries of the House of Commons.

He then ran accounts of speeches and MPs sarcastic remarks. Soon MPs gave Cave transcripts of their speeches, possibly making this the first time that politicians leaked flattering information to the press.

Ultimately, the magazine's reporting infuriated the House. Cave refused to back down. He continued publishing its debates, but with a twist. Now he ran them under the heading "Debates in the Senate of Lilliput." He attributed speeches to Lilliputian leaders whose fanciful names readers would have easily deciphered. Readers were most amused, and the magazine's renown and circulation rose.

Cave's most scandalous moment came in 1738. He dared to publish remarks King George II had sent to Parliament. The problem was he ran them before MPs heard them. The House of Commons denounced Cave, passing a resolution advising him of its "high indignation."

An even more chilling moment came when Cave dared run articles about the trial of Simon Fraser who had conspired to return England to Roman Catholic rule. Convicted of treason, he was the last man to be beheaded in England. As a result of his magazine's reporting, Cave not only paid a fine but had to beg forgiveness on his knees.

Scholars say Cave's magazine was remarkably fair in its coverage of controversial events. After all, Cave wanted as many cash-paying readers as he could get, and experience had taught him to be wary of upsetting the powers that be, except when covering juicy treason trials and tidbits from the King.

His coverage of the colonies (and their grievances) was thorough and sympathetic. For this, Americans may thank Cave's fellow publisher Ben Franklin. They were friends, and in 1741 Franklin started his own magazine *The General Magazine and Historical Chronicle*, though it only lasted for six monthly issues.

Cave reported on Franklin's experiments with lightning rods and published his pamphlet *Experiments and Observations in Electricity*. He put a lightning road on top of his London office building, a fitting place for such a courageous publication. And when lightning struck it, sure enough Cave published an article about that.

MORAL: Ready, fire, aim.

Chapter 86

Eilmer of Malmesbury

Prayer on a Wing

This monk had faith, but gravity was stronger.

"Hazarded a deed of remarkable boldness"

Move over, Orville and Wilbur Wright. You were bold and tenacious inventors, but you have nothing on Eilmer of Malmesbury. Sometimes known as Oliver of Malmesbury due to a misreading of ancient documents, this 11th century Benedictine monk was the first man to fly.

What is known of him and his exploits was written by his brother monk William of Malmesbury, a historian who lived in the same abbey at the same time. Scholars agree that the story is true, due to William's reputation. He is regarded as one of the most learned men in Europe during his lifetime. He wrote the majestic work *Gesta Regum Anglorum* (Deeds of the English Kings) which covers English history from 449 A.D. to 1120 A.D.

Here is how William immortalized his fellow monk:

"He was a man learned for those times, of ripe old age, and in his early youth had hazarded a deed of remarkable boldness...

"He had by some means, I scarcely know what, fastened wings to his hands and feet so that, mistaking fable for truth, he might fly like Daedalus, and, collecting the breeze upon the summit of a tower, flew for more than a furlong [about 200 yards]...

Violence of the wind

"But agitated by the violence of the wind and the swirling of air, as well as by the awareness of his rash attempt, he fell, broke both his legs and was lame ever after. He used to relate as the cause of his failure, his forgetting to provide himself a tail."

Little else is known about the courageous Eilmer. Scholars have, however, surmised certain facts.

His flight took place sometime around the year 1010. We know this because Eilmer saw Halley's Comet in 1066 and remarked that he had seen it swing past Earth in 989 when he was a youngster 76 years earlier. He is quoted in the *Anglo-Saxon Chronicle*, a collection of ancient accounts, saying, "You've come, have you?...You've come, you source of tears to many mothers, you evil. I hate you! It is long since I saw you, but as I see you now you are much more terrible, for I see you brandishing the downfall of my country. I hate you!"

The English saw the comet as a portent of ill fate. After seeing it for the first time, Vikings invaded destroying many towns, include Malmesbury. Shortly after Eilmer saw the comet a second time, England's last Anglo-Saxon king Harold II died at the Battle of Hastings later that year, and William the Conqueror became the first Norman (or French) king of England.

So, if Eilmer had been a child in 989, he would have been an "early youth" in his 20s around the year 1010.

Eilmer was an educated man for his day. He knew the myth of Icarus, the young Greek inventor who flew by affixing wings to his arms. He fell to his death when he soared too close to the sun, its heat melting the wax that held the feathers to his wings. His true crime was that of *hubris*, foolish pride which led to his demise, making his story a cautionary tale that Eilmer failed to heed.

It is also possible that Eilmer had heard stories of flight spread by Crusaders returning from the Middle East and Europe. Some say the Muslim inventor Ibn Firnas built and flew a glider in Cordoba, Spain, in 985. (Most historians discount this tale, because no account of it was put to paper until 600 years later.)

Eilmer had the mechanical skills to build his flying machine. According to a U.S. Air Force website, his wings would likely have been made of cloth attached to a wooden frame. The frame would have had hinges to allow Eilmer to flap the wings.

His airfoil, based on William's account, also included material fastened between or around his legs.

Kingdom's first capital

But could the flight have actually taken place and could Eilmer have flown 200 yards, a distance which experts say might take 15 seconds?

The answer is a yes.

There has been an abbey at Malmesbury, about 100 miles west of London, since around 676 A.D., and the original structure had an 80-foot tower. Today's magnificent Romanesque and early gothic abbey is the third to be built on this site. Around 1500, a storm destroyed the original structures.

The abbey has a treasured history. Its spire once made it England's tallest building. Historians say the abbey was the kingdom's first capital and home to its first King, Athelstan the Glorious. It also had the realm's second largest library.

Today the abbey's church remains in use and is stunning. Its sides, the clerestory, have towering walls mounted with rows of high-set massive windows which allow light to stream into the church. The church's 122-foot-long nave sports a vaulted ceiling so steep visitors must crane their necks to take it in.

The church was a prized possession during the English Civil War of the mid-16th century. It changed hands seven times. Many of its walls show signs of ruthless fighting. Many spots are pockmarked with places where bullets went astray.

Life was far more peaceful when Eilmer and William were its residents. The abbey was an institute of theological learning. It kept safe mighty relics—pieces of the cross on which Jesus was crucified and fragments of the Crown of Thorns.

But is there enough wind at the site? Would there have been enough room for Eilmer to make his flight?

The abbey sits atop a hill. "The toun of Malmesbryi stondith on the very toppe of a great slaty rok, and ys wonderfully defended by nature," wrote the 16th century writer Leland.

On one side, the hill descends abruptly for about 60 feet before sloping to the Avon River about 600 feet away. Today crows soar around the tower, and if they have inhabited the area since Eilmer's day, he undoubtedly would have observed them and learned something, but not all, of their amazing abilities.

MORAL: God is in the de-*tail*-s.

Chapter 87

Henry Ford

Man in Gear

He heeded his mother's advice and changed the world.

"You must earn the right to play."

When the 20th century rolled to a close, *Fortune* magazine decreed him the "Businessman of the Century."

Of his childhood inclinations, he would write, "My father was not entirely in sympathy with my bent toward mechanics. He thought that I ought to be a farmer."

When Henry Ford he left his father William's farm at the age of 16 to seek his fame and fortune in nearby Detroit, he wrote, "I was all but given up for lost."

Indeed, his father was fond of saying, "Oh, Henry ain't much of a farmer. He is more of a tinkerer."

As a child, he enjoyed taking apart and reassembling his classmates' pocket watches. He and some other boys built a steam engine using a beat-up 10-gallon can for a boiler. When it exploded, it sent tin shrapnel flying at the boys, and one of the whizzing metal shards tore into Ford's face, leaving a scar on his cheek.

An early biographer of Ford's wrote that "he worked with his tools always against the wishes of his father." The young Ford made pocket money by repairing neighbors' watches. He would wait until his father went to sleep before stealing away to neighbors' farm house to pick up broken watches.

When Ford built a prototype car a few years later, his father disapproved of it, saying "he thought it was something that would scare all the horses off the road." It's said that he even called his son "an awful fool."

Other family accounts say that the father and son got along well. For example, relatives say Ford didn't exactly run off to Detroit. It was only nine miles away, and he went to live with an aunt. When his first job didn't pan out, his father came to town to assure his new employer that he was a fine young man.

There is agreement, though, the Ford doted on his mother Mary. "I have tried to live my life as my mother would have wished," he said.

He always remembered the maxims she taught him: "Life will give you many unpleasant tasks to do; your duty will be hard and disagreeable and painful to you at times, but you must do it" and "You must earn the right to play."

Mary was also something of a fiend for doing things efficiently. A half-century after her passing, Ford said that "Mother believed in doing things and getting things done, not in talking about things and wishing they might be done. She was systematic and orderly and thorough, and she demanded that from us."

Sensible words. Considering that her son would become famed for his skill at mass-producing vast numbers of automobiles, her lessons clearly made a difference.

By the end of the 1880s, Ford was obsessed with the thought of building a horseless carriage. He experimented with designing and building gasoline-powered engines at a time when other entrepreneurs were focused on trying to perfect steam-powered and electric vehicles. He was far from alone in his interest in commercializing the horseless carriage. Between 1900 and 1908, 501 American companies vied for dominance in the emerging car industry.

In 1896 created (and drove) his first vehicle, the Quadricycle. It had a two-cylinder engine, a steering bar, bicycle tires mounted on a frame, a top speed of 20 miles per hour, and not much else.

He wasn't the first inventor to drive a car in Detroit, but he wasn't far behind. Literally. When that first car made its debut in March of that year, Ford was there and engaging in industrial espionage. He followed behind it on his bicycle.

He later became the second inventor to drive a car in Detroit. When it came time for Ford to hit the streets, he had to knock down part of the wall of his one-room factory/laboratory.

In his zeal to build a car, he failed to realize that the door to his shed was too narrow to accommodate an exiting vehicle.

A month later a decisive moment came in Ford's life. He wangled his way into a fancy dinner party for prominent local business leaders. The guest? Thomas Edison.

During a discussion of how batteries for electric cars would be charged, someone mentioned that Ford had driven a gas-powered car. Edison expressed curiosity.

Ford then moved down the table to sit next to the great man. He did this partly because Edison was deaf and partly because he knew that the best way he could communicate his engineering designs would be to draw diagrams.

Some might have thought the wizard of electricity would have scoffed at the notion of powering a vehicle with a dangerous substance like gasoline, but after hearing Ford's description of his invention, Edison replied "You have it. Keep at it!....Your car is self-contained—it carries its own power-plant—no fire, no boiler, no smoke, no steam. You have the thing. Keep at it."

Edison's words of praise cheered Ford mightily. This marked the beginning of a lifelong friendship between the two great inventors.

After several failed business ventures in the early 1900s, Ford vowed to change American life. His goal? To make internal-combustion powered vehicles to everyone.

"I will build a motor car for the great multitude," Ford said. "It will be large enough for the family but small enough for the individual to run and care for. It will be constructed of the best material, by the best men to be hired, after the simplest designs that modern engineering can devise. But it will be so low in price that no man making a good salary will be unable to own one—and enjoy with this family the blessing of hours of pleasure in God's great open spaces."

He made his mark with the Model T. Only a few days after his first cars left his factory in 1908, they became a sensation. Orders for more than 15,000 more deluged the company. The price was right—$850 (or $22,000 in 2018 dollars), and when production ramped up, their cost in 1914 fell to $360 (or $7,000).

It was the everyman's car. It was easy for anyone with modest mechanical aptitude to take apart or repair. By end of World War I, half of all cars on the road in America were Model T's. Ford built 82,000 of them in 1908, and in 1923, his massive Rouge Plant in Detroit turned out two million. By the time the last one came off the assembly line in 1927, Ford had built 15 million flivvers.

It's a myth that the car was only available in black. Ford did joke that "You can have it in any color you want, so long as it's black." But customers could buy models in in green, gray, blue, red until 1914. Thereafter, Model T's only came in black. It was a cost-saving measure.

Later, Ford became thoroughly controversial. He used violence to suppress labor unions. He sympathized with the "efficient" Nazi regime in the 1930s, and he mistreated his eldest son Edsel to such a point that emotional distress may have contributed to his early death at the age of 49.

On the other hand, Ford astonished America in the early 1900s when he decided to pay his factory workers twice the going rate. And he only required a 40-hour work week. Although conditions in his factories were slave-like by modern standards, he wanted his employees to be well-compensated for their hard work and have time home with their families. A cynical view would be that he wanted his workers to have enough money to buy his cars.

Ford lived his dreams. Said the great automaker: "To make a sensation, be one."

MORAL: Get in the driver's seat.

Chapter 88

The Faithful Dog

Scalped and left to die, the soldier
had once chance to survive.

"Prevailed on them to follow him to the fatal spot..."

Consider this account from the diary of Dr. James
Thatcher, a surgeon in the Continental Army during the
Revolutionary War. The events below occurred near Saratoga,
New York, in October or November 1777. They are taken from
his book *A Military Journal During the American Revolutionary
War*.

"Among the most remarkable occurances which come
under my observation, the following is deserving of particular
notice.

"Captain Greg, of one of the New York regiments, while
stationed at Fort Stanwix, on the Mohawk river, went with two
of his soldiers into the woods a short distance to shoot pigeons; a
party of Indians started suddenly from concealment in the
bushes, shot them all down, tomahawked and scalped them, and
left them for dead.

"The captain, after some time revived, and perceiving his
men were killed; himself robbed of his scalp, and suffering
extreme agony from his numerous wounds, made an effort to
move and lay his bleeding head on one of the dead bodies,
expecting soon to expire.

In the tenderest manner

"A faithful dog who accompanied him, manifested great
agitation, and in the tenderest manner licked his wounds, which
afforded him great relief from exquisite distress. He then
directed the dog, as if a human being, to go in search of some
person to come to his relief.

"The animal, with every appearance of anxiety, ran about a mile, when he met two men fishing in the river, and endeavored in the most moving manner, by whining and piteous cries, to prevail on them to follow him into the woods; struck with the singular conduct of the dog, they were induced to follow him a part of the way, but fearing some decoy or danger, they were about to return, when the dog, fixing his eyes on them, renewed his entreaties by his cries, and taking hold of their clothes with his teeth, prevailed on them to follow him to the fatal spot.

"Such was the remarkable fidelity and sagacity of this animal. Captain Greg was immediately carried to the fort, where his wounds were dressed; he was afterward removed to our hospital and put under my care.

"He was a most frightful spectacle; the whole of his scalp was removed; in two places on the fore part of his head, the tomahawk had penetrated through the skull; there was a wound on his back with the same instrument, besides a wound in his side and another through his arm by a musket ball.

Kind and over-ruling Providence

"This unfortunate man, after suffering extremely for a long time, finally recovered, and appeared to be well satisfied in having his scalp restored to him, though uncovered with hair.

"The Indian mode of scalping their victims is this—with a knife they made a circular cut form the forehead quite round, just about the ears, then taking hold of the skin with their teeth, they tear off the whole hairy scalp in an instant, with wonderful dexterity.

"This they carefully dry and preserve as a trophy, showing the number of their victims, and they have a method of painting on the dried scalp, different figures, and colors, to designate the sex and age of the victim, and also the manner and circumstance of the murder."

In the consideration of this tale, one must also pause to consider the bravery of Captain Greg and his compatriots, as well as that of Dr. Thatcher whose diary begins in January 1775 with this entry:

"I shall venture, I hope not rashly, to enlist, and trust my destiny in the hands of a kind and over-ruling Providence. My contemplated enterprise, it is true, requires the experience and resolution of riper years than twenty one...."

After leaving the service in 1783, Dr. Thatcher practiced in Plymouth, Massachusetts. He died at the age of 90 in 1844.

MORAL: Be dogged.

Chapter 89

Elijah McCoy

The Real McCoy

Ignoring insults, he greased the wheels of civilization.

George and Mildred McCoy could have remained as slaves in Kentucky. Instead, they found the courage in 1837 to flee to Ontario, Canada, via the Underground Railroad. They had 11 children, and they certainly picked the right name for their son Elijah, whom they named after the prophet in the Bible.

He grew up to be a modern-day miracle worker, an inventor who held 57 patents.

When he was about 15, his family moved to Ypsilanti, Michigan. Seeing promise in Elijah, his parents sent him to the University of Edinburgh in Scotland, where he studied to become a mechanical engineer.

When he returned home degree in hand, the only job he could find was as a Fireman-Oiler on the Michigan Central Railroad. He shoveled coal into the locomotive's steam engine and tended to its boiler to make sure it didn't explode. But being an oiler was what truly inspired McCoy.

In those days, trains had to make regular stops so that their bearings, cylinders, and levers, and other moving parts could be lubricated by hand. This meant that every train had a man aboard like McCoy whose job it was to walk from one end of the train to the other carrying a long-necked oil can and applying oil where it was needed. This meant delays and extra labor costs for railroad companies. What's more, other industries also needed oilers to regularly service their machines.

McCoy had a workshop in his home, and in 1872 he won patent #129,843 for an automatic lubricator. It could be used to oil all manner of steam engines in trains, ships, factories, mines, oil-drilling rigs, and elsewhere.

Other inventors had created similar devices. These were basically containers that had tiny stopcocks that insured a regular, continuous flow to oil to gears and axles in motion. McCoy's proved far superior, so much so that it was derided as a "n*gger oil cup."

Such cruel talk did not last long, for McCoy's invention rapidly won acclaim. He was often called on to personally supervise its installation. Soon enough when engineers and mechanics bought or examined lubricating equipment, they would ask "Is this the real McCoy?" The highest praise, though, came when competitors studied his design and copied it.

Today there is some dispute over whether the expression began with McCoy's invention. Suffice it to say that no less of an authority than the Smithsonian Institution believes McCoy's ingenuity is the source of the expression. In 1989, it named an exhibition on African American Invention and Innovation, 1619-1930 — "The Real McCoy."

McCoy went on to patent improved tire treads, rubber heels, automatic lawn sprinklers, and the collapsible ironing board. (His wife had complained to him about how hard it was to iron clothes on uneven surfaces.)

He stayed active in his field into old age. When he was 72, he filed a patent for a graphite/oil lubricating system to service modern engines which ran at far higher speeds than steam engines. (It allowed for a solid lubricant such as graphite to be suspended in a lubricating liquid without clogging under high temperatures.) He also served as a consultant to major corporations and offered career counseling to young men.

MORAL: The squeaky wheel gets the inspiration.

Chapter 90

Henry Kaiser

"Start Swinging!"

He could build anything. And through force of will he did.

"Live daringly, boldly, fearlessly. Taste the relish to be found in competition— in having put forth the best within you."

The son of an immigrant cobbler from tiny Sprout Brook in upstate New York, Henry Kaiser had a huge knack for putting things together—big things, industrial things. He made waves, literally. His fearlessness in the pursuit of the American dream made him a role model to millions in the 20th century.

He left school at the age of 12 or 13 to become an errand boy. It was a sign of things to come. Here was a young man who was restless, always on the move. Between 1898 and 1900, he worked at not one but three photography studios. He became a traveling salesman. Then he owned his own photo store in Lake Placid, New York. Then he owned four more in Florida.

Bess Fosburgh saw what a catch he was. They married in Boston in 1907. She was from a well-to-do family, and her father may have urged his new son-in-law to find more substantial employment.

The on-the-go Kaiser got into the construction industry in the Pacific Northwest. He sold heavy equipment and building supplies. That led to work managing road construction and public works projects. He was the right man in the right place. The northwest was still fairly wild territory, and there was much money to be made putting in roads.

Smaller jobs got bigger. Soon all his construction deals were in the millions. He got a big break that vaulted him into the big leagues. He was invited to become part of a group of six companies that had wangled a deal to build 750 miles of roads and 400 bridges in Cuba, all in a three-year period—A $20 million project ($250 million in 2018 dollars).

It was a huge challenge in a foreign country, and he excelled at it. "Problems are only opportunities in work clothes," said Kaiser who one biographer called an "imaginative pragmatist."

That was just the beginning. This consortium of companies known by the meat-and-potatoes name of "The Six Companies" in 1931 won the deal that truly put Kaiser on the map. They built a massive dam on the Colorado River—Hoover Dam. Between 1931 and 1936, as many 20,000 men labored to build this 726-foot-tall structure. Today this legendary landmark supplies power to 20 million people in three states.

By the late 1930s, it seemed as though there was nothing Kaiser couldn't do. His conglomerate employed 250,000 workers. They made steel and cement. They dug coal. And they built ports, blast furnaces, and airplane parts, and made weapons.

He also built a few ships. That would swiftly change. To win the war and to help its allies Britain and the Soviet Union, America had to build troop ships and freighters—lots of them and fast.

In his country's moment of need, Kaiser rose to the challenge. "I always have to dream up there against the stars," he said. "If I don't dream I will make it, I won't even get close."

Ship building had once been fairly leisurely. It might take six months to construct a ship from the keel up. Kaiser threw that strategy out the window. He adapted techniques of mass production to shipbuilding. For example, the home building industry uses modular construction techniques. It puts together parts of homes off-site and assembles them where the house is being built. That's what Kaiser did with ships. And instead of painstakingly riveting steel panels together in drydock, his workers welded them, saving much time.

His labor policies were new and different, too. He hired women and African-Americans in large numbers. What's more, Kaiser became known as one of the nation's most enlightened employers. He offered the world's first pre-paid health insurance program to his employees in 1938. He became famed for his ability to work closely and peacefully with unions.

When Kaiser got into shipbuilding, it typically took 230 days to build a substantial ship. He cut that to 45 days and then to less than 20 days. One of his crews even built a ship in less than five days. (It was a wartime publicity stunt.)

He never took credit for all his innovations. Kaiser knew that to be successful he had to surround himself with the best people. "I make progress by having people around me who are smarter than I am and listening to them," he said. "And I assume that everyone is smarter about something than I am."

Uncle Sam named the freighters EC2 ships. All were 441-feet-long and nearly identical. They weren't made to look pretty. People dubbed them 'Ugly Ducklings.'

That changed when President Roosevelt attended the christening of the first 14 of these ships in September 1941. The first ship to slide down the ways was the *Patrick Henry*. In his speech, Roosevelt recited the climax of Henry's legendary speech, saying "Give me liberty or give me death."

Just as Henry and the other Founding Fathers brought liberty to America, Roosevelt told the world that these ships would bring liberty to Europe. Thus, the 'Ugly Ducklings' became known as Liberty Ships.

Between 1941 and 1945, Kaiser built 2,751 Liberty Ships at 18 shipyards ranging from Portland, Oregon, and Richmond, California, to Baltimore, Maryland. By 1943, those yards completed three ships a day.

Kaiser so impressed Roosevelt that he put the industrialist on his short-list of possible vice-presidential candidates in 1944, even though Kaiser had never been in politics, never campaigned for anyone, and didn't belong to the Democratic Party.

He was a man who simply got things done and feared no challenge.

And he enjoyed a good joke. It's said that on one occasion when a woman was visiting his office, he asked her if she'd like the honor of christening a Liberty Ship.

When she said she would be delighted to do so, Kaiser found a bottle of champagne. He led her through the clanging hustle-and-bustle of the busy shipyard to an empty dry dock.

Once there, he handed his puzzled guest the bottle.

"But there's nothing there!" she exclaimed

"Never mind," replied Kaiser, looking at his watch. "Start swinging!"

MORAL: Build on your successes, no matter how small.

Chapter 91

Charb

Likeness of the Truth

Killers came for the brave cartoonist.

"I prefer to die on my feet than to live on my knees."

Coco is Corinne Rey's pen name. She's a cartoonist, a French cartoonist. It was 11:30 a.m. on Wednesday, January 7, 2015. She was late for a 10:30 staff meeting at the Paris-based magazine where she was a contributor.

She had just picked up her daughter from a nearby nursery school. She was taking her little girl to the meeting.

Two young men stood at the locked outside door to the lobby. They wore black from head to toe. Black hoods covered their heads. Black masks hid their faces. They both wielded Kalashnikovs—AK-47 Russian assault rifles. They wore bulletproof vests.

The two al-Qaeda terrorists told the terrified Rey words to the following effect: "If you don't enter the security code that opens this door, we'll kill your little girl."

Rey punched in the numbers. Upon entering the lobby, the terrorists shot and killed a maintenance man at the front desk. They dragged Rey and her little child upstairs. She flung herself under a desk and lay on top of her daughter.

"Where is Charb?" the gunmen shouted (or words to that effect). They shot and killed him, firing at his head. Over the next 10 minutes, they blasted the offices, murdering eight cartoonists, editors, and writers and wounding three others.

Police on bicycles

By this time, police on bicycles had arrived outside, probably unaware of exactly what was happening. The terrorists killed two of the officers. One whom they injured lay on the sidewalk begging for mercy. A terrorist stood above him and shot him dead. Other police officers were also injured.

Who was Charb? Charb's full name was Stephane Carbonnier. He was 47. He was an atheist with Communist sympathies. His courage knew no bounds.

He was a cartoonist and editorial director of *Charlie Hebdo*, a French satirical magazine. His long-running comic strip Maurice et Patapon featured Maurice, a left-wing bisexual man, and Patapon, a conservative cat.

For years he and his little magazine (It had a circulation of only 50,000) delighted in making fun of everyone and everything. It once called Buddhism "the most stupid religion ever." It ran a cartoon of Pope Benedict XVI in Nazi regalia. (As a teenager, he had to enroll in the Hitler Youth. It was mandatory, even though he was a seminary student.)

In 2006 *Charlie Hebdo* republished Dutch cartoons of Muhammad, the prophet of Islam. The Qur'an says nothing on the issue of depictions of Muhammad. He was often painted in Islam's first centuries. Today, however, most Muslims disapprove of this. Radical Muslim terrorists use violence to enforce this custom as part of their strategy to subjugate non-Muslims.

"We publish caricatures every week, but people only describe them as declarations of war when it's about the person of the prophet or radical Islam," Charb said in 2012. "When you start saying that you can't create such drawings, then the same thing will apply to other, more harmless representations."

Over the years Charb's magazine had run several of his cartoons, often on its covers, satirizing Muhammad and Islam. A 2006 cover showed Muhammad weeping below the headline "Muhammad overwhelmed by fundamentalists." A 2011 cover emblazoned with another cartoon of Muhammad had that headline "100 lashes if you don't die of laughter." A second 2011 cover cartoon showed Muhammad kissing a man. The caption? "Love is stronger than hate."

No concealed carry permit

"Muhammad isn't sacred to me," said Charb. "I don't blame Muslims for not laughing at our drawings. I live under French law. I don't live under Qur'anic law."

In response to the cartoons and such statements, al-Qaeda in 2011 firebombed *Charlie Hebdo's* offices. After that, Charb lived under police guard. French police denied his application for a permit to carry a concealed handgun.

Al-Qaeda also put him on its "Wanted: Dead or Alive" list. That list includes the Somali activist Ayaan Hirsi Ali who has denounced Muslim oppression of women; the Texan Molly Norris who founded "Draw Mohammed Day" (She now lives in hiding); and novelist Salman Rushdie.

"I've got no kids, no wife, no car, no credit cards," said Charb. "Perhaps what I'm going to say sounds a bit pompous, but I prefer to die on my feet than to live on my knees."

Two days before Charb was murdered, he completed an 82-page manifesto on Islamophobia titled "Open Letter: On Blasphemy, Islamophobia, and the True Enemies of Free Expression." His murder came the day before *Charlie Hebdo* was to publish an issue titled *Sharia Hebdo* in which Muhammad served as its mock "editor."

"It should be as normal to criticize Islam as it is to criticize Jews or Catholics," said Charb. "Do we want to live in fear and terror and practice self-censorship?"

In response to the murders, French prime minister Francois Fillon said, "Freedom of expression is an inalienable right in our democracy, and all attacks on the freedom of the press must be condemned with the greatest firmness. No cause can justify such an act of violence."

British Prime Minister David Cameron agreed, saying, "We stand united with the French people in our opposition to all forms of terrorism and stand squarely for free speech and democracy."

The others who died that day were:

Frederic Boisseau, 42, maintenance worker
Franck Brinsolaro, 49, police officer
Elsa Cayat, 54, psychiatrist and columnist
Jean Cabut, 76, cartoonist
Philippe Honore, 73, cartoonist
Clarissa Jean-Philippe, 26, police officer
Bernard Maris, 68, economist and journalist
Ahmed Merabet, 40, police officer
Mustapha Ourrad, 60, proofreader
Michel Renaud, 69, travel industry figure and journalist
Bernard Verlhac, 57, cartoonist
Georges Wolinski, 80, cartoonist

MORAL: Stand up for what you believe.

Chapter 92

Xernona Craig

Dragon Slayer

A black woman helped a white man join
the clan of humankind.

"I won't run away from people."

It takes courage to sit down and talk with someone you
loathe. It's even more remarkable when two people who should
despise each other will sit and listen to each other. And it's
astonishing when such a dialogue opens someone's heart.

That's what happened in 1968 in Atlanta when Ku Klux
Klan Grand Dragon Calvin Craig and civil rights activist Xernona
Clayton had the courage to start talking to each other.

During the 1960s, Clayton worked for the Southern
Christian Leadership Conference. Among other duties, she
planned civil rights marches for Dr. Martin Luther King. (She
later became the first black woman in the South to host an
evening TV talk show, and after that, she was an executive at
Turner Broadcasting.)

In 1966, she became the community affairs director for
the Model Cities program in Atlanta. The goal of this federal
initiative was to improve the quality of life in newly
desegregated neighborhoods.

The following year Mayor Ivan Allen Jr. warned her that
Craig lived in one of those neighborhoods.

"I don't know how you're all going to get along," the
mayor sighed.

"Well, I won't run away from people," Clayton replied.

Craig was a heavy equipment operator who had joined
the Klan sometime between 1957 and 1960. His official title was
Grand Dragon of the Georgia Realm of the United Klans of
America, Knights of the Ku Klux Klan. He was "the most courtly

nineteenth century gentleman," according to one reporter, and Clayton remembers him as being tall, handsome, well dressed. He also had a great sense of humor, according to her.

Looks can be deceiving. For her book *The Klan*, author Patsy Sim interviewed Craig. He told her "I can take five men in a city of 25,000, and that is just like having an army....five can almost control the political atmosphere of that city."

One day at one of her local meetings, Clayton met a man who wouldn't shake her hand. He would only touch her fingertips. She suspected that he was Craig. (In fact, at the Model Cities meetings he attended, if a black person sat next to him, he would move to another seat.)

Change a man's heart

The next day he came to her office. "Every day he would come by and make it his business to get into a discussion with me about race," said Clayton. "Every time I asked him a question he didn't want to answer, he just laughed."

He baffled her. He was a deacon at his Baptist church. He went twice a week to services, yet he also attended evening Klan meetings. "I did want to change his attitude, because I was listening to Dr. King preach, saying that you've got to change a man's heart before you can change his behavior. I never forgot that," said Clayton.

Upon learning he was a deacon, she asked him. "What part of the Bible are you reading? Where does it say to treat someone differently because they don't look like you" She told him he had too much intelligence to be "so ignorant."

Clayton surprised Craig when she told him white people often came to dinner at her home. When he said that he would never do so, she knowingly replied, "You'll not only be eating at my house, you'll be eating out of my hand."

The most charitable thing to say about Craig was that he was a complicated man. James L. Townsend, the founding editor of *Atlanta* magazine, offered this peculiar analysis: "Calvin Craig is not a killer, and most assuredly he's not a nut. It's just that he's got a few killers and a few nuts in his organization, and he, personally, doesn't have the moral courage to repudiate them....It's too bad. He's a nice guy."

In early April 1968, Clayton drove Dr. King to the Atlanta airport for his flight to Memphis, Tennessee, where he would lead a march on behalf of striking sanitation workers. On April 4, 1968, King was assassinated there.

Strangely, that night Craig came to Clayton's home. He would not come in but instead stood in her front yard to show his respects.

Four days later he held a press conference. He denounced the Klan and said he was leaving the organization. "Black men and white men can stand shoulder-to-shoulder in a united America," he told the media.

Clearly, Clayton's gentle patience had paid off. "Extremists of both the black groups and the white groups [must] sit down at the conference table and work out the problems so we can have peace in America today," he said.

A good streak hidden

Three months later he ran for sheriff of Fulton County (where Atlanta is located). He said that if elected he would hire black law-enforcement officers and jail matrons and would have no compunctions against arresting Klansmen.

Craig's conversion became national news. Clayton won the moniker of "the Dragon slayer."

Mail for Craig poured into Atlanta by the sack. No one knew where to deliver it. One day the mayor called Clayton and asked if she would give Craig his mail.

"Only in Atlanta could the contact to a Klansman be through a black woman," the mayor joked.

Atlanta's newspaper *The Journal Constitution* published a strangely worded editorial about Craig's conversion. It reflected the era's morally conflicted notions: "Just supposing that we have to have a Ku Klux Klan—which we emphatically and categorically deny, but just suppose—we couldn't have had a much less objectionable Grand Dragon for one than Calvin F.

Craig. We always suspected that he had a good streak hidden in him some place."

During the months when Clayton got to know Craig, she sensed that underneath his Southern courtliness and good cheer lay a great deal of anger. "He was more at peace," after quitting the Klan, according to her. This unlikely duo even traveled around the United States giving joint interviews on civil rights.

Craig was indeed complicated and troubled. Though he attended and led rallies in which crosses were burned, he claimed he was opposed to violence. "When I seen the men were kind of restless, I would always go out and promote some type of activity to let them get a lot of the steam off," he told Sims. "I think it helped on both sides because long as you got people organized that feels the same way, you got control of them and you can keep violence down."

That wasn't always the case with Craig. In 1960 blacks protested school segregation in Crawfordsville, Georgia, according to Sims. A black teenage boy attempted to board a school bus. According to her, news articles said Craig grabbed him, twisted his arm behind his back, and slammed him on the hood of a police car. All the while, white protestors shouted, "Kill him! Kill him!"

Craig admitted to Sims that he had run two bomb-making schools. In a 1970 interview, Craig said, "I trained most of my people for some of the most violent..." leaving his sentence unfinished.

The House Un-American Activities Committee said that he had previously attended such training sessions himself in October 1961. Craig was never convicted or accused of any violent crimes. Congress did hold him in contempt in 1966 when he refused to provide one of its committees with Klan records.

Craig's daughter Gail met with Clayton for a joint interview in 2011 for *Atlanta* magazine. "My grandmother—my father's mother—was in the Klan," she said. "She invited my mother to join the Klan. So my mother went into the Klan first, and then my father [in 1960]. It was all around the same time.

"I was five when he first told me. He brought me his robe, those green robes of the Grand Dragon, and he showed it to me.

He talked to me a little bit about the Klan, but the main thing was the secrets. I should never tell anyone." By the time, her father quit, Mayes was 18, and she hated the Klan.

For the rest of his life, Craig's heart wavered. In 1970 he helped found the Christian American Patriotic Society. Five years later, he led efforts to revive the KKK in Georgia.

But in 1984, he had a change of heart again. He left both groups and donated his robes and other artifacts to Emory University.

MORAL: Love conquers all.

Chapter 93

Ignatz Semmelweis

Clean Hands, Clean Conscience

This doctor rescued new mothers from
certain death, and his peers hated him.

*"When I look back upon the past, I can only dispel the
sadness which falls upon me by gazing into that happy future
when the infection will be banished."*

Imagine lying in a maternity ward bed in the throes of
labor in the Vienna General Hospital's First Obstetrical Clinic in
1847. Your doctor walks in, blood smeared on his smock. His
hands are filthy. He smells like an open grave.

Doctors in those days did not wash their hands. It took
too much time. Sinks and faucets were not in every room.
Besides, everyone knew disease was spread by mysterious
miasmas ("ill winds" in the air) or by a person's "humoural
imbalances."

What's more, doctors viewed themselves as sort of sacred
figures imbued with special healing powers. It would be utterly
inconceivable if they were causing illness, not curing it. How
preposterous. To suggest otherwise—particularly for a doctor to
do so—would have been an unspeakable insult.

That's exactly what Dr. Ignatz Semmelweis did. He figured
out the cause of hospital infection. He was courageous enough to
confront his peers. Sadly, he also was a genius at insulting other
physicians so severely that most refused to listen to him.

Semmelweis was the chief resident in his hospital's
obstetrics department. It was then regarded as a lesser medical
specialty. Most doctors aspired to be surgeons. It's possible that
because Semmelweis was Hungarian and Jewish, prejudice
blocked his entry into that field.

Begged on their knees

His hospital had two wards where babies were delivered. In one ward, midwives handled that responsibility. In the other ward, doctors were in charge. Semmelweis could not help but notice that the mortality rate among new mothers in his First Clinic was about 10 percent and less than four percent in the midwives' ward.

Pregnant women knew this, too. Admittance to each clinic was random, as they each admitted new patients on alternating days.

Viennese women knew which ward was safer. Semmelweis knew that some women had begged on their knees in the street to be admitted to the safer clinic. death rates were lower among women who gave birth at home than in his own ward.

"What protected those who delivered outside the clinic from these destructive unknown endemic influences?" he asked himself.

Death following childbirth was an ugly affair. Known then as puerperal fever, today it is called sepsis, a bacterial blood infection. Death was typically accompanied by a high fever, pus, and abscesses and occurred within about 24 hours of birth.

Semmelweis rigorously examined each clinic to figure out what could be causing the different death rates.

He ruled out many things. He determined that religious beliefs had nothing to do with the death rate. In his doctor-run clinic, women gave birth lying on their backs; in the midwives' clinic, however, they did so lying on their sides. Perhaps that was the reason, so Semmelweis had women in his clinic deliver babies on their sides. The death rate remained unaffected.

When a new mother died in the doctors' clinic, a priest walked through the ward ringing a bell. Maybe it so frightened the women, the tolling of the bell killed them. He told the priest not to ring a bell and to walk elsewhere. This made no difference either.

He went on vacation. Upon returning, he learned that one of his friends and colleagues Dr. Jakob Kolletschka had died after performing an autopsy on a woman who had died of the fever. While conducting the autopsy, he had cut his finger.

Now Semmelweis had it. In his clinic, doctors performed autopsies and went directly to delivery rooms without washing their hands. He concluded that doctors were unwittingly transporting germs or what he called "cadaverous particles" to patients. A "morbid poison" he called it.

He immediately instituted a policy wherein all doctors were wash their hands in a chlorinated lime solution. Today we would call it a dis-infectant, something that stops infections. He also insisted that all medical instruments be washed in this disinfectant, too.

The result? In two months, the death rate fell to two percent.

Peers urged Semmelweis to publish his findings. For unknown reasons, he declined to do so, and a friendly colleague published a paper summarizing his findings. It took him 13 years to publish the results of his research.

As insightful and courageous as Semmelweis was, he lacked insight about human relations. His bull-headed insistence on improved hygiene insulted other physicians. Worse, he offended the head of his hospital. As a result, Semmelweis was passed over for promotion.

A medical Nero

An angry Semmelweis returned to his native Budapest where he became head of obstetrics at a hospital there. History repeated itself, and he made a habit of haranguing its doctors and nurses, too.

To one colleague he said, you have been "a partner in this massacre." A second doctor got this tongue-lashing: "Should you...without having disproved my doctrine, continue to train your pupils [in ways contradicting my principles], I declare before God and the world that you are a murderer and the 'History of Childbed Fever' would not be unjust to you if it memorialized you as a medical Nero."

Finally, in 1861, Semmelweis published a paper under his own name. By then it was too late. He reputation was destroyed. He had also started behaving strangely. He drank heavily and was seen with prostitutes. His reputation was ruined.

Fearing for his sanity, his family and medical associates tricked him into visiting a mad house. They told him he should visit to learned about its new treatments. After arriving, he was forced into a straitjacket and tossed into a dark cell. He may also have been beaten by guards.

He died 14 days later. He was 47. The cause? Gangrene, possibly due to the assault he suffered. He died of sepsis, the disease he worked to prevent.

"When I look back upon the past, I can only dispel the sadness which falls upon me by gazing into that happy future when the infection will be banished," he once said, "The conviction that such a time must inevitably sooner or later arrive will cheer my dying hour."

Today Semmelweis is renowned by doctors around the globe as "the father of infection control" and "the savior of mothers."

The same year that Semmelweis died the Scottish surgeon Joseph Lister conducted his first experiments regarding antiseptic surgery. He ordered surgeons who reported to him to glove their hands and wash them in a disinfecting solution before and after surgery. "Without Semmelweis, my achievements would be nothing," Lister once said.

The truth is both men were latecomers to germ theory. As early the 16th century B.C., the ancient Israelites knew, as it is written in the Book of Numbers, that "He that toucheth the dead body of any man shall be unclean seven days....Whosoever toucheth the dead body of any man that is dead, and purifieth not himself, defileth the tabernacle of the Lord."

MORAL: Don't defile yourself.

Chapter 94

Frank Gehring

Saintly Coincidence

The priest was only doing his job, and that included
reuniting a girl with her mother thousands of miles away.

"Where else would I be?"

The battle of Guadalcanal marked the first decisive Allied
victory against the Japanese in World War II. For six-long grisly
months, the Japanese and American armies battered each other
to the bloody death on this jungle island in the southern
Solomons.

From August 1942 to February 1943, in the thick
underbrush at night, death could come at any moment. Men
leapt on each other like crazed animals. They beat each other to
death. They strangled each other.

"It was a darkness without time," said Marine Pfc. Robert
Leckie. "To the right and left of me rose up those terrible
formless things of my imagination.... I dared not close my eyes
lest the darkness crawl beneath my eyelids and suffocate me."

When the fighting at sea and on the land ended, the
Japanese had been roundly defeated. They had suffered
brutally—as many as 30,000 of their men lay dead. "Guadalcanal
is no longer merely a name of an island in Japanese military
history," said one Japanese commander. "It is the name of the
graveyard of the Japanese army."

Allied forces had been outnumbered by the Japanese at
sea and on the land, yet they won. "Before Guadalcanal, the
enemy advanced at his pleasure," said one American leader.
"After Guadalcanal, he retreated at ours."

Into the thick of this horror came a Brooklyn-born
Catholic priest, the Reverend Frederic Gehring. A Navy chaplain
and lieutenant, he accompanied the First Marine Division into

combat on Guadalcanal, landing there a few weeks after they made their beachhead. He would remain with them through six months of unspeakable fighting.

Endowed with the right stuff, Gehring was the first Navy chaplain to be awarded the Presidential Legion of Merit for conspicuous gallantry. His citation proclaimed that he was "brave under fire, cheerful in the face of discouragement, and tireless in his devotion to duty"

Good luck or grace

Good luck or the grace of God seemed to follow Father Gehring everywhere. In the early 1930s he successfully raised money for three years in the U.S. to help orphans in China. He then lived in China from 1933 to 1939 running several homes for children.

When Japanese planes attacked and strafed one of his orphanages on Christmas Day in 1938, others dove for cover. Instead, Gehring grabbed a huge American flag, ran outside, and waved it at the swooping fighters. (At that time America was a neutral country; Father Gehring figured that his orphanage should be immune from attack.)

To his delight, the fighters swung away, ending the assault. He presumed it was God's will (and good fortune) until someone suggested that perhaps the pilots left only because they had spent all their ammo.

Two days after Pearl Harbor, Father Gehring volunteered. On Guadalcanal, he astonished the GIs with his bravery. Fearless, he would go to the front and leap into fox holes, so he could be near soldiers. After all, that was where the need for his services would be the greatest.

"Padre, what are you doing here?" a shocked GI asked him.

"Where else would I be?" he replied.

Without a gun or any weapon, this priest made three highly dangerous expeditions through enemy-occupied areas. The reason? To evacuate trapped 27 missionaries by motorboat. The GIs felt lucky to keep him on their side of the battle.

When the Japanese blew up Gehring's chapel tent before Christmas 1942, he put up a new one, and 700 bone-weary GIs gathered there for Christmas Eve services.

There was a problem, though. No one knew how to play his beat-up hand organ.

Then Barney Ross stepped forward. He was Jewish and unfamiliar with Christmas carols, yet he mastered each one. The service concluded with Father Gehring accompanying him on the violin for a finale of "My Yiddishe Mama."

(Ross was the sole survivor of a patrol ambushed by Japanese soldiers. All the other GIs were either killed or wounded. Ross held off 24 attacking Japanese soldiers for 12 hours until help arrived.)

Father Gehring's greatest feat of courage came off the battlefield.

GIs found a six-year-old Chinese girl dying in a ditch. She was burning with malaria. That was the least of it. Japanese soldiers had carved her arms and legs with a sword or bayonet and left her to die. They had also fractured her skull, apparently with a rifle butt. (Its imprint was plain to see.)

Little Treasure

Navy doctors told Father Gehring her injuries were so grave she would die before dawn.

But Father Gehring knew illness, and he knew children. Most of all, he had faith. He wouldn't give up on her. Hour by hour and day by day she got better.

He gave her the name Pao Pei, which means "Little Treasure" in Chinese. When GIs complained that they couldn't pronounce that, they agreed to change her name to Patsy. (Even though Father Gehring spoke several Chinese dialects, Patsy responded to none of them.) He gave her the last name Li, which was the Chinese name he had chosen for himself before the war started.

When Patsy was well enough, the time came for Gehring to send her to an orphanage run by French nuns in the New Hebrides islands. By this time, however, Patsy had become attached to her savior. When he tried to put her on the airplane that would take her away, she wept and hugged him and begged to stay with him.

A *New York Times* reporter writing an article about Father Gehring witnessed this heart-wrenching farewell. He wrote a dispatch about the father's good works. He devoted some of the article to discussing how Gehring had saved the child and how emotional their parting was. The article said the girl's name was Patsy Lee, a name the priest chosen out of thin air.

A Chinese woman in New York City read the article and was astonished. She cut the story out of the newspaper and mailed it to her sister Ruth Li. She was a refugee from Japanese-occupied Singapore.

She forwarded the article because the name of the child in the story had the same name as her sister's six-year-old daughter—Patsy Li.

Ruth Li had lost her child when the Japanese torpedoed and sank their ship 4,000 miles from Guadalcanal.

Here is what happened: On February 13, 1942, as the Japanese were advancing on Singapore, Ruth and hundreds of other terrified residents of Singapore boarded the *S.S. Kuala* with her two children, along with hundreds of others trying the escape.

Ruth Li had her two children with her—one-year-old Lotie and six-year-old Patsy (or Pai-Ti Li whose name means 'white plum blossom.')

That morning Japanese dive bombers plunged towards the ship. Their bombs ripped into it. Amid explosions and fire, women and children rushed to the ship's railing to clamber down ropes to lifeboats.

Patsy screamed when she saw the last lifeboat pull away. Her mother told her to swim to a piece of wreckage and wait.

Then another explosion hammered the ship. The shock sent Ruth and Lotie flying into the ocean. When Ruth came to the surface, her baby was gone. So was Patsy. In shock, Ruth finally made it to a lifeboat and after a day later was rescued by the Japanese.

When she read the newspaper story, she became convinced that the Patsy on Guadalcanal was her Patsy. She began corresponding with Father Gehring.

When he got her letter, Gehring thought, "Merciful Father, help me! How can I tell this poor woman that the girl cannot possibly be her child?'

Nonetheless, he told her that miracles happen. He encouraged her to adopt the child. In 1946 Li visited the orphanage in the New Hebrides. Upon seeing the little girl, she instantly knew that she was her daughter. But Patsy didn't recognize her.

Then Ruth saw her daughter's smallpox vaccination scar. Surely that was proof. But the child also had a blemish, and her daughter had had no such mark. Then Patsy noticed a scar on her eyelid. It was identical to a scar her child had. The nuns were unconvinced.

Finally, Ruth gave Patsy a writing test. She had a sample of her earlier handwriting in which she had written all her capital E's backwards. When Patsy handed Ruth her new writing samples, sure enough, she wrote those new E's backwards, too,

Later, a survivor of the shipwreck said that he thought a little girl had saw been put on a freighter heading for Guadalcanal. In 1950, Patsy immigrated to the U.S. (soon followed by her mother) and became a nurse.

As for Father Gehring, the Padre of Guadalcanal, he contracted Dengue fever on the island and was evacuated in February 1943. He died at the age of 95 in 1998.

MORAL: Blossom where you are planted.

Chapter 95

Theodore Roosevelt

"If I've Got To, I've Got To."

The weakling turned he-man took a slug
in the chest and kept on talking.

"Do what you can, with what you have, where you are."

The poor thing had asthma. Little Teedie, as he was called, often had to sleep sitting up. Sometimes his father drove their carriage as fast as he could through the streets, so the onrushing wind would be forced into his tiny lungs.

His parents did everything possible. They tried to rule out household allergies. They took him to the mountains, to the beach, to the country, all in the hope that fresh air would help him.

They even had him smoke cigars. And they induced vomiting with syrup of ipecac. That's what some doctors said would help.

Nothing helped. (Perhaps avoiding church might have done the child good. One historian noted that most of Teedie's attacks came on Saturday nights and on Sundays.)

This pathetic child yearned for a robust life. He devoured adventure stories and tales of "manliness."

"I was nervous and timid," Theodore Roosevelt remembered. "Yet upon reading of the people I admired, ranging from the soldiers of Valley Forge to Morgan's riflemen, to the heroes of my favorite stories, and from hearing of the feats performed by my Southern forbears and kinfolk, and from knowing my father, I had a great admiration for men who were fearless and who could hold their own in the world and I had a great desire to be like them."

He loved wild animals. He wore frogs under his hat on the streetcar. His parents indulged him and let him have a snapping turtle. He kept it chained to the legs of a sink in the back hall. "How can I do the laundry?" groaned the maid.

Teedie also had a pet woodchuck, and it stank. "Either I leave, or the woodchuck does," the cook grumbled. Houseguests inspected water pitchers carefully before pouring, for fear he might be storing snakes in them.

One day after a severe asthma attack, the doctor told Teedie's father that he was "bright" and "precocious" and that "more exercise" would do him a world of good.

"I know you will do it."

With that wise counsel in mind, his father sat his son down and said, "Theodore, you have the mind but you have not the body, and without the help of the body the mind cannot go as far as it should. You must make your body. It is hard drudgery to make one's body, but I know you will do it."

"With a flash of white teeth," recalled a witness, young T.R. gave a grin and snarl of enthusiasm. He swore to his father, "I'll make my body!"

That he did. He took to lifting weights and working his chest muscles on the parallel bars. Progress was slow. It didn't help that he was also horribly nearsighted. When he went shooting one day with friends, he couldn't understand why they hit their targets when the fast flying birds were blurs to him.

"Soon afterwards, I got my first pair of spectacles, which literally opened an entirely new world to me," he wrote, "I had no idea how beautiful the world was until I got those spectacles."

At Harvard, Roosevelt rowed a one-man shell on the Charles River. He worked out in the gym. He loved boxing and was a runner-up in a college competition. (His habit of amateur zoo keeping continued. He kept lobsters, snakes, and a tortoise in his off-campus room.)

Given his penchant for all things wild and smelly, he considered becoming a scientist in the field of natural history. Instead he entered law school. Finding it maddening, he went into politics, announcing, "I intended to be one of the governing class."

Whirlwind would be the most apt word to describe Roosevelt's life. On his 22nd birthday, he married the beautiful socialite Alice Lee. A year later he was elected a New York State Assemblyman.

Four years later in 1884, Roosevelts courage would be severely tested.

A day after Alice gave birth to their first child, his mother died of typhoid fever in her bed at home. Eleven hours later Alice followed her to the grave, also at home, dying of Bright's Disease, a kidney disorder whose symptoms had been masked by her pregnancy.

"When my heart's dearest died, the light went from my life for ever," he wrote.

He was not one to sit in a dark room and mourn. He moved to Medora, North Dakota, and at the age of 26 became a rancher and deputy sheriff. He chased down outlaws who stole his boat. After nabbing them, he decided against hanging them. While a cowboy went for help, he stood guard over them for 40 hours without sleep.

In the Bighorn Mountains, he and a fellow hunter saw grizzly tracks. "It gave me rather an eerie feeling in the silent, lonely woods, to see for the first time the unmistakable proofs that I was in the home of the mighty lord of the wilderness."

There, suddenly, was the bear 10 feet in front of them. It stood more than nine feet tall and weighed 1,200 pounds.

"Then he saw us, and dropped down again on all fours the shaggy hair on his neck and shoulders seeming to bristle as he turned toward us," Roosevelt wrote. In an instant, he raised his rifle, and looking into the beast's "small, glittering evil eyes," he pulled the trigger.

Rearing back, "the huge beast fell over on his side in the death throes, the ball having gone into his brain, striking fairly between the eyes as if the distance had been measured by a carpenter's rule."

Roosevelt also faced down the most dangerous animal of all—the human animal. As he would later recount, "It was late in the evening when I reached the place [a hotel bar in present day Wibaux, Montana]. I heard one or two shots in the bar-room as I came up, and I disliked going in. But it was a cold night, and there was nowhere else to go.

"A shabby individual in a broad hat with a cocked gun in each hand was walking up and down the floor talking with strident profanity. He had evidently been shooting at the clock, which had two or three holes in its face."

Seeing Roosevelt's glasses, the drunk said, "Four eyes is going to treat!"

Roosevelt smiled, thinking the drunk's mood would pass, and he took a seat. Then the man leaned over Roosevelt with "a gun in each hand."

Pretending to be intimidated, Roosevelt said, " 'Well, if I've got to, I've got to.' "

Roosevelt, the boxer, went into action. "As I rose, I struck quick and hard with my right just to one side of the point of his jaw, hitting with my left as I straightened out and then again with my right."

The drunk collapsed, his guns accidentally firing as he went down. No one was hurt, and the bully hopped a freight train out of town the next morning.

Recalling his days out west as a rancher, he said, "We led a free and hardy life with horse and rifle...We knew toil and hardship and hunger and thirst; and we saw men die violent deaths as they worked among the horses and cattle, or fought in evil feuds with one another, but we felt the beat of hardy life in our veins, and ours was the glory of work and the joy of living."

A man in a hurry, he ran for mayor of New York City a year later, married again the year after that, and later became a New York City police commissioner and then Assistant Secretary of the U.S. Navy.

"The great day"

At age 39, he earned his nickname as a "Rough Rider," as Colonel of the First U.S. Volunteer Cavalry in the Spanish-American War. On Kettle Hill in Cuba, he was the only man on horseback. He rode from position to position, defying whizzing bullets, urging his troops up the hill. When the shooting (and the war) stopped, the Spanish empire was defeated. "The great day of my life," he called it.

He served two successful terms as president. After a four-year hiatus, he left the Republican Party and ran for president in 1912 in his nearly formed Bull Moose party

At a stop in Milwaukee before delivering a speech, a deranged saloonkeeper shot him in the chest at close range. The bullet's impact rocked Roosevelt. But the slug slowed substantially, passing through his steel eyeglasses case and a 50-page speech folded in his breast pocket. Nonetheless, it entered Roosevelt's chest.

After collecting himself, he noticed he was not coughing blood. As a hunter, he knew that if the bullet had hit his heart, he would have been doing so and would soon be dead. Realizing he only had a flesh wound, Roosevelt ignored pleas to rush him to the hospital.

Instead, he delivered his remarks, speaking for 90 minutes, blood oozing onto his shirt. He began his address by saying, "Ladies and gentlemen, I don't know whether you fully understand that I have just been shot, but it takes more than that to kill a Bull Moose."

MORAL: Give it your best shot.

Chapter 96

Roger Ebert

Thumbs Up

This critic smiled at the most painful tragedy.

"We must try to contribute joy to the world."

For a generation of moviegoers, film critic Roger Ebert of *The Chicago Sun-Times* was famous for talking about movies. Then cancer took away his ability to speak (and to eat and drink through his mouth). His courage to continue working inspired his fans as though he were one of the film heroes he wrote about.

He was arguably the nation's best known and most respected film critic. For 24 years, Ebert and Gene Siskel, the reviewer for the competing *Chicago Tribune*, playfully argued about new films on their half-hour TV show *Siskel and Ebert at the Movies*. They became famous for their "thumbs up" or "thumbs down" way of voting, so much so that they had the expression "Two Thumbs Up" copyrighted.

Ebert lived and breathed movies. He wrote 15 books, most of which were film criticism, and in 1975 he became the first movie reviewer to win a Pulitzer Prize.

From 1967 to 2013, he saw about 500 films a year and reviewed about half of them. Out of those more than 20,000 or so movies, his top 10 favorites were *2001: A Space Odyssey; Aguirre, the Wrath of God; Apocalypse Now; Citizen Kane; La Dolce Vita; The General; Raging Bull; Tokyo Story; The Tree of Life;* and *Vertigo*.

In 1999, Siskel died suddenly of a brain tumor. Ebert soldiered on with other TV partners. Then in 2002 he had surgery to remove his cancerous thyroid gland. The next year he lost part of his salivary glands to cancer.

Then in 2006 cancer attacked his jaw, and part of it was removed. Two weeks later as he was packing to leave the hospital, his carotid artery, weakened by cancer and surgery, burst. He was rushed back into the operating room. Most of the rest of his jaw had to be removed.

Having lost the ability to eat or drink, he was fed a special paste through a tube in his stomach. Ebert constantly fantasized about the taste of food—everything from orange soda and Good & Plenty to an entire meal at Steak & Shake.

"What I miss [most about not being able to eat] is the society," he wrote. "Meals are when we most easily meet with friends and family. They're the first way we experience places far from home. Where we sit to regard the passing parade. How we learn indirectly of other cultures. When we feel good together."

Through all of his trials, Ebert did everything he could to continue to write. He lost himself in his work. "When I am writing," he said, "My problems become invisible, and I am the same person I always was."

Surgeons performed three additional surgeries to try to reconstruct his jaw. None succeeded. The cancer was too powerful. It was one thing after another. It began eating away at his right shoulder. He broke his hip. He passed away in 2013. His last words to the public were, "I'll see you at the movies."

Near the end of his life Ebert said, "What I am grateful for is the gift of intelligence, and for life, love, wonder, and laughter....I believe that if, at the end of it all, according to our abilities, we have done something to make others a little happier, and something to make ourselves a little happier, that is about the best we can do....We must try to contribute joy to the world. This is true no matter what our problems, our health, our circumstances. We must try."

One of Ebert's heroes was fellow Chicago writer Studs Terkel who penned best-selling oral histories of Harry Truman and everyday working people. "The lesson Studs taught me is that your life is over when you stop living it."

Ebert never stopped living his life.

MORAL: Real heroes are in real life.

Davy Crockett

What a Crock!

This backwoods politician fought for
what was right—in Congress and in war.

"Be always sure you're right—then go ahead!"

French scholar Alexis de Tocqueville visited America in the 1830s. To this day, he is renowned for his shrewd insights into the American character. But he got at least one thing wrong. He was horrified to learn that western Tennessee voters had sent to Congress "an individual named David Crockett, who has no education, can read with difficulty, has no property, no fixed residence, but passes his life hunting, selling his game to live, and dwelling continuously in the woods."

Even today, that sort of fellow might have more appeal to some Americans than most current Congressmen. Americans have long had a fondness for rough-hewn tough guys with true grit. There's no better example of such a man than the legendary Davy Crockett, immortalized forever by Walt Disney's TV miniseries (which later became a hit movie). Its title song crowned Davy "the King of the Wild Frontier."

Crockett was a true American jack-of-all-trades and master of all. He was a formidable hunter possessing a deadly aim, a never-say-die pioneer farmer, a husband and father, an entrepreneur, a soldier, but, most of all, a politician. It's surprising to learn that he spent most of his adult life in the Tennessee legislature and in Congress and was even a potential presidential candidate. He was a soldier fewer than six months.

Born almost exactly a decade after the signing of the Declaration of Independence, Crockett grew up in near poverty on the frontier in and around present-day Greeneville,

Tennessee, in the eastern part of the state. His was his parents' fifth son in six years.

The Disney song says he was "born'd on a mountaintop in Tennessee,/Greenest state in the Land of the Free." Sadly, there are no mountains in Greeneville, though the Volunteer State is acclaimed for its natural beauty.

The song goes on to say he was "raised in the woods so's he knew ev'ry tree,/Kilt him a b'ar when he was only three." While Crockett was a master scout, nothing in the historical record indicates the age at which he first took down a bear.

Hickory switch

He did grow up fast. At the age of 12, he became a cowboy. His father hired him out to accompany a rancher herding cattle on a 400-mile odyssey. He had only a few months of schooling, and he didn't enjoy it. On one occasion when he dawdled on the way to school, his father chased him there, wielding a hickory switch. At age 14, he made another 400-mile trip, this time to Baltimore, also accompanying cattle.

While still in his teens, he moved away from home, renting himself out as a hired farm hand. He swiftly married. By the time he had two children, he concluded he was "better at increasing my family than my fortune."

Crockett was always on the move—and always in a westerly direction. By 1812, he located his family in southeastern Tennessee near Lynchburg. Indian tribes there and throughout the southeast rose up against settlers, massacring nearly 500 settlers who had taken refuge in a fort. (A hundred of the victims were children.)

Along with other farmers, Crockett volunteered to fight. He served under an officer who reported to General Andrew Jackson. Serving as a scout, Crockett located the Indian war party's whereabouts, but his account was ignored because he wasn't an officer. "I was no great man, but just a poor soldier," he recalled.

When the battle finally came, Crockett and other soldiers massacred nearly 50 Indians who refused to surrender and had taken refuge in a house. (There was no love lost between settlers and Indians; Indians butchered Crockett's grandparents in 1777.) When new volunteers arrived, Crockett went back to his wife and family, missing the decisive battle in which Jackson put down the uprising.

"This closed my career as a warrior," he wrote. "And I am glad of it, for I like life now a heap better than I did then, and I am glad all over that I lived to see these times, which I should not have done if I had keep fooling along in war and got used up at it."

His first wife died of a sudden illness leaving him with five children. As was the custom, Crockett promptly remarried and moved further west to the Lawrenceburg, Tennessee, area, where he was appointed a magistrate to help bring law and order to the frontier.

"I gave my decisions," he said, "on the principles of common justice and honesty between man and man, and relied on natural born sense, and not on law [and] learning to guide me; for I had never read a page in a law book in my life."

Soon enough his good-humored personality inspired his neighbors to ask him to run for the state legislature. He did so saying he had "never read even a newspaper in my life, or any thing else on the subject."

Strongly built, Crockett had a robust head of black hair, an easy smile, a gift of storytelling, and an earnest friendly character. One newspaper reported that he was "just such a one as you would desire to meet with, if any accident or misfortune had happened to you on the highway."

As was the custom in the day, the candidates traveled together from one village to another, giving speeches back to back. On one occasion, when Crockett's opponent went to speak, he found that Crockett had already invited voters to get drunk (another custom of the day), thus robbing him of his audience. Crockett won the election.

Later, when running for Congress, he heard his opponent's speech so many times that he memorized it. When the candidates came to the next town, Crockett spoke first, delivered the man's oration for him, leaving him dumbfounded and speechless when his turn to speak came.

Neck or nothing

During those days, Crockett still lived the life of a frontier farmer and business man. He had a scheme to make barrel staves and float them down the Mississippi to sell. When his riverboat sank, he became trapped and had to be yanked to safety through the porthole. "Neck or nothing, come out or sink!" he said.

In a day when a man's ability to hunt meant the difference between life and starvation for his family, Crockett was fearless.

One time in west Tennessee, his dogs treed a bear. After shooting it, the bear fell, landing amid the howling hounds. Then the lot of them dropped into a crevasse created by the colossal New Madrid earthquakes of 1811 and 1812. (The shocks ranged from 7.4 to 7.9 on the Richter scale. They were so titanic the Mississippi ran backward, and the ground sank creating the 13,000-acre Reelfoot Lake.) Crockett leapt into the tussle. While the bear was battling the dogs, he plunged his blade into its heart, killing it.

That's the way he approached politics, too. "Independent and fearless" is how one Tennessee political opponent described him. Henry Clay, Jackson's prime rival, said Crockett was "the only man that I know now in Tennessee that could openly oppose Genl. Jackson in his own district and get elected to congress."

In Washington, Crockett became known for three things. First, he steadfastly supported his frontier constituents. He once said both cynically and in jest, "We should occasionally legislate for the poor." On another occasion, he remarked, "The children of my people never saw the inside of a college in their lives, and never are likely to do so."

Second, he stood up for what was right, even though it sometimes ran contrary to what most of his constituents would have preferred. He opposed President Jackson's forced removal of peaceful Indian tribes from southeastern states, thinking it inhumane. This from a man who years earlier had given no quarter to warring Indians.

Most of all, Crockett became famed in Congress for his opposition to Jackson, a Democrat, who he saw as favoring moneyed Eastern interests over those of struggling western settlers. Thus, he became a favorite of the Whig party. He said he'd rather be "politically dead than hypocritically immortalized" by acting as a lap dog to his fellow Tennessean.

After being defeated for re-election, Crockett found himself in the enviable position of being idolized in the theatre. He was America's first media superstar. In 1831, a popular play about the fictional *Nimrod Wildfire* told tales of a backwoods military hero running for office. Lightning struck again in 1833 when he became the centerpiece of a book of mostly tall tales titled *Sketches and Eccentricities of Colonel David Crockett of West Tennessee.*

Offended that both the book and the play made him look like a bumpkin (and that he profited from neither) he went on a speaking tour to cash in on his fame. No less an authority than *The New York Sun* said he was "a gentleman, his speech flashing with wit, but never vulgar or buffoonish." He didn't go about in society wearing a coon skin cap but instead toured the northeast "wearing fashionably cut pantaloons and a loose calico hunting shirt, ruffled around the collar."

Crockett got his own word out in 1834 with his book *A Narrative of the Life of David Crockett of the State of Tennessee.* A best seller, it flew off store shelves. He then went on a 19-city book tour organized and paid for by the Whig Party—It wanted him to run for president and was testing his appeal.

In Jersey City, he proved his aim was true. At a shooting contest, firing a rifle he'd never held before, he hit a target only two inches off center at a range of 100 yards. Then at 40 yards, he put a bullet through a quarter.

Ultimately, the Whig party lost interest in Crockett. During his time in Congress, he was unable to pass a single bill. All he was known for was his adamant opposition to anything Jackson favored.

Tired of politics, Crockett headed to Texas. It wasn't necessarily to fight. It was to scout the territory with an eye on relocating his family. "I...have enrolled my name as a volunteer," he said. "I am in hopes of making a fortune yet for myself and family bad as my prospect has been."

At the same time, the Mexican army attacked American settlers. Even though Mexico had opened its northern territory to American pioneers in 1821, tensions had grown between the newcomers and the government.

Crockett heard that 150 of his armed countrymen were trapped in a 90-year-old mission in San Antonio, the Alamo. He naturally wanted to help. His feud with Jackson had something to do with it. The Texas settlers were divided between Whigs and Democrats. Those following Jackson had been ordered to withdraw by their leader Sam Houston, while others following Col. William Travis chose to stay and fight.

Surrounded and hopelessly outnumbered, the defenders were massacred on March 5, 1836. The Mexican commander Santa Anna had told his troops in writing, "In this war you know there are no prisoners."

How did Crockett die? The most reliable account says that true to his nature, Crockett died fighting. Eualia Yorba, a woman who had previously met him, entered the Alamo with a priest after the battle. "He lay dead by the side of a dying man, whose bloody-and powder-stained face I was washing," she said. "His coat and rough woolen shirt were soaked with blood so that the original color was hidden, for the eccentric hero must have died of some ball in the chest or a bayonet thrust."

Davy Crockett went to his reward at age 49. "His land is biggest and his land is best,/From grassy plains to the mountain crest," goes the Disney song. "He's ahead of us all meeting the test,/Following the legend into the West."

MORAL: Die fighting.

Chapter 98

Buzz Aldrin

Buzzing Around

He went to the Moon only to come home to hell.

"We have the universe at our fingertips."

The second person to do something never gets as much attention as the first person. The example-to-end-all-examples of that would be Buzz Aldrin, the Lunar Module Pilot on Apollo 11, the second man to walk on the Moon. His courage is equal to that of Neil Armstrong.

Born Edwin Eugene Aldrin Jr., he got his nickname Buzz not from his flying exploits but because one of his young sisters could only pronounce the word "brother" as "buzzer." His name actually is Buzz. He had it legally changed in 1988. (Interestingly, the maiden name of Aldrin's mother is Moon.)

And Aldrin knew how to fly. After graduating third in his class at West Point in 1951, he was commissioned in the Air Force and flew 66 combat missions in Korea where he shot down two MiG-15 fighters.

Besides being a nerves-of-steel flier, Aldrin also knew a little bit about the science of spaceflight and orbital docking maneuvers. He earned his PhD from MIT in 1963. His thesis topic? *Line-of-Sight Guidance Techniques for Manned Orbital Rendezvous.*

A rather important switch

He was America's best, a fitting partner to stand beside Armstrong as they descended to the Moon's surface on July 20, 1969. The Lunar Module (LM, formerly called the LEM, Lunar Excursion Module) was stripped to the bones to keep its weight light for liftoff.

There were no seats. The astronauts slept in hammocks. Its walls were not much thicker than aluminum foil, and there were no covers on their circuit breakers.

As a consequence of this weight-saving design, one circuit breaker switch snapped off when Armstrong and Aldrin dressed or undressed. Aldrin noticed it on the floor when he was undressing after the Moon walk. He had to wedge it back in place with the plastic cap of a felt-tip pen. It was a rather important switch. It was the circuit breaker for the ascent engine. Had it not worked or gone missing, they would have been stranded.

After detaching from the Command Module, the LM descended from its orbit eight miles above the Moon.

"If you read, you are go for powered descent," said astronaut Charlie Duke in Houston. He was serving as Capcom, the Capsule Communicator.

Five minutes into the descent an alarm flashed.

"Program alarm," Armstrong radioed Houston. "It's a twelve-o-two," he said referring to the numbers on the screen.

Neither Aldrin or Armstrong had seen this alarm during their training sessions.

However, the Apollo 12 astronauts had been given this alarm during a simulation. When they saw it, they aborted their 'flight.' "You should not have aborted," the trainers told the crew.

The alarm meant that the computer was being overloaded with data. Aldrin had left on the LM's rendezvous radar on as a safety precaution in case he and Armstrong had to abort the flight. Nonetheless, their Apollo Guidance Computer (AGC) was still functioning perfectly. It had been designed to be crash-proof and to focus its computing activities on the highest priority tasks.

Though Apollo's computers have been derided as primitive, they represented a giant leap, so to speak, in computing technology. Engineers had fit what once required a room into a container the size of a briefcase, and this was the first time computers had performed real-time navigational problem-solving. Ten years would pass before the technology in the AGCs would be used in "real world" applications in computers like the Apple II desktop.

Somehow Armstrong and Aldrin went through years of training—and the Apollo 12 snafu—without ever knowing what a "1202" alarm was.

By the time this crisis was averted, the LM had dropped to 750 feet above the Moon, its engine controlling its gradual descent.

NASA had carefully picked the landing site. Photos showed it to be free of craters and large rocks. This proved not to be the case.

"Pretty rocky area," Armstrong radioed.

"Six hundred, down at 19," he added, meaning that the LM was now only 200 yards above the surface and descending at 19 feet-per-second.

At this point, Armstrong said, "I'm going to..." and took control of the LM away from the computer and began to fly it manually.

"I've got a good spot."

"Okay," said Aldrin. "Four hundred feet. Down at nine. Fifty-eight forward." That meant that instead of descending vertically, Armstrong was flying the LM forward at 58 feet per second, going 40 miles an hour, shooting across the lunar surface like a helicopter.

"Three hundred," said Aldrin.

"Okay, how's the fuel?" Armstrong replied.

"Eight percent."

At 200 feet above the surface, Armstrong said, "I've got a good spot."

The astronauts now had only 94 seconds of fuel left. If the LM was higher than 70 feet above the surface with only 20 seconds of fuel remaining, they would have had to abort. They would not have had enough fuel to make a safe landing and would have come down too hard and crashed.

If they aborted at 70 feet, they would have jettisoned the lower half of the LM (which was designed to remain on the Moon's surface) and then fire the rocket on the top half of the LEM, shooting them back into orbit.

"Sixty seconds," warned Houston, telling the astronauts they had one minute to get to 50 feet above a landing site.

"Sixty feet, down two and a half," said Armstrong.

"Two forward," said Aldrin. "Forty feet....Picking up some dust."

If the LEM ran out of fuel now, it would crash before the ascent engine could gain enough thrust to hurl it to safety.

"Four forward," said Aldrin. "Drifting to the right a little."

"Thirty seconds," said Duke.

At about that moment, a vertical probe jutting from the bottom of one of the LM's four footpads touched the surface.

"Contact light," said Aldrin, and Armstrong settled the LM to a perfect landing.

"Shutdown," said Armstrong.

"Okay, engine stopped," replied Aldrin.

They had landed with less than 20 seconds of fuel remaining.

"We copy you down, Eagle."

"Houston, Tranquility Base here. The Eagle has landed," said Armstrong

"Tranquility, we copy you on the ground. You got a bunch of guys about to turn blue. We're breathing again. Thanks a lot."

"Thank you," Aldrin replied.

One landing danger remained. As the astronauts completed a post-landing checklist, Houston noticed that pressure was abnormally high—and rising—in one of the descent fuel tanks. The remaining fuel should have been venting out. It wasn't.

"Tranquility, Houston," said Duke. "We have an indication that we've frozen up the descent-fuel helium heat exchanger— and with some fuel trapped in the line between there and the valves...And the pressure we're looking at is increasing there. Over."

"We were ready to leave if we had to," Armstrong later said, "And we were listening carefully to their instructions."

Then the gauge read normal again, and no action was required.

Everyone knows what Armstrong said when he set foot on the Moon. What did Aldrin say? "Beautiful view."

After returning to Earth, Aldrin struggled with depression, alcoholism, and divorce. "Having been to the Moon, I plummeted into my own personal hell on Earth," he wrote in his autobiography.

Aldrin conquered his demons, and at age 87 remained a tireless advocate of space travel. Says Aldrin: "I believe we have the universe at our fingertips."

MORAL: Trust your internal guidance system.

Chapter 99

Michelangelo

Mr. Renaissance

He worked in pain to paint the most beautiful art.

*"The greatest danger for most of us is not
that our aim is too high, and we miss it,
but that it is too low, and we reach it."*

Michelangelo di Lodovico Buonarroti Simoni never gave up. Through pain, disease, hardship, and possibly mental illness, he made art. His tenacity and vision won him the nickname Il Divino, the Divine One. A poet, sculptor, painter, and architect, along with DaVinci, he was *the* Renaissance Man par excellence.

His mother died when he was only six. When he was a boy, his banker father did not want him to become an artist. To him, it was no different than being a common laborer. After all, artists also worked with their hands. To dissuade his son (and because he refused to do his schoolwork), his father hit him when he caught him drawing.

No matter how many times his father struck him, the boy kept at it. Eventually, when he was 13, his father apprenticed him to a painter. A year after that his talent was such that when Florence's ruler Lorenzo di Medici asked the painter to send him his best pupils, away went the young Michelangelo.

Beauty radiates throughf his art, especially his sculptures David and the Pieta which he completed before he was 30. There may be no finer example of handsomeness in all of the history of sculpture than the 17-foot-tall marble David.

"Such a punch"

Yet Michelangelo was tormented by his own ugliness. When he was 14, another art student Pietro Torrigiano punched him in the face, breaking his nose. It may have been because Torrigiano was jealous of Michelangelo's skill or because the Divine One had a devilish habit of insulting other students.

"Clenching my fist, I gave him such a punch on the nose that I felt the bone and cartilage smush like a biscuit," said Torrigiano. "He will carry my mark with him until he dies." (Torrigiano was banished. He became a soldier and later died in a Spanish dungeon.)

As for Michelangelo, his nose was flattened for life, and he felt his looks were freakish. "I see myself so ugly," he wrote in a poem. "My face has the shape that causes fright."

He had what today people would call poor self-esteem. Very poor. "His domestic habits were incredibly squalid," his biographer wrote. (Such was Michelangelo's fame that he was the first artist who ever had a biography written about him while he was alive.)

He wore his clothes to bed, sometimes not even taking off his booth. He stank. He once he kept his boots on for months, and when he finally took them off, his skin came off with them—like a snake's, his assistant remembered. His behaviors were so extreme that some scholars think he suffered from autism or obsessive-compulsive disorder. If a conversation bored him or he didn't know what to say, he would walk away.

Since he could not make his face and body more pleasing perhaps that motivated him to paint and sculpt human figures who were the quintessence of beauty.

He worked in agony. The ceiling of the Sistine Chapel measures 128 feet by 45 feet and is 65 feet from the floor. It took Michelangelo four years to paint it, and he painted it alone, after firing assistant painters who he deemed incompetent.

The great Biblical figures on the ceiling twist and strain in all manner of ways, perhaps reflecting Michelangelo's miseries at work. In another poem he wrote, "My beard toward Heaven, I feel the back of my brain/Upon my neck, I grow the breast of a Harpy."   Paint fell in his face. (Despite what most people believe, he painted standing, not lying down.) The poem continues, "My brush, above my face continually,/Makes it a splendid floor by dripping down." For months after completing the ceiling, he couldn't see well when he looked down.

Throughout his adult life he suffered from gout and kidney stones, both of which may have caused depression and insomnia which plagued him.

Nothing would keep him from his work, such was his obsession with his art. He would continue to sculpt even at night. He did this by fashioning a hat made of thick paper. In the center of the hat he would fix a candle made of goat tallow. It cast enough light to let him work—and keep his hands free. To create.

MORAL: Find your ceiling and paint it.

Chapter 100

Margaret Moncrieffe

Runaway to War

This gutsy girl crossed enemy lines, desperately
searching for her father—a British officer.

"...Made it their study to show me every mark of regard."

Impetuous might be a good word to describe Margaret
Moncrieffe. A 14-year-old runaway, she dined with George
Washington on the eve of the British invasion of New York City
in 1776.

Washington did not attend the Continental Congress in
Philadelphia that year—and therefore did not sign the
Declaration of Independence—because as commander of the
continental army , he had taken residence in Manhattan,
spending his days not with the complexities of political
philosophy but struggling with a far more tangible and fearful
problem—how to defend the island from a British armada that
had filled New York City's harbor in preparation for a
Normandy-style landing of thousands of battle-hardened
soldiers.

Washington's task was far from promising. On July
12—only three days after he ordered the Declaration read aloud
to his troops—two British warships left the main body of ships
arrayed at anchor. Together they sailed up the Hudson River.
One of the vessels had 40 guns, the other 20. Together, as they
glided by unscathed, they pounded the city with barrages of
cannon fire, smashing buildings and sending cannonballs
whizzing down Manhattan's side streets causing people to flee in
terror.

That the feisty Miss Margaret would find herself at
dinner with Washington is all the more remarkable because she
was the daughter of Major Thomas Moncrieffe of the British

Army, and she desperately wanted to be at his side.

Born in Nova Scotia in 1762, she was a dark-haired beauty. Her "eyes [were] full of witchery," people said. When she was three, her mother died. For a time, she came under the protection of General Gage who commanded all the King's armies on the continent. She even lived in his home. But her father decreed that she and her brother should be educated at Miss Beard's boarding school in Dublin, so off she went across the Atlantic, still only three years old.

The next time she saw her father she was eight, and he had a new wife. She hailed from one of New York City's most prestigious families, the Jays. "I did not like my new mother," Margaret later said. She would not see either parent for another two years, when her father had her shipped to New York City where he was stationed.

"The heart-cheering smile"

Life was sweet for the next two years, as her father was often at home, and she could "bask in the heart-cheering smile of paternal fondness." When her stepmother died, her father remarried six months later as was often the custom.

Unfortunately for Margaret, when her father went away, she had to live in the home of her first stepmother's brother Frederick Jay. He supported the Revolution. This was intolerable to a teenage girl who adored her soldier father and all the British Empire stood for. She wrote that she could not abide being "forced to hear my nearest and dearest relations continually traduced."

With the invasion looming, the Jay family fled Manhattan to the comparative safety of Elizabethton, New Jersey, and then to another village a further 10 miles inland. Margaret could stand the patriot taunts and the separation from her father no more, and when the family was at church, she stole a horse and fled back to Elizabethton where she stayed with family friends.

Desperate to cross back over the river to be closer to her father, she wrote Israel Putnam, a general in the colonial army. She knew that he and her father had been friends years before when they were both loyal to the King.

At about the same time, the British commander Lord Howe wanted to engage Washington in peace talks. A small British vessel under a white flag came to shore. Its officer found Washington's aide Colonel Henry Knox waiting, and he said, "I have a letter, sir, from Lord Howe to Mr. Washington."

"Sir, we have no such person in our army with that address," Knox replied, refusing to accept correspondence unless the British acknowledged Washington's rank, thus implying at least tacit recognition of the legitimacy of his cause.

The next day a second British boat came to shore, also under a white flag. This time the letter was addressed to "George Washington, Esq." Again, Knox refused to touch it.

On the third day, the boat, again under a white flag, came to shore, and this time the letter was addressed, not to Washington, but to the astonishment of the colonial officers, its recipient was someone they had never heard of— "Miss Margaret Moncrieffe."

While preparing for battle, Major Moncrieffe had received word from the Jay family that his daughter had run off. He was desperate to see to her safety and had written the colonials inquiring as to her whereabouts.

Both letters landed on Putnam's desk at nearly the same time, and he wrote Margaret saying that although he and her father were on opposing sides, he would "with pleasure, do any kind office in my power for him or any of his connexions."

A day later, Margaret was taken to 1 Broadway, Putnam's home which also served as the headquarters of the continental army.

The Putnam family gave her a spare bedroom, and the next day an unusually tall man with a most dignified bearing and his plump and cheerful wife came to visit—George and Martha Washington.

Margaret wanted dearly to proclaim her loyalty to King George III, but she thought the better of it, and she later wrote that the Washingtons "made it their study to show me every mark of regard."

A few days later she found herself invited to a formal dinner hosted by General Washington—this in the midst of the pending invasion. Someone proclaimed a toast to the Continental Congress. Amid much clinking of glasses, Washington noticed that Margaret had not lifted her glass. He said to her, "Miss Moncrieffe, you don't drink your wine."

Margaret, true to her father and his country, declared "General Howe is the toast."

This did not go over well. There was much fussing. Stern reproachful stares were likely directed at her until General Putnam said to Washington "everything said or done by such a child ought rather to amuse than affront you." Washington turned again to Margaret and said, "Well, Miss, I will overlook your indiscretion on condition that you drink my health, or General Putnam's, the first time you dine at Sir William Howe's table, on the other side of the water."

Thus, the future president proved his leadership skills, averting a minor diplomatic crisis with his Loyalist teenage guest.

Fearing that she was a spy, the Americans moved her to another home, and there she met and fell prey to that most terrible of teenage afflictions—the romantic crush. The object of her adoration? The ever-so-dashing twenty-one-year old Colonel Aaron Burr.

"To him I plighted my virgin vow," she later recalled, calling him "the Conqueror of my soul." Destiny tore them apart, and on August 7 she a delegation led by Colonel Knox rowed her over to Admiral Howe's flagship, the *Eagle*.

That evening she was invited to yet another formal dinner, this one hosted by General William Howe, the brother of Admiral Richard Howe. As many as 50 of the most prominent British military leaders and their wives were there. To honor her dramatic arrival, her hosts asked Margaret to make a toast.

True to her word, she raised her glass and asked everyone to toast to General Putnam's health. As before, this startled and offended all present, but General Howe made light of her remarks. Knowing that Putnam was elderly and portly, to everyone's amusement, he said, "If he be the lady's sweetheart, I can have no objection to drink his health."

What lay in store

If this were a Hollywood story, Margaret would have somehow remained united with her father through military campaigns, dressing his wounds, only to later be reunited with the charming Col. Burr, and they would marry, have children, and through many trials live to old age together on a technicolor farm.

This is not what lay in store for Margaret Moncrieffe, as Russell Shorto tells the tale in his book *Revolution Song*. Her father, not knowing what to do with her and following the practice of the times, arranged for her to be married to John Coghlan, a soldier whom she had briefly met at a dance. She refused. To help her see the error of her teenage ways, he locked her in her bedroom.

At last, against her wishes, she married Coghlan, and he went away to fight. A year later he returned, saying that he had sold his commission, was leaving the army, and they would return to England via Ireland.

Margaret was the only woman on a troop ship carrying 600 or 700 men. Coghlan a drunken lout. The captain threatened to toss him in the brig if he could treat his wife better, such were the ravings that came from their tiny cabin.

When she learned that her husband, like her father, also planned to imprison her until she reformed, she ran off into the Irish countryside. Ultimately, she found her way to London, but her behavior had become something of a scandal. Soon she found General Gage, the former commander of British forces in North America, at her door. He told her that it had been decided that she would be shipped to a French convent where she would live for three years.

With the aid of Lord Clinton, a distant friend in whose home she had briefly lived, she talked her way out of the nunnery and returned to London. She then received a letter from the general's wife saying that her father had disowned her. He would no longer pay her expenses, and she was out of his will.

Resourceful—and beautiful—she became the mistress of a prominent politician. She bore his child. Then he left her. She took up with an aristocrat who squired her around Europe. When that dalliance ended, she became the lover of yet another society gent. He also abandoned her, leaving her with another child who died shortly after birth.

She had two children with her next lover, an army captain. For a time, she thought he would propose to her, but, no, he advised her that he was engaged to wed an aristocratic lady and that, of course, his bride would raise their two children.

Another lover followed as did massive debts. Facing debtors' prison, to evade her creditors, she placed her own obituary in the newspaper and fled to Paris. The year was inauspicious—1787, just before the French Revolution. Again, her bills mounted. She was put in a French debtor's prison— along with her two-year-old son. And she was seven months pregnant.

Returning to England, she was locked in debtor's prison in London. There she gave birth, the delivery aided by a young inexperienced doctor. She and her infant lay naked for two days before being cared for.

Upon being released, she learned her father had passed away. Now more creditors pursued her, thinking she had an inheritance. Her beauty long gone, she knew only one way to make enough money to pay her bills—She wrote a tell-all autobiography, naming names, and sharing unseemly details.

Appearing in 1794, it was titled *Memoirs of Mrs. Coghlan*, and it was a hit. However, she did not sell enough copies to pay her bills, and in 1797, she was again imprisoned. Six years later, she was freed. And still in debt. She wrote various luminaries, including the King, seeking aid. None was given.

Again, she was imprisoned. After that, nothing is known of her and her fate.

MORAL: Let prudence temper courage.

Chapter 101

Alfred Wegener

Jigsaw Man

He said the earth moved under his
feet, and everyone laughed.

*"Why should we hesitate to
toss the old views overboard?"*

Albert Wegener was not satisfied with being a
meteorologist, astronomer, physicist, an arctic explorer, and a
balloonist. (In 1906 he and his brother set a new world's record
for the longest balloon flight, remaining aloft for 52 hours.) He
figured out how the Earth is put together.

At Christmas in 1911, a friend showed him one of his
presents—a lavish world atlas. Wegener looked at a map that
showed Africa and South America. He though it looked as though
both continents once fit together. He noticed that North America
and Europe appeared as though they could nestle together, too,
if Greenland fit between them.

This wasn't the first time a scientist (or thousands of
school children) had noticed this, but Wegener did his research.
Before doing so he attended military training in the German
army and went on a second expedition to Greenland, making the
longest ice cap crossing up to that time. He spent the winter on
the ice and traveled 750 miles.

Upon returning, his investigations revealed that the
coasts of South America and Africa had the same types of
limestone formations, and the ocean floors off of both coasts had
contours suggesting that they had once been closer together. He
discovered that many plants and animals (and especially fossils)
showed remarkable similarities across various continents. For
example, marsupials in Australia and South America looked

similar. What's more, they both shared the same flatworm parasites.

"A conviction of the fundamental soundness of the idea took root in my mind," he wrote. He shared his suspicions with his future father-in-law, a noted climatologist, writing "If it turns out that sense and meaning are now becoming evident in the whole history of the Earth's development, why should we hesitate to toss the old views overboard?"

Being a speedy worker, the next year in 1912, Wegener published a lengthy treatise *Die Heraushebung der Großformen der Erdrinde (Kontinente und Ozeane) auf geophysikalischer Grundlage* (The Geophysical Basis of the Evolution of the Large-Scale Features of the Earth's Crust (Continents and Oceans).

World War I intervened. Wegener was lucky to survive. He was shot twice—once in the arm and again in the neck.

Upon being discharged and while recuperating, he followed up his pamphlet in 1915 with a slender volume that further detailed his conclusions. He postulated that the continents were once one land mass which he named Pangaea. ("All the Earth" in Greek) and that over a period of 300 million years the landmasses had gradually moved apart due to "continental displacement." (Today geologists believe that in 250 million years the continents will once again coalesce into the mega-continent, Pangaea Ultima.)

The son of an evangelical minister, Wegener preached his beliefs with a passion. He was mocked by his German colleagues, but the abuse grew much worse in 1922 when his book was translated into English.

The ruling theory was that continents were stable or fixed in place. Adherents to that belief were known as fixists and stabilists. Wegener literally challenged the foundations of their long-held beliefs.

A Chicago professor told Wegener he was promoting a "footloose" hypothesis and taking "considerable liberties with our globe." The head of the American Philosophical Society said his notions were "utter, damned rot!" One "expert" called his ideas "delirious ravings." Another said his pronouncements proved he lived in a "state of auto-intoxication." "Geo-poetry" another scientist sniffed.

Wegener wasn't right about everything. He thought centrifugal forces created by the Earth's rotation caused continental motion (or drift). He also incorrectly thought continents zipped along at eight feet annually when their real rate of motion is about an inch a year. And he was wrong when he asserted that the continents themselves move; in reality, the plates on which the continents rest move, not the landmasses themselves.

It also didn't help that Wegener had no degree in geology. Plus, he was German, and following World War I, a great deal of anti-German bias existed

Yet he correctly concluded that "the forces that displace continents are the same as those that produce great fold-mountain ranges. Continental drift, faults and compressions, earthquakes, volcanicity, [ocean] transgression cycles and [apparent] polar wandering are undoubtedly connected on a grand scale."

After years of struggle, Wegener finally earned an appointment in 1924 as a professor of meteorology, not geology.

Sadly, he did not live to see his theories proved true. In 1929 at the age of 50 he went on yet another expedition to Greenland, this time to bring supplies to remote weather stations. He and two other men ventured off from the main party. They knew that a far off station desperately needed food and other supplies.

Months later a rescue team found Wegener's body in his sleeping bag in his tent. It is believed he died of a heart attack. They built a mausoleum out of blocks of ice around his body. It remains there today, moving ever gradually westward.

Wegener wrote that he felt he had an "obligation to be a hero" and lived his life accordingly. He said he thought the stakes of life were high. He believed that to accomplish anything worth doing one must take the attitude "accomplish it or die."

MORAL: Keep moving.

George **Spencer** is the Executive Editor
of the *Dartmouth Alumni Magazine*.
He lives in Lebanon, New Hampshire.

***

stgeorge777@gmail.com

***

www.365courage.blogspot.com

***

Cover art "Megalopsychia" by St. George

www.stgeorgeart.net

Made in the USA
Las Vegas, NV
25 November 2022

60281705R00224